Preparing Stuart Kings and Princes to Rule

Preparing Stuart Kings and Princes to Rule

The Men and Women who Trained the Royals

Julia A. Hickey

PEN & SWORD
HISTORY

First published in Great Britain in 2026 by
Pen & Sword History
An imprint of Pen & Sword Books Limited
Yorkshire – Philadelphia

ISBN 978 1 03612 389 5

A CIP catalogue record for this book is
available from the British Library.

Typeset by Mac Style
Printed in the UK by CPI Group (UK) Ltd, Croydon, CR0 4YY.

FSC
www.fsc.org
MIX
Paper | Supporting responsible forestry
FSC® C013604

The Publisher's authorised representative in the EU for product safety is Authorised Rep Compliance Ltd., Ground Floor, 71 Lower Baggot Street, Dublin D02 P593, Ireland.
www.arccompliance.com

For a complete list of Pen & Sword titles please contact:

PEN & SWORD BOOKS LIMITED
47 Church Street, Barnsley, South Yorkshire, S70 2AS, England
E-mail: enquiries@pen-and-sword.co.uk
Website: www.pen-and-sword.co.uk
or
PEN AND SWORD BOOKS
1950 Lawrence Road, Havertown, PA 19083, USA
E-mail: uspen-and-sword@casematepublishers.com
Website: www.penandswordbooks.com

Contents

Simplified Table of the Stuart Family

The name Stewart, coming from the office of High Steward of Scotland, changed to Stuart during the sixteenth century when Mary, Queen of Scots, adopted the French spelling of the name making it easier to pronounce. She retained the form after her return to Scotland, and it became the official royal spelling when her second husband, Lord Darnley, and their son James VI/I continued to use the same form.

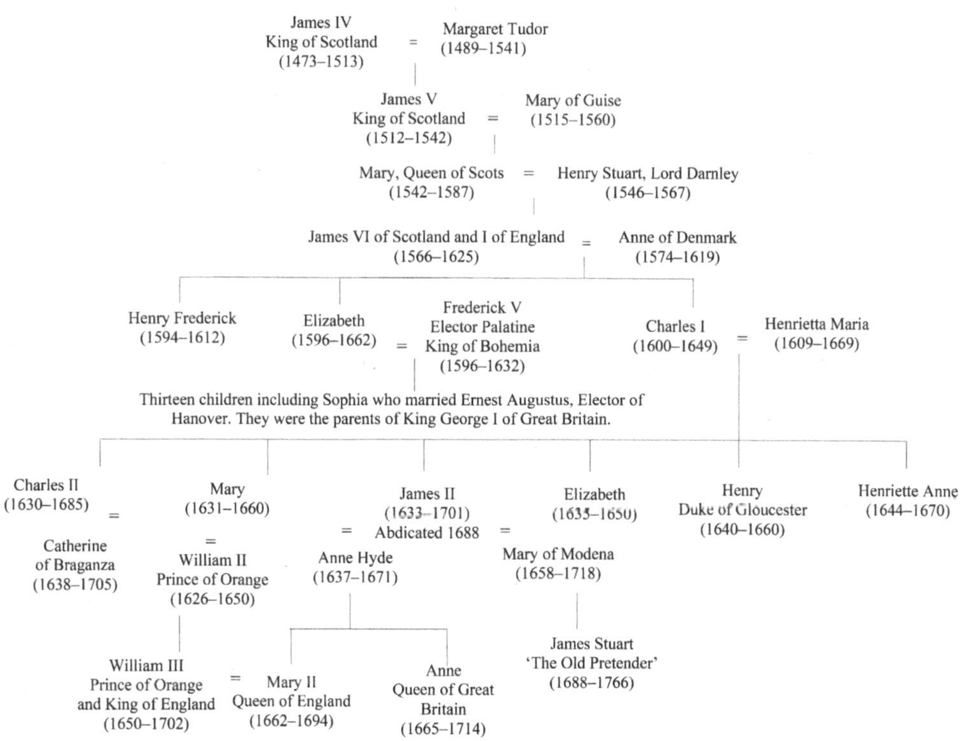

Chapter One

The Infancy of Mary, Queen of Scots

On 24 November 1542, a Scots army met 3000 English borderers led by the deputy warden of the West March, Sir Thomas Wharton, in battle at Solway Moss about five and a half miles north of Carlisle. Not realising how small the English army was, the Scots fled the field leaving more than a thousand prisoners behind them. Following the defeat, James V, who was already ill, took to his bed at Falkland Palace in Fife. He was still there when word arrived on 8 December that his queen had given birth to a daughter at Linlithgow instead of the boy that they both hoped might replace their two young sons, the Dukes of Rothesay and Albany, who perished within hours of one another in April 1541. The king died on 14 December, possibly from a contagious diseases like cholera that plagued all armies at the time.[1] His infant daughter became Mary, Queen of Scots, the first queen regnant of Scotland.

For the first six to twelve months of her life the queen was kept swaddled in fine linen bands from head to foot to ensure that her bones, which were thought to be soft, were prevented from growing crooked. It was believed that careful swaddling could shape a baby's posture and prevent physical deformity. She was rocked in her cradle, sung to, fed and cared for by servants. There was no question of Mary of Guise nursing her daughter herself even though the recently published *The Byrth of Mankynde* by Richard Jonas, which was a translation of an earlier German text dating from 1513, recommended that women should feed their own children. The topic, covered in the third part of the book, identified that the mother's breast milk would offer 'remedies for manye and sundry diseases, which oft times chaunce unto infantes after theyr byrth'.[2] Instead, the royal baby was handed to a wet nurse who was selected from a good family, had recently given birth to a child of her own, and was of a wholesome disposition. Queens and aristocratic women did not usually suckle their own children because it was thought to inhibit further pregnancies and women of Mary of Guise's rank were expected to produce as many heirs as possible for their husbands. Even though James V was dead, and there was a growing anti-wet-nursing lobby, it was inconceivable that his widow should flout convention.

Wet nurses were carefully selected since it was believed that a nurse transferred her character with her milk. It was essential for the chosen women to be good humoured and cheerful, and not inclined to be quarrelsome, sad, unduly worried or dishonest. It was even thought that the wet nurse's manners and moral attitudes could be transmitted to her charge. The woman's behaviour, health and diet were carefully monitored by the doctors responsible for Mary's care to ensure that she produced a steady supply of milk, the quality of which would ensure the infant's health. If the wet nurse's milk failed and the baby was switched to another nurse it was possible that Mary might become unwell, as had happened to her elder brother James, Duke of Rothesay in 1541. In an era with a high infant mortality, where one in five babies died before their first birthday, every precaution was taken to ensure Mary's survival.

The new queen's day to day care and the management of the royal nursery was in the hands of Jean, or Janet, Sinclair. King James V had previously paid Sinclair and her husband, John Kemp, £40 for their services. The couple were also gifted with life-rent of lands in Newtonlees, Berwickshire by Mary of Guise[3] for Jean's charge of the royal couple's short lived elder son. Cardinal Beaton, who aspired to becoming regent during Mary's minority, presented Janet with £11 on 29 December in order to ensure her favour. He recognised that she had the dowager queen's ear and that Jean would be an important influence on the new queen, Mary, as she grew up. The gift is listed among the costs of paying for suspected witches to be transported from Edinburgh to St Andrews as well as men and equipment to fight the English.[4]

Beaton was not the only one with his eye on the future. For the time being, the queen's mother, Mary of Guise, decided that she and her daughter would both remain at Linlithgow, which was a sumptuous residence designed along the same lines as a French Renaissance chateau, rather than establishing a separate household for the queen elsewhere, as was the custom. The dowager queen, alone in a foreign country, recognised that she was in a difficult position, surrounded by courtiers and politicians who wished to exploit her and her child for their own ends. She understood that physical possession of Mary was essential if she was to play an active role both in the queen's life and the rule of her adoptive country. Her son, François, by her first husband, Louis II d'Orléans, Duc de Longueville, had already been left in France to be raised by his grandmother, Antoinette de Bourbon, when Mary of Guise came to Scotland as James V's bride. Of her five children, three of whom died in infancy, only Mary remained close by.

The new queen's mother might also reasonably have expected to become regent, despite Beaton's pretensions. There was a precedent for it: Margaret Tudor, ruled on her son's behalf when James V first became king after the death of his father at Flodden in 1513. Mary of Guise, a pragmatist, sought to influence the outcome of the Scottish council's deliberations upon the matter with the aid of Guise finances but she was denied the role. Cardinal Beaton, who had exercised sway over Mary's father, maintained that James V wished him to rule as regent and provided the late king's will as evidence to support his claim. Men opposed to the cardinal's continued dominance asserted that the document was forged. James Hamilton, 2nd Earl of Arran, who was the queen's heir until she had children of her own, was among the most vocal of the cardinal's opponents. Arran's grandmother was Mary Stewart, the sister of King James III, although there was some question, raised by the Earl of Lennox who was the next in line after Hamilton, about Arran's legitimacy as his father may not have properly divorced his first wife, Elizabeth Home, before marrying the earl's mother, Janet Beaton. Despite this difficulty, the earl was voted into office as regent, with the title Lord Governor, by the royal council with the cardinal being nominated as chancellor.

It was the earl's responsibility to reconcile the Catholic faction led by Cardinal Beaton (who was irritated that he was not regent), the pro-French party led by Mary of Guise, and the reform-minded Lords of the Congregation with his own pro-English stance. His difficulties were exacerbated by his inability to arrive at a firm decision. His contemporaries described him as inconsistent, even timid, in both his political and religious views which depended upon the circumstances in which he found himself at any given time. By September 1543, rather than using his extensive wealth and power to remove opposition to his rule, Arran found himself in the shadow of Cardinal Beaton who remained determined upon a French alliance and the end of Protestantism.

Parliament decreed that in addition to the regency council, officials should take turns as royal guardians so that none of the men selected became too influential. On 15 March 1543 they nominated three nobles to care for the queen during her minority. John, 5th Lord Lindsey of Byres who had been at Falkland with James V when he died was appointed as was William Keith, 4th Earl Marichal. The latter's father had filled the role of James V's governor at Edinburgh Castle for a period in 1520. The whole family benefitted from the relationship which looked set to continue into the next generation.[5] The third man, Alexander, 5th Lord Livingston of Callendar, also claimed hereditary guardianship of underage Stuart monarchs. Following the assassination of James I in 1436, it was Sir Alexander Livingston who became James II's guardian and regent during the new king's minority. Alexander's son, James, also served as one of the monarch's guardians. Their reward was the lordship of Callendar. The 5th lord was a personal friend of James V and a fierce opponent of the English. At the time, Linlithgow Palace was in the charge of Lord Livingston and while the queen was resident in the palace, he was her custodian or Lord Keeper.

Parliament decided that it should be Mary of Guise who determined her daughter's diet and the practicalities of her upbringing rather than her governors. They did, however, appoint John Erskine, Prior of Inchmahome[6] to be the queen's director of education. Erskine was a younger son of the 5th Lord Erskine who had been appointed as James V's Lord Keeper in 1522, when the 10-year-old king was sent to Stirling. In all, Mary would have eight Lord Keepers, including the 5th Lord Erskine, during her early years. The tradition of particular families safeguarding Stuart monarchs during their minorities would ensure that the noble families remained at the heart of Scotland's unsettled politics during the queen's minority and beyond.

Since Mary of Guise remained with her daughter, and effectively retained physical custody of her, she preserved political leverage as well as enjoying more regular contact with her daughter than most royal mothers. It meant that the dowager was able to give Mary early lessons in manners as well as reading and writing and teaching the child her first prayers. Even though she was a reigning monarch, it was essential that the queen, who was raised as a devout Catholic, was taught to be a good and obedient wife. Faith, piety and education were all bound together. Mary of Guise also set about ensuring that her daughter was raised to know that she was a queen in her own right and that the men and women whom she ruled recognised her as such rather than the daughter of a foreign consort. The French Mary of Guise spoke fluent Scots and seems to have ensured that her daughter spoke only that language from her infancy.

Arran was alarmed by Mary of Guise's influence over the queen. He began to have her correspondence to and from France intercepted as well as placing spies in her household. A letter from Mary of Guise's uncle, Cardinal Lorraine, revealed that the dowager's father, Claude, Duc de Guise, a professional soldier, was so worried by the events in Scotland that he planned to bring an army to assist her. The disturbing news about the growing possibility of French interference added to the political imperative not only for Arran but also for Henry VIII, who remained anxious to prevent the expansion of French influence to the north of his kingdom.

In the meantime, the Stuart succession depended on the survival of a small girl who, rumour whispered, was unlikely to survive. Sir Ralph Sadler, the English ambassador to Scotland, who visited the queen in her nursery at Linlithgow, where Jean unwrapped the swaddling from around Mary, laid the gossip to rest when he described her as 'as goodly a child as I have seen of her age, and like to live'.[7] Sadler, working on behalf of Henry VIII, convinced Arran of the personal advantages of the union between Mary and the Henry's 5-year-old son, which would unite England and Scotland under the rule of Edward VI when he ascended to the throne. The marriage would resolve the centuries-old hostilities between the two nations and have the added benefit of reducing the influence of Catholic France on England's neighbour. A payment of £1000 helped to secure the regent's backing. Arran's initial stance in favour of the marriage was as a supporter of religious reform in Scotland. He furthered the chances of a wedding between Mary and Edward by arranging for Cardinal Beaton, who besides being Catholic and favouring a French alliance was the earl's most dangerous rival, to be arrested at the end of January 1543. Meanwhile, Arran gave a further practical demonstration of his intentions when he issued a statement supporting the English break from Rome and dissolution of the monasteries.

Mary of Guise, still refused to be parted from her daughter and unless Arran was able to remove her from her mother's care, he would find it difficult to achieve his ends, despite the dowager's seeming acquiescence to the proposed match for her daughter. She even went so far as to tell Sadler that all she wanted was the best outcome available for Scotland and that the queen's marriage to Edward would surely be God's work. They might not have trusted the dowager but the ambassador and Arran's biggest failure was to underestimate Mary of Guise's skill for intrigue. She did not seek to gain the regency for herself or to ferment resentment among the Scottish nobility against Arran. Instead, she concentrated her considerable talents on persuading Sadler, over a period of several months, that Arran was entirely self-interested and totally untrustworthy.

The idea that a woman might rule in her own right was inconceivable to most sixteenth-century minds. A female monarch, no matter how capable, did not govern – she provided her husband with heirs. The little queen would bring a kingdom to her spouse when she married. For the Scots the matter was more of a conundrum. If Mary wed abroad, then there was every danger that Scotland's independence would be diminished at the hands of a foreign ruler, but if she married into a Scottish family, the ensuing rivalry and jealousy could trigger a civil war. Whoever controlled Mary would control the future direction that Scotland's foreign policy and religious practices would take. While the various factions on the council vied for political power and domination of the future of Scotland's religion, Arran trod the political tightrope between the almost equally divided lords.

On 8 April 1543, Sadler reported that Matthew Stewart, 4th Earl of Lennox, who had returned from France where his mother had sent him to be educated, presented himself as an alternate candidate for the regency through his own royal ancestry. He was gathering a force to 'surprise and get into their hands the said young queen'[8] so that they could take her from the regent's control to Edinburgh. Mary was so well guarded by Arran at Linlithgow that it seemed unlikely that they would achieve their goal.[9] The best that Lennox, who had signed a 'Secret Bond' with other pro-French nobles, could achieve was an agreement that Arran would rule with the advice of a council.

In the meantime, Henry VIII opened further negotiations with Arran by suggesting that his own younger daughter, Elizabeth, should marry Arran's heir, James Hamilton. Arran did not accept the English offer, recognising its dangers. However, he was eager to see his family advance so Sir Ralph Sadler was able to report that the earl was willing to make peace with England. The result was the Treaty of Greenwich, agreed on 1 July 1543, which would have united the warring kingdoms. Prisoners captured at the Battle of Solway Moss were released, without payment of ransom, upon their undertaking to promote the match and a subsidy paid to some Scottish nobles to achieve the same end. Under the terms of the treaty Mary would remain in Scotland until she was 10-years-old and be married the year afterwards to Edward.

In Scotland the bargain was not as cut and dried as Henry VIII, or Arran, liked to believe. Mary's mother, Mary of Guise, opposed the match as did many of the Scottish nobility who objected to the idea of an alliance to an old enemy. Throughout 1543 there was a struggle between Protestant pro-English sympathisers and the Scots, usually Catholic, who favoured a continuation of the 'auld alliance' with France. As early as July 1543, Sadler reported that the French navy lay off Arbroath.[10] The ambassador also reported that Arran could not remove Mary from Linlithgow to Edinburgh as Henry VIII wished because she was teething, Sadler added, somewhat sardonically, that 'he tendeth as much her health, preservation, and surety, as if she were his own natural child'.[11] The letter speculated as to the reasons behind the regent's sudden prevarication. The truth was that the lords who were part of the Secret Bond would not let Arran place Mary where he would control her future.

Sadler and his wife, who was expecting a child when the ambassador wrote to the king, were ordered to remain with the Scottish queen throughout her childhood.[12] Henry wanted to ensure that Mary was raised speaking English rather than Scots. The ambassador, who was reluctant for his wife, Ellen, to travel while she was pregnant, reflected on the importance of Mary being provided with a suitable household to guide her. He added that Ellen had no experience of life at court. Instead, the ambassador identified the need for a 'grave and discreet woman, of good years and experience; and the better if she were a widow'. [13] He suggested that Lady Katherine Edgcumbe would be a more suitable candidate to fulfil the role of English governess to the young queen.She was distantly related to the Tudors through the St John family and had experience serving in the household of Katherine of Aragon at Ludlow as well as being a lady-in-waiting to Anne of Cleves. The proposal came to nothing and in October 1543, the king granted Sadler's friend an annuity instead.

The French threat to an Anglo-Scottish alliance did not diminish with the Treaty of Greenwich. Those loyal to the dowager and the Catholic Church continued to agitate against the newly signed agreement. Mary of Guise remained wary of Arran, whose first actions on being appointed regent included the seizure of the royal castles and the advancement of his own family. She might have been denied a place in the council chamber but so long as Mary was in her hands, she could protect not only her daughter but her own interests as well. With that in mind, Mary of Guise persuaded Sadler of the advantages of a move from Linlithgow to Stirling Castle, which was an impregnable fortress as well as being part of her own dowry. Amid tales that Lord Bothwell was threatening to kidnap the young queen, heightened security was an essential. On 26 July 1543, the royal retinue, escorted by Lennox, made its way to Mary of Guise's preferred residence.

At Stirling the queen's new Lord Keeper, John Erskine, 5th Lord Erskine, who had also been James V's guardian during his minority[14], was predisposed to an Anglo-French alliance rather than a Protestant match, even though he was a reformer himself. Like many of the men and women who surrounded the queen, he was part of her extended kinship network. His daughter, Margaret Erskine, had been one of James V's mistresses and was the mother of Mary's half-brother, James Stewart. It was his task to order the queen's nursery household, to manage its costs and its servants according to the direction of the queen's mother and the regent. The move meant that Arran was at even more of a disadvantage than he had been while the queen was housed at Linlithgow.

The Catholic elements of the regency council gradually gained the upper hand with the aid of the French, who sent funds to subsidise their campaign. Mary of Guise was able to arrange for Cardinal Beaton to stay at Stirling and advocated his return to power both with Sadler and the queen's council. In England, Henry VIII agitated against the dowager's continuing presence at Stirling Castle. He wished for her to reside in the town and have limited access to her daughter; his demands came to nothing. Eventually, Arran was forced to address his increasing isolation by coming to an agreement with Cardinal Beaton and acquiescing to the French marriage proposal. He was also obliged to make a public confession of his renunciation of faith and receive pardon for his transgression. As an added precaution to ensure the regent's future compliance, Arran was required to give his eldest son, James, into the cardinal's care with the promise that there might still be a royal match for the boy. It meant that, for the time being, Henry VIII's plans were thwarted, although the English monarch did not become fully aware of the situation until the autumn, by which time it was too late in the year to begin an armed conflict.

Having dissembled successfully in the matter of her daughter's marriage to Prince Edward, Mary of Guise was finally able to discredit Arran in the eyes of Henry VIII by sharing the rumours that the regent sought to promote himself and his own family by a marriage between his eldest son, who was some five years the queen's senior, and Scotland's sovereign. As a consequence, the earl found himself facing difficulties both at home and in his relationship with the English. His problems were compounded by the claims of Lennox to the regency and title of heir apparent.

Sadler was threatened with violence and Arran, who realised he had misjudged the situation, distanced himself from the ambassador whose reports went on to describe ordinary Scots as 'rude, ignorant and beastly.'[15] Political power was shifting away from those men who favoured an English alliance. Cardinal Beaton and the Earls of Argyll, Huntly and Moray became the queen's protectors, appointed according to the terms of the document that Beaton claimed to be James V's will. Mary of Guise would have to wait another twelve years before she could obtain control of Scotland, despite an attempt in 1544 to have the regency transferred to her. In December 1543, the Scottish Parliament renounced the Treaty of Greenwich blaming English contraventions of the agreement. Sadler was recalled from Scotland because Henry VIII, who no longer trusted the pro-English Scottish party, intended to claim his son's intended bride by force. The south of Scotland went up in flames once more as an English army visited their king's displeasure upon the people who lived there. The campaign would come to be known as the Rough Wooing.

For the next four years, Mary remained at Stirling, playing in its gardens and growing from infancy into a child under the supervision of Jean Sinclair who ensured that nursery routines were maintained. She was weaned at about the age of 2 and Jean, overseen by the dowager, taught Mary to make the sign of the cross and to know her prayers, the most important being the *Pater Noster*, *Credo* and *Ave Maria*. The daily routine included attendance at services held in the Chapel Royal and practical lessons of piety, including the giving of alms and making offerings to the Church.

Political, as well as martial, conflict was never far from the surface during Mary's childhood at Stirling. While the court paid their dues to their little queen, the dowager played the Earls of Lennox and Bothwell off against one another as suitors for her hand. Whoever married Mary's mother would have sufficient leverage to force Arran from office and rule as regent in his place. The two rivals for the dowager's hand were accomplished in the art of courtly love but James V's widow was an equally talented player in the game of fair words, and she had no intention of taking another husband. When Lennox understood the reality of the situation he left Scotland, allied himself to the English and was wed to Lady Margaret Douglas, the daughter of Margaret Tudor from her second marriage to the Earl of Angus. Henry VIII even paid his niece's dowry to facilitate the union and was, conveniently, persuaded that it was Lennox who was rightful heir apparent rather than Arran while the Scots' queen was without children of her own.

The Rough Wooing gathered momentum under the command of the Earl of Hertford. The palace of Holyrood was ransacked by the English before they left Edinburgh in flames. Arran was blamed for the disaster, giving Mary of Guise the opportunity to negotiate a seat on the privy council for herself. She continued to promote a pro-French policy and gained assistance against Hertford's army from King François I. But events did not play out entirely in her favour. As the violence escalated, Cardinal Beaton became progressively more unpopular, not only with the lords who supported an English marriage but also with the increasingly vociferous Protestant reformers, who objected to his burning of George Wishart, a reformer, in March 1546.

Beaton was murdered at St Andrews Castle on 29 May 1546 and his remains displayed from the castle walls there. Arran's heir, the Master of Hamilton, who had been in the cardinal's care, was now in the hands of a group of Protestant lords and reformers. The Scottish Parliament hastened to exclude young James Hamilton from the succession whilst he was a captive for fear that someone might attempt to make him king in Mary's place. The castle at St Andrews was placed under siege and eventually captured by the French. The assassination was followed by a brief hiatus in the war between the English and the Scots because Henry VIII erroneously believed that the cardinal's death marked a break in the 'auld alliance'.

The deaths of Beaton in 1546, Henry VIII in January 1547 and, François I of France on 31 March the same year did not end the hostilities about whose consort the Scottish queen would become. François' successor, King Henri II, advised by the Guise family, declared himself to be Scotland's protector, sent more troops and confirmed that he wished its queen to marry his own son, the dauphin, François, who was born in 1544. Hertford, elevated to the dukedom of Somerset, as Edward VI's protector during the first years of his minority, continued the Rough Wooing on behalf of his nephew and sent a reminder via the Norroy King of Arms that 'the invasion of Scotland is only to bring to good effect the godly purpose of the marriage between King Edward VI and Queen Mary'.[16] Like Henry VIII, Somerset wanted to ensure that there would be no marriage alliance between Scotland and France. The queen's mother and advisors were not convinced by the tactics and continued to resist the duke's attempts to capture Mary, who remained at Stirling.

In September 1547, the Scots were defeated for a second time in five years by an English army of 18,000 men under Somerset's command at the Battle of Pinkie near Edinburgh. Arran badly misinterpreted English manoeuvres at the start of the battle and gave up his strategic advantage to pursue his enemy, believing that they were in retreat. Among the men who died was Lord Livingston's eldest son, John, who was married to a daughter of Malcolm, Lord Fleming. The Scottish capital and Leith both fell to the invaders but Somerset did not follow up on the victory himself. Instead, he returned to England, leaving his troops to secure southern Scotland and to advance on Stirling.

Mary, who was now 4-years-old, was moved for her own safety to the Augustinian priory on the island of Inchmahome, some fifteen miles west of her home. The priory's commendator, Robert Erskine, who was one of

Lord Erskine's sons, was killed at Pinkie and so John Erskine, the prior, was appointed commendator in his brother's place. Mary and her mother would have been given Erskine's own chambers and it is thought that while she was there, she began her formal education under Erskine's guidance. It is likely that she learned a few words of Latin during her three weeks on the island before returning to Stirling where Alexander Scott, the parson of Balmaclellan, and one of the canons at the Chapel Royal took over her daily lessons under the commendator's direction. She was joined at her studies by her cousin, Mary Fleming, whose father Malcolm was also killed at Pinkie.

Janet Stewart, Lady Fleming, Mary Fleming's mother, joined the queen's household as its governess. Mary was growing too big for a nurse but Jean remained by her side. The dowager understood that when the queen left Scotland to marry, her nurse would go with her as a surrogate parent. As well as being the half-sister of King James V, Janet Stewart was the mother of eight children and known for her short temper as well as her beauty. Her relationship to the queen, her experience as a mother and her personal friendship with Mary of Guise equipped her to fulfil the role of governess. It also helped that two of her daughters were married to the two eldest sons of Lord Livingston, who remained one of the queen's joint custodians. It was her responsibility to oversee the royal nursery, and the queen's lessons and to teach her how to conduct herself. In reality, she shared the role with Mary of Guise.

The regency council, which met on 2 November 1547, determined that their queen would only be safe from the English in France, as the bride of the Dauphin. Arran was sent to negotiate with Henri II, gaining the dukedom of Châtellerault for himself in the process, an income of 12,000 livres, and another promise of marriage for his son.[17] In February 1548 the Scottish Parliament agreed the terms of Mary's marriage to Henri II's son. The queen was moved to the coast at Dunbarton Castle, with her guardians, Lords Erskine and Livingston, in readiness for her departure. On March 2, Robert Moffet reported Mary's presence at the port as well as the arrival of French troops to defend her.[18] In June, the French recaptured Haddington in East Lothian from the English and at the beginning of July a formal treaty was signed there between the 'auld alliance'. This safeguarded the Scots from

English aggressors, as well as offering underpinning safeguards for Scottish self-government, and was cemented by the marriage pact.

On 7 August 1548, Mary, who was not yet 6-years-old and recently recovered from the measles, said farewell to her mother and sailed for France, according to the terms of the Treaty of Haddington, with her household. This included her guardians Lord Erskine and Lord Livingston; her governess; Jean Sinclair and her husband John Kemp; the Commendator of Inchmahome; ladies-in-waiting and several other children, including three of her own illegitimate half-siblings, who served as her companions. James Stewart Mary's 17-year-old half-brother travelled with the group on his way to university at Paris. In total, four ships were required to carry the queen and her retinue to France. Mary of Guise was determined that no one should forget that Mary was Queen of Scots and that she should be served by her own people.

In Scotland, Arran, the new Duke of Châtellerault, remained as regent, but his son had been sent to France before the queen. Mary of Guise stayed on Scottish shores, bereft of her beloved daughter, but determined to ensure the success of the French alliance. Encouraged by her uncles and by Henri II, she set about undermining the regent's position in the interests of her own increasing power.

Chapter Two

Mary's French Education

King Henri II sent Mary to be raised alongside her future husband, François, at the royal nursery at Carrieres-Sur-Seine, near St-Germain-en-Laye, which was overseen by Henri's long-term mistress, Diane de Poitiers. The officials in day-to-day charge of the nursery were Jean d'Humières and his wife, Françoise, who was the governess to the French royal children. It was their responsibility to follow the instructions of Diane de Poitiers and to manage the household's staff, which comprised about 250 people. There were a number of junior governesses including Marie-Catherine Gondi who was a personal friend of Henri II's queen, Catherine de Medici.

Since Mary was already a queen, she took precedence over the king's daughters, Elizabeth and Claude, and was honoured by the whole court. Her education would endow Mary with the accomplishments of a Renaissance princess but it would not equip her to govern. Salic law prevented a woman from ruling France in her own right. Mary's responsibilities would be as a wife and a mother to French kings. Her father-in-law and, in time, her husband, would govern Scotland through Mary's privy council on her behalf.

The remainder of Mary's childhood was spent surrounded by cousins, tutors, an array of pets, including a bear, and an army of French servants. Henri II was a solicitous father and Catherine de Medici, who waited a decade for the birth of her first child, was deeply concerned for the welfare of her seven surviving children. The French queen laid down ordinances for meals and insisted that Jean d'Humières keep her informed about the nursery's occupants, while Marie-Catherine Gondi, who was placed to spy upon Diane de Poitiers, provided additional information. The Scottish queen's upbringing was also monitored by her maternal grandmother, Antoinette of Guise, as well as her Guise uncles – François, Duc de Guise and Charles, Cardinal of Lorraine – who sought to use Mary as a pawn to extend their influence at the French court as well as reporting to Mary of Guise.

The curriculum, as well as being humanist in its origins, reflected an Italian influence which valued the importance of educated women in a sophisticated society. Mothers were, after all, people with the most influence on the early lives and educations of their sons. It was they who instilled civic virtue and morality on their families. It was also their responsibility to support their husbands politically and socially. A well-educated woman could be an asset to the fortunes of her family. Northern European humanists including Erasmus and Sir Thomas More, advocated the importance of female education, while Juan Luis Vives wrote a text on the education of women at the behest of Katherine of Aragon to direct Mary Tudor's learning. It was widely agreed by the scholars, who emphasised the importance of piety, that female education improved a girl's Christian virtues and instilled moral values.

By contrast, Anne of France's *Lessons for my Daughter*, written for Suzanne of Bourbon and printed in about 1517, impressed the importance of education for princesses and queens, to shape strong-minded, independent women. The lessons of Anne's book created the portrait of an ideal Renaissance princess, able to successfully manoeuvre her way through the male dominated world of politics in much the same way that Mary of Guise was required to do in Scotland. *Lessons for my Daughter* was written from the viewpoint of a woman who ruled France from 1483 to 1491 as her brother, Charles VIII's, regent. It was based upon her experiences, on the lessons she learned as a child from her mother, Charlotte of Savoy, and on the books Anne read in the royal library, which included texts like those of Christine de Pizan's, *The Treasure of the City of Ladies* written a century earlier. Anne's original manuscript, given to her daughter, found its way along with the rest of the Bourbon library to Fontainebleau and was then given as a present to Diane de Poitiers, who had been educated by Anne of France.[1] Both women were ambitious, politically powerful and worldly-wise. In addition to the traditional advice for the proper behaviour of a woman, it would have been as well for Mary to take to heart Anne's guidance that 'There is no man of worth, however noble he may be, who does not use treachery'.[2] It might perhaps have saved her from the flattery of Lord Darnley or given her some insight into her council's behaviour when she returned to Scotland in 1561. At the time though there was no consideration of Mary ruling her kingdom for herself, let alone ever returning to it.

Mary's Scottish retinue numbered about thirty people. John Erskine and Alexander Livingston remained in attendance on their queen; the latter died sometime between July 1549 and January 1551. His eldest son, John, was killed at the Battle of Pinkie in 1547 so it was his second son, William, who became the 6th lord, and like his father before him, William would serve his queen faithfully. Alexander's daughter, Mary Livingston, was one of the queen's companions. John Erskine of Inchmahome, the third of Lord Erskine's sons, was raised to enter the Church but his circumstances changed with the deaths of his elder brothers by 1551, and the death of their father in 1552. It meant that he succeeded as the 6th Lord Erskine and assumed with it the hereditary mantle of Governor of Stirling Castle. He resigned his office in Mary's household in favour of a nephew, David Erskine, and returned to Scotland where he took over the governorship of Edinburgh Castle.

Now though, the majority of the young queen's Scottish retinue were regarded as uncouth and, even, unwashed. Nor did it help that Henri was expected to pay for the household. It made more economic and political sense for Mary to be raised alongside Henri's daughters. The majority of the queen's Scottish servants were dismissed and sent home apart from her governess, Lady Fleming, who Mary of Guise insisted must remain. Jean Sinclair, Mary's nurse since infancy, had no intention of abandoning her charge either. She wrote to Antoinette de Bourbon asking to remain and when that failed, Jean wrote to Mary of Guise describing low wages and irregular payment as well as being deprived of her authority. The dowager intervened on Jean's behalf. Mistress Sinclair remained with the queen, as did her husband, John Kemp, described by Mary as her foster-father.

Also permitted to stay in France were the queen's four companions, Mary Beaton, Mary Fleming, Mary Livingston and Mary Seton, although they were sent to a Dominican convent school at nearby Poissy to learn French and to dissuade the queen from conversing in her native tongue. When Mary arrived in France, she spoke very little French, demonstrating her mother's determination that Mary should be viewed by her people as Scottish. The queen's remaining household merged with the dauphin's and Diane of Poitiers set about turning the Scottish queen into a French one. At first Mary shared Elizabeth of France's lessons and was required to spend two hours every day studying French.[3] She and Elizabeth became close friends and would remain so when they became adults. Diane and Henri were determined that the queen would prefer French to other languages. Although Mary was able to speak Scots, she never spent much time writing it during her childhood and she did not begin to study English until 1568, following her deposition from her throne.

Henri II regarded his court as the most cultured in Europe and Mary would benefit from having the best teachers available. Claude Millot, Antoine Fouquelin and Jacques Amyot who taught the dauphin and his brothers assumed responsibility for educating Mary. As well as French, she learned Latin, which was associated with classical learning, and according to Sir Thomas More, the development of good moral character. She read Cicero, Plato and Aristotle's *Politics and Rhetoric*. The Scottish queen was required to translate texts from Latin into French and back again, the so-called double translation, in order to learn vocabulary, grammar and style from classical writers. The same authors provided lessons in history, philosophy and rhetoric. The dauphin needed to be adept in the art of public speaking and since Mary shared his curriculum, she also learned the skill. In England, Vives saw no reason for Mary's cousin, Mary Tudor, to learn the subject because he believed that hers would be an entirely domestic role. Elizabeth Tudor, tutored by Roger Ascham, was subject to no such restrictions.

The children within the royal classroom were expected to write compositions mirroring the grammar and constructions of the classical scholars they read. Claude Millet, who was also Elizabeth of France's tutor, required Mary, when she was aged 11, to write a series of letters in notebooks addressed to her companion and other members of the court, over a period of six months in 1554. The right-hand page contained the Latin work while the left-hand side was written in French. Not only did Mary develop an understanding of Latin grammar and vocabulary but she was also required to focus on the virtues required by educated women. In total sixty-four of Mary's letters survive. Their original source was a letter written in 1491 by the Florentine scholar Angelo Ambrogini to Cassandra Fedele.[4] Cassandra, a letter writer and orator, gave a famous lecture to the Venetian doge in which she advocated female education. A copy of the letter was contained in a volume of Ambrogini's work held by the library at Fontainebleau.

As well as writing essays in the form of letters to Elizabeth, Mary also wrote letters to her mother. At first the correspondence reflected its classroom origins but swiftly took on a more personal content as the bond between mother and daughter reasserted itself across the sea that separated them. Mary of Guise's correspondence was the most direct advice on ruling a kingdom that Mary ever received. Any other guidance was gleaned from the histories that Mary studied and from her study of Greek under the tutorship of Pierre Danès who may have used *L'Institution du Prince* by Guillaume Baudé, which drew on classical authors for its contents. Whether she studied it in the schoolroom or not, Mary owned a copy of the text which she brought back to Scotland with her.[5]

Her teachers drew on Aesop, Cicero, Plato, Aristotle, Quintilian and Plutarch. Having grasped Latin, Mary moved on to Greek, Italian and Spanish. She was also required to study Erasmus and Ptolemy's study of geography which claimed that the earth was at the centre of the universe while everything else, including the sun, revolved around it. The texts were a Renaissance primer in princely education.

As well as her school books, Mary was expected to excel at music and dancing with François, who was a year younger than her. She sang and played the lute, clavichord and harp. Her first public appearances at the French court required her to dance a measure with the dauphin, who she was encouraged to befriend and talk of in courtly terms. Lady Fleming and Diane de Poitiers coached the princess in posture, etiquette and manners so that she knew how to conduct herself and could take her place on the public stage. Dancing was an essential part of an aristocratic girl's education despite what Vives, who wrote a book advising on Mary Tudor's education, concluded in *The Instruction of a Christian Woman* published in 1532. The Spanish educator believed that exposure to music, dancing and tournaments would lead to immorality. It was an impossible stricture to place upon gently born girls who would be expected to take their place at a royal court. From her first appearance on the dance floor, it was clear that Mary was a talented dancer and Henri II found her an Italian dance master. In later years, John Knox would complain that the queen was more interested in 'fiddling and flynging' and 'immoderate dancing' than in religion.[6] In France, court entertainments were not equated to moral failure; rather musical skills added to a woman's perceived attractiveness and Mary's love of dancing was no greater than her cousin, Elizabeth I's. Mary also became proficient at falconry soon after she arrived in France and later enjoyed hunting larger game, riding in a pair of breeches under her skirts according to the Italian fashions introduced by Catherine de Medici. It meant that she could ride astride rather than the more usual side saddle.

The Scottish queen and her aristocratic female companions were expected to demonstrate piety through attendance at Church and knowledge of the Bible. It was also anticipated that Mary and her companions would know how to run a household. It was a woman's responsibility as a wife to manage her husband's estates in his absence and have oversight of its finances – it mattered not one jot that Mary was a regnant monarch or that she would have trusted servants to undertake these tasks for her. A special kitchen was created where the queen and the French princesses learned how to make confections and preserves.[7] It was unlikely that a queen would ever need to make her own jam but domestic skills were regarded as essential qualities in a woman, whatever her rank. Vives also emphasised the importance of feminine occupations; he believed that they were essential for a virtuous wife and that idle hands led to sinfulness or to gossiping.

Mary was also taught how to knit and to embroider. She learned plain sewing first, including sewing handkerchiefs and shifts, before advancing to decorative techniques, the most basic of which was a double running stitch. This is known today in Britain as Holbein stitch after the artist Hans Holbein, who portrayed so many of Henry VIII's court attired in clothing decorated by blackwork embroidery which employed a double running stitch to make intricate patterns and designs. As an adult, during her imprisonment in England, she created many canvas works, showing a preference for French fashions, using techniques she learned as a child. Her teacher in the royal nursery was Pierre Danjou, who was Henri II's personal embroiderer. In addition to her tutor, Mary would also have learned, at least by observation, from Catherine de Medici who was a skilled embroiderer. Catherine even arrived from Italy, when she married the king, with her own designer, Fredico de Vincola, who created starched lace ruffs that Catherine made fashionable and published pattern books for aristocratic embroiderers who wished to emulate the style. Catherine spent her afternoons and evenings embroidering, listening to the conversations that swirled around her as she worked.[8]

Mary's mother-in-law was something of an expert at a form of needle lace known as *lacis*. This technique might be best described as darning netting to create a pattern by filling in the meshes or leaving them open. An inventory of her possessions made after her death shows that Henri's consort also enjoyed canvas work stitched with '*gros poinct*'. In total there were more than 200 canvases itemised.[9] She learned her skills as a child at the Convent of the Murate in Florence famous for its goldwork embroidery. In England, there was a flowering of embroidery in the aftermath of the Reformation for secular use; in France, embroidered gifts made to the Church was a display of piety as well as wealth and education.

In about 1549, François Clouet drew a portrait of Mary, who was in her eighth year. It was made by the court painter to celebrate her forthcoming marriage to the dauphin. She was becoming progressively more French in her tastes as well as becoming used to the grand spaces and magnificent pageantry of her new home. The following year, Jean d'Humières died and was succeeded by Claude d'Urfé who took over as governor. Claude, who was French ambassador to the Papal States prior to his appointment, was a patron of the arts. It was he who appointed Joachim du Bellay, a poet who promoted French as an equal of both Latin and Greek.

The new appointments were not the only changes to the household in which Mary lived. Lady Fleming, Mary's governess, spoke fluent French and kept control of Mary's female staff, much to Diane de Poitiers' irritation. In 1550, it was rumoured that Constable Montmorency was courting the governess. He was a rival of Diane's for the ear of the king. When it became clear that Lady Fleming was not beyond reproach and that she was entertaining her lover in her chamber, Diane, thinking to rid herself of both adversaries, provided Mary's uncles with a key to enter the rooms next to Lady Fleming's quarters in order to catch the pair. But when they arrived on the scene, they discovered the king.

Diane, who feared that she might be losing her hold over him, argued that Henri was bringing the Queen of Scots into disrepute by sleeping with her governess. In the midst of the scandal, Lady Fleming became pregnant and gave birth to a son, Henry of Angoulême, which turned the affair into a public rather than private scandal. Sir John Mason, writing to the council from Amboise on 29 April 1551, reported that Janet was 'brought a-bed of a child, wherat the women around her do not much rejoice'.[10] Henri recognised his son but Lady Fleming made the mistake of believing that she might become an official mistress and announced her situation without any thought for the feelings of the king's wife, Catherine de Medici. The queen, who gave birth to a son who was also named Henri three months after Lady Fleming, felt humiliated and, although she resented the influence of Diane over her husband, arranged for the governess to be sent back to Scotland. Mason speculated that Mary's former governess would return to France as soon as she was able[11] but Mary of Guise, who was Scotland's regent in fact if not name by that time, forbade it.

In 1550, Mary of Guise took the opportunity to visit her beloved daughter and to finalise the arrangements for her marriage to the dauphin. The dowager remained in France for a year, during which time she kept Mary with her and superintended her education. She also took the opportunity to visit Mary's elder half-brother François, Duke of Longueville. The boy had written regularly to his mother and corresponded with his half-sister throughout his separation from his immediate family. By the time Mary of Guise was reunited with her son, he was almost 15-years-old and already ailing; Mary of Guise would end up nursing her son through his final illness. When she left France to return to Scotland she must have wondered if she would ever see her daughter again.

By the end of 1551, Mary, who was 9-years-old, was outgrowing the nursery and it was time to focus more closely on court etiquette and household management. It was at about this time that Jean Sinclair and her husband returned to Scotland, where Jean died in 1557. The loss of another familiar face from her nursery marked the fact that Mary, no longer a child, should be provided with a staff appropriate for a queen. At the beginning of 1553, Henri II established an independent household for the dauphin now that he was too old to be in female care and it raised questions about Mary's status. As a reigning monarch she ought to have had her own household but the removal of the dauphin made financing Mary's household more difficult, and there were no additional funds forthcoming from Scotland for the purpose. A further indicator of Mary's newfound maturity was demonstrated in December 1553 when the French *parlement* decreed that the Scottish queen was of age and should choose her own regent to rule in her stead. Châtellerault, formerly 2nd Earl of Arran, finally resigned and Mary of Guise was officially appointed to the role.

Lady Fleming's replacement, Françoise d'Estamville, was a woman known for her devoutness. She lacked warmth or the social skills necessary to avoid friction either with her charge or the household that served her. These problems were exacerbated by the financial constraints she faced running the queen's household. Despite the protestations of her Guise uncles that the Scottish queen needed up to 60,000 francs a year, her servants often remained unpaid for months. In 1555, worn down by the household's financial difficulties and her own quarrels with the staff, Françoise became unwell and that Christmas argued with Mary who had given two dresses to her aunts who were both abbesses. The gowns were to be cut up and used as altar cloths but Mary's governess took exception, believing that the dresses should have been gifted to her. When the young queen wrote to her mother, she explained that Françoise refused to allow Mary to give any of her possessions to her servants in order to reward them for their service, as was usual at the time. The Scottish queen, who often exchanged correspondence with her mother, knew the importance of appearing generous and being a good employer.

It was a fashion at the French court to use emblems, puns and riddles to create these identifiers or *impresas* and the Scottish queen took the symbol of the marigold, which was both a play on her name and was associated, through folklore, with the Virgin Mary. The queen's needlework, completed in captivity, reflects her delight in playing with words and the puns that were popular at the French court during her youth. She used books that she asked servants and friends to purchase for her to aid her designs and began to rebuild the library that she left behind in Edinburgh. Among the texts she is known to have used were Erasmus' *Adages* in Latin and English, containing an annotated collection of proverbs.

More tutors were appointed including Pierre de Ronsard, a writer of French poetry, described by his countrymen as 'the prince of poets', who in 1556 published a collection of poetry at Mary's request. The queen was learning about the importance of patronage and that a Renaissance sovereign had many ways of demonstrating their learning. After she returned to Scotland, the poet dedicated a sonnet to Mary and criticised the French for not defending her from the trials and tribulations in her own country. He also implored his former pupil to find better advisers before her situation became any worse.

In 1558, when Mary was 15 years old, her uncles taught her about the importance of security and sending the most important of her letters in cipher. Her mother had been sending her letters about the way to rule Scotland since 1554, when she became regent in Châtellerault's place. She discussed what policies she adopted and often asked Mary to approve them, as well as encouraging Mary to make her own suggestions about the way her kingdom should be run. Mary, who learned to write with a fashionable Italic script that was the mark of a Renaissance prince, penned her responses but did not fully appreciate the difficulties her mother faced on her behalf. If the queen was becoming ever more French, so too was her homeland where government positions were readily given to Frenchmen and strategic fortresses, with the exception of Edinburgh, were garrisoned by Henri's troops.

Scotland was an increasingly Protestant country and its inhabitants were resentful both of the French and the controls that Mary of Guise sought to exert on her daughter's behalf. Catholicism was becoming associated with the French. It meant that to be Protestant was to oppose foreign rule.

On 24 April 1558, Mary married the dauphin, François, at the Notre Dame in Paris. She had already secretly agreed that in the event of her own death without children that the French would keep Scotland for themselves and succeed to her rights and titles to the English throne. This was in contravention to the rights of Châtellerault, who had yielded the regency to Mary of Guise on the understanding that if Mary died without heirs, he would inherit the throne by right of his bloodline. Mary also agreed to pay the French for their continuing defence of her realm from the English and to cover the costs of her own education. A third clause disabled the rights of the Scottish Parliament to pass any laws contrary to the agreements made by Mary with the French. Mary's lack of experience, her upbringing in France and even her trusting nature meant that the 15-year-old effectively signed away her kingdom.

When Queen Mary I of England died in November 1558, Henri II was quick to proclaim his daughter-in-law queen of England, Scotland and

Ireland and added the heraldic arms of England to those of France and Scotland on all of the Scottish queen's plate and cloth of state. Mary Stuart was the granddaughter of Margaret Tudor, the elder sister of Henry VIII, and should have been next in line for the Tudor throne after her cousin, according to the Catholic Church, rather than Henry VIII's younger daughter, Elizabeth, whose legitimacy was questionable. The decision made by the French king and Mary's uncles, not to mention the demands made by the papacy to declare in her favour, would cast a long shadow over Mary's relationship with Elizabeth I, who had endured a much harder and more dangerous childhood than Mary, who had lived a cossetted life. At court, James Hamilton, Châtellerault's heir, who had known Mary since she was a baby, resented that the queen was married to François rather than himself. A French ambassador in Spain commented that 'he had persuaded himself that the Queen of Scotland was to be no one else's wife but his'.[12] It is thought to be one of the reasons that he adopted Protestantism, which he chose to flaunt with the establishment of a Protestant congregation at Châtellerault in February 1559, and an alliance with Elizabeth I when, fearing arrest, he was forced to flee.

In 1559, the French court celebrated the marriage of Mary's schoolroom companion Claude, the second daughter of Henri II and Catherine, to Charles III, Duke of Loraine. Six months later, in June, Elizabeth, Claude's sister, was married by proxy to Mary Tudor's widower, Philip II of Spain. The union was followed by three days of festivities which included a tournament. On 30 June, Henri issued a jousting challenge, open to all comers. Gabriel de Montgomery took up the challenge and struck the king on the shoulder with his lance. The wooden weapon shattered, sending shards in all directions. One of them penetrated the king's visor and entered his eye. Mary's father-in-law died in agony on 10 July. By then Catherine de Medici had issued orders for Diane de Poitiers to be denied access to the king's bedchamber and that she should leave the court.

Mary's husband became King François II and was crowned at Reims in September. The seal of François II and his queen bore his title to England and Ireland as well as France and Scotland. Inevitably, Elizabeth I's view of her cousin was soured by the claim. Catherine de Medici was temporarily side-lined while Mary's uncles took up the reigns of office. The dowager queen, who was often in her daughter-in-law's company, kept her own counsel about the course which French politics took during the following year, although she ensured that she remained a presence at court.

In Scotland, rebellion against French rule coalesced into an alliance with Elizabeth I. Mary's half-brother, James Stewart, a representative of the Lords of the Congregation, signed the Treaty of Berwick with the English on 27 February 1560, to ensure mutual support against the French. On 11 June 1560, Mary's mother, Mary of Guise, increasingly troubled by the Protestant reformation in Scotland and the Lords of the Congregation, died in Edinburgh, having first begged the Scots to be obedient to their queen. The dowager's involvement with Scottish politics began almost immediately after her daughter's birth and ended only with her death. Another woman might have returned to France with her daughter, but Mary of Guise chose to stay in her adoptive country to protect the interests of her daughter. She proved to be a capable ruler but her death was the precursor to rapid religious and political change.

On 6 July 1560, the Guises, with their eyes on power in France, and the debts left by Henri II, negotiated the Treaty of Edinburgh with the English, and withdrew French troops from Scotland. They also agreed to revoke Mary's claim to England and Ireland. The Scottish Parliament made Protestantism the official religion of the country on 24 August.[13] No one consulted Mary to find out what her views might have been on either matter and she never agreed with the terms of her uncles' negotiations. The Guises had betrayed her political interests in Scotland and rather than the queen imposing her own religious beliefs on her people, as happened in other countries at the time, the Scottish Parliament made its own decision.

Most disastrous of all, François became ill with an ear infection and died on the evening of 5 December. He had been king of France for just seventeen months. Mary was not yet 18-years-old. The new king was Mary's brother-in-law, 10-year-old Charles. Catherine de Medici took steps to ensure that the ascendency of the Guises was at an end and that it was she who ruled on her son's behalf. Until that time Catherine had been queen in name only but like Mary of Guise, she was an astute and capable politician. Although she loved her husband, Henri was entirely devoted, throughout his life, to Diane de Poitiers who was twenty years older than him. She had bided her time and removed her at the first possible opportunity. Now, she decided that all connections with the Guises must be removed unless they became a threat to her newfound power. The suggestion that Mary marry Charles was quickly dismissed. Mary's uncles subsequentially tried to negotiate a Spanish match to Don Carlos. The thought that she might marry the son of Philip II of Spain was one doomed to failure. Philip was an ally of Catherine de Medici through his marriage to Mary's schoolroom companion, Elizabeth. There was, it seemed, no place for Mary who handed over the queen of France's jewels to her mother-in-law the day after she became a widow. Then, clad in white, she withdrew into forty days of official mourning where she began to decide what she would do next.

Chapter Three

A Stuart Heir to Scotland and England

On 19 August 1561, Mary returned to Scotland. Before she arrived back in her homeland, the queen gave her people assurances that Calvinism would continue to be the country's official religion and that she would practice her own religion in private. Her older half-brother, James Stewart, to whom she granted the earldoms of Moray and Mar in 1562, supported her stand despite being in the pay of the English and having tried to persuade her to renounce Catholicism. Moray, who converted to Protestantism in 1556, recognised the need for moderation and Mary sensibly turned down the plans of the Catholic faction who wished to see a Counter-Reformation. The queen chose Moray and William Maitland of Lethington as her chief councillors as well as James Douglas, 4th Earl of Morton as her lord chancellor. This calmed fears about a Catholic resurgence even though her reliance on her half-brother and Morton's distrust of papacy meant that she would never be fully in control of her realm.

The queen soon discovered that despite her attempts to mollify her people, domestic affairs were not straight forward. The difficulties of Scottish politics were not confined to religion; it was shot through with feuds, personal rivalries and ambitious men seeking power for themselves. Mary was unfamiliar with the different nuances other than through her mother's correspondence and the men who presented themselves to her in the artificial setting of the French court. She knew about some of the changes that had happened in Scotland while she was growing up but she was reliant on Moray's support and advice about how to best manage her country, its people and her neighbours. Intelligence and her famous charm could only carry her so far. Besides which, many of Mary's subjects were suspicious of her because she was female, had been raised in France since the age of 5 and was, to all intents and purposes, culturally and linguistically French. She maintained her French customs, retained some of her French servants and advisors and even worse, was Catholic.

As queen it was also her duty to remarry and provide Scotland with an heir. The question of Mary's second marriage remained as fraught as it was during her infancy. It was all too evident that the Scottish aristocracy would not allow one from their own number to gain ascendency over the rest by means of a royal marriage. James Hamilton, the eldest son of Mary's former regent, the Duke of Châtellerault, who was a candidate for Elizabeth I's hand, began to court Mary before she returned to Scotland. She had known him since childhood; his father managed to gain a significant number of pledges in support of the union prior to Cardinal Beaton's assassination in 1546 and he remained next in line to the throne after his father until the queen had children of her own. Hamilton, styled as Earl of Arran soon after his father's elevation to a dukedom, had always believed himself to be Mary's rightful husband but Moray, who recognised the Hamiltons as rivals to his own power, managed to convince the queen that they were a threat to her crown. The queen turned Arran down and did not include him in her privy council. Her distrust was not without justification. Her rejection drew the disappointed earl into treason and madness. By 1562 Arran was confined first at St Andrews and then in Edinburgh Castle.

On 29 July 1565 Mary married Henry Stuart, Lord Darnley, who was also her second cousin and three years younger than her. Mary's new husband was both tall and handsome but the union displeased the English queen, Elizabeth, as it appeared to her that Mary was consolidating her claim to the English throne by marriage to Darnley, whose mother was Lady Margaret Douglas, the daughter of Margaret Tudor through her second marriage to the Earl of Angus. The former was known to be Catholic while Darnley's father, Matthew Stewart, 4th Earl of Lennox's, allegiances shifted with the political climate. The shift to Stuart from Stewart reflected the influence of the French language. Whatever the spelling of her new surname, it wasn't long before Mary found herself mired in a moral and political dilemma occasioned by the inequality of her marriage.

Darnley, denied the crown matrimonial by Mary, descended into jealousy and drunkenness. He was able to persuade a number of Scottish lords, who felt that their own power was decreasing, that Mary relied more on her foreign servants than on them. Matters were not helped when the queen insisted that all official documents must be signed first by her and then by her husband, or at least by a stamp that was made bearing his signature and which she gave to her Italian secretary, David Rizzio. On 9 March 1566, by which time Mary was five months pregnant, having accused Rizzio of unwarranted familiarities with the queen and, at Darnley's prompting, a group of men burst into her private chamber in Holyrood. They dragged Rizzio screaming from Mary's presence and murdered him before throwing the body down the stairs. The principal plotters, the lords Morton, Ruthven and Lindsey, held Mary captive in her own chambers at Holyrood that night in fear of her, and her unborn child's, life.

At some point during the time that Mary remained at Holyrood, Darnley was persuaded that his co-conspirators had no intention of giving him any real power. The queen, still believing that she was in danger, fled to Dunbar Castle, taking her husband with her despite her aversion to the man she married through choice such a short time previously. Mary knew that Darnley had to acknowledge the child she carried was his, if the infant was to be recognised as her heir. She refused to allow Darnley's father, Matthew Stewart, to accompany them as he had also been part of the group responsible for Rizzio's death. Rizzio was mourned by very few apart from the queen but it did not take long for men loyal to the rightful monarch to gather troops on her behalf. Mary was able to return to Edinburgh on 18 March 1566, accompanied by the earls of Bothwell and Huntly, while Lennox was banished from court. Mary chose to stay behind the protective walls of Edinburgh Castle and to make a will that left her kingdom to her child in the event of her death during its delivery. She did not name Darnley as one of the three designated regents.

At the beginning of June, the queen withdrew to her lying-in chamber with her midwife, Margaret Asteane, to await the arrival of her first child. Here, she gave birth to a son, named James, on 19 June. Having been forced to confront rumours that the baby was Rizzio's rather than Darnley's, the queen was quick to summon her husband to view his son for the first time. When she demanded that her ladies bear witness to the truth of the matter, she knew that no one could dispute the resemblance of her son to his father. Mary predicted that the boy would rule over both Scotland and England. She sent Sir James Melville to Greenwich with the news. His memoirs describe a meeting with the English queen amid a scene of merriness, which was laid to one side with his news, causing her to exclaim that she was 'but of barren stock'[1] while Mary was 'lighter of a fair son'.[2] Elizabeth recognised that even if she chose not to name an heir, James' bloodline and gender ensured that he would succeed her as king. In Scotland, Mary had not yet realised that her own throne was now at risk for the very same reasons.

The arrival of an heir provided dynastic continuity and the fact that he was a boy suggested, to Mary, that God smiled upon her rule. Before the queen's customary month of being retired from the world was complete, she took James to Stirling Castle along with his wet nurse, Helen Little, who was provided with a new taffeta gown by the queen's tailor.[3] The queen rewarded the wet nurse for her service with lands at Kingsbarns in Fife which yielded an income of £20 each year, as well as 60 capons, which were part of the rental terms from her tenants.[4] Little's daughter, Sarah Graym and two servants assisted her but James' day-to-day care lay in the hands of the wife of Arthur Forbes of Rires, or Reres, who was the keeper of Falkland Palace, a role he inherited from his own father. Margaret Beaton, Lady Rires was one of the queen's ladies in waiting. In addition to being the niece of the assassinated Cardinal Beaton, she was also aunt to one of the queen's famous 'Four Marys' – Mary Beaton. The whole family were fiercely supportive of the Queen of Scots who was fearful that Darnley might attempt to kidnap her son, as heir to the throne, and rule as James' regent. Five more young women, from noble families, were appointed, at different times, to rock the king's cradle.

It was the duty of James' staff to provide care for the king under the direction of a governess who oversaw the nursery and reported to Mary. At Stirling, this task was allotted to Annabell Murray, Countess of Mar and wife of John Erskine, the custodian of the castle. Annabell was one of Mary of Guise's ladies-in-waiting, as well as a personal friend of the queen, while John, Mary's first tutor, had accompanied her to France. She created him Earl of Mar in 1565, taking the title from her half-brother, James Stewart who remained Earl of Moray. The earls of Mar claimed an ancestral right to raise the kings of Scotland. For Mary the appointment may have offered a sense of stability and personal security. She knew that if her son fell into the wrong hands, that he would provide any rebellion designed to place him on the throne a veneer of legitimacy.

The great medieval fortification at Stirling offered protection and familiarity. It meant that Mary did not have to pretend that her relationship with Darnley was mended. She sought advice from Moray about the inconvenient matter of her husband. Also included in discussions about Darnley were the Earl of Bothwell and Lord Huntly. There was a possibility that Mary might divorce Darnley, but if her marriage was annulled questions would arise about Prince James' legitimacy. She had no intention of permitting her son's right to the throne to be questioned so the idea was unthinkable.

Mary returned to Edinburgh on 6 September 1566 but was back in Stirling when James was baptised on 17 December 1566. His godparents were Elizabeth I of England, Charles IX of France and the Duke of Savoy; they were all represented by proxy. The baptism was carried out according to Catholic rites by the Archbishop of St Andrews which meant that the Earl of Bedford, a puritan, who delivered Elizabeth's baptism gift of a gold font did not witness proceedings although her proxy, the Countess of Argyll, held the baby whilst the bishop named him. Bedford was joined in the courtyard outside the medieval chapel at Stirling Castle by the Earls of Huntly, Moray and Bothwell, until they were able to re-join the celebrations, which included a masque created by George Buchanan who would be appointed as the king's tutor. The festivities lasted for three days, concluding with a fireworks display, during which time there was no sign of Lord Darnley, who preferred to be absent from a gathering that refused to recognise him as Scotland's rightful king.

The king's aunt, Jane Stewart, Countess of Argyll, an illegitimate daughter of James V, had been raised in the household of Mary of Guise. She was in France for at least part of Mary's childhood, being known as *Mademoiselle la bâtarde d'Eccosse*[5], and was at her half-sister's side when Rizzio was murdered. It was a sign of the times that the General Assembly was later able to force the countess to make a public penance for her part in the baptism, which demonstrated a falling away from the Protestant faith.

After the celebrations were over, Darnley travelled to his father's estates near Glasgow where he became ill with smallpox or the effects of syphilis. The queen's enemies spread the rumour that he was being poisoned. Meanwhile,

Mary, having considered the alternatives, knew that even if she did not trust her husband that she had to appear reconciled with him. And for a time when she persuaded him to return to Edinburgh to convalesce, the queen's marriage appeared to improve. It was not wise for him to stay with the court if he suffered from a contagious disease, so he stayed at the nearby Old Provost's Lodgings at Kirk o'Field where Mary could visit him every day.

On the evening of Sunday, 9 February 1567, there was an explosion that destroyed the lodging and the nearby Prebendaries' Chamber. The bodies of Darnley and his servant were found dressed in their nightclothes in a nearby orchard. The pair survived the explosion, tried to escape and were strangled as they fled. Suspicion fell on the queen and James Hepburn, 4th Earl of Bothwell. Guzman de Silva, the Spanish ambassador, informed his master that he had no doubt as to Mary's complicity in the crime.[6] It is impossible to know whether the queen was complicit or if she narrowly escaped assassination herself. She was in the habit of sleeping at Kirk o'Field, on another floor to her husband, when she visited him. It was only because she was attending the wedding celebrations of one of her pages that she was not present on the evening of the explosion.

Three months after the assassination Mary married Bothwell, who remained the prime suspect for Darnley's murder despite being acquitted by a jury the previous month. The circumstances of the wedding added to the widespread belief that the queen was involved in the death of her second husband. Many people considered the queen's third marriage, made on 15 May 1567 according to Protestant rites, unlawful because they were Catholic. Or if they were Protestant they questioned the validity of Bothwell's divorce from Lady Jean Gordon, his wife of just over a year, less than a fortnight prior to his wedding to the queen. Even now historians are divided as to whether Mary married the earl willingly or not. It is certain that on 21 April, Mary spent the day at Stirling with James. It was a private visit so she only took a small escort with her. From there she travelled to Linlithgow intending to return to Edinburgh on the 23 April. However, when Bothwell and a force of approximately 800 armed men waylaid her, she agreed, willingly or not, to accompany him to Dunbar Castle which was a royal residence. Once there, Mary was locked in, with Bothwell's wife and sister to act as chaperones, and the castle surrounded by Bothwell's men. The earl stated that his actions were to protect Mary from her enemies. Sources are divided as to whether the kidnap was real or pretended but it seems certain that while at Dunbar that Bothwell shared the queen's bed. In the sixteenth century rape was a crime, but when an unwed queen was abused it allowed her attacker to pursue a crown. For Mary to seek justice after being sexually assaulted was, perhaps, unthinkable. To complicate matters still further, Bothwell possessed an agreement made by many Protestant lords known as the Ainslie Tavern bond which agreed to him marrying Mary, and by 1567 there were few people that she could trust. The queen recognised that she needed to make the best of a bad situation. So, she pardoned the earl for kidnapping her, elevated him to a dukedom, waited for him to divorce his wife, Jean Gordon, and then prepared for her third marriage. Cecil's spies reported, even before Bothwell was tried and found innocent of Darnley's murder, that the queen intended to wed him. Even more difficult than the rumours, was the fact that as a Catholic, Mary must have understood that Bothwell could never truly be divorced for his former wife and, even if it was the case, her marriage by a Protestant priest would not be recognised by the papacy. She chose, instead, to argue that her new husband's former union with Jean Gordon was invalid even though Jean, who was a Catholic, was in possession of a papal dispensation permitting it.

A group of Protestant nobles, known as the Confederate Lords, including men who previously supported Mary, took up arms claiming that they wished to punish Darnley's murder and free the queen from Bothwell. A rumour spread that the duke intended to gain custody of the prince and that the queen had effectively deserted James, as well as placing him in danger through her ill-considered marriage. A month after she married Bothwell, the queen and her supporters faced the Confederate Lords at Carberry Hill near Edinburgh in a stand-off. Bothwell escaped while Mary was made prisoner at Lochleven where she miscarried twins. A week after her capture, the so-called Casket letters were discovered, containing Mary's letters to Bothwell. Public opinion, inflamed by John Knox (the leader of Scotland's Reformation), turned against the queen and, in the face of intimidation, she was forced to abdicate in favour of her son on 24 July 1567. One of the leaders of the Lords, Archibald Campbell, 5th Earl of Argyll and estranged husband of Janet Stewart, was horrified by the idea of deposing Mary from her throne and changed sides.

Argyll's defection was not sufficient to alter the course of events. James was crowned at Stirling on 29 July 1567. James Douglas, 4th Earl of Morton, who played a leading part in the murder of Rizzio, and the reformer, John Erskine of Dun, swore to defend the realm and the Protestant faith in his name. John Knox preached the sermon but Moray was absent from proceedings. He had taken no part in his half-sister's deposition and had left Edinburgh the day before Lord Darnley's murder. He had a knack for avoiding the public gaze while being involved behind the scenes. The coronation was no different. Moray was nominated as Regent on 22 August, even though the former regent, Châtellerault, made his own claim to the regency, as heir to the throne, just as he had done when Mary was an infant. The Earl of Lennox, James' grandfather, was also considered to have legitimate grounds to claim the position, being the king's nearest male relation. In England, Moray's regency was encouraged by William Cecil because the new regent was committed to an Anglo-Scottish accord. The earl, whose title was not hereditary, was also reliant upon English support. It helped that Moray was prepared to appear in the guise of a reluctant regent to overcome Elizabeth I's antipathy for the state of affairs.

Mar was now responsible for the safekeeping of a king who was also a potential heir to the throne of Elizabeth I of England. De Silva, the Spanish ambassador, reported to his master, Philip II, that the earl was taking no chances and was keeping the infant king under a strong guard.[7] At Stirling the nursery turned into the king's household but it remained largely unchanged, even though its staff were now carefully itemised to include Helen Little's servants Helen Blyth and Gilbert Ramsay.[8] Mar and his countess ensured that their kin were close to the king but the servants who cared for him stayed with him throughout his childhood years, ensuring that despite the political turbulence that marked the politics of Scotland, his nursery and household provided a stable home for James. As Mar was respected by all sides there was no question of appointing a new governor. Sir James Melville described the earl as 'well-loved and liked of every man for his good qualities and great discretion'.[9] Knox was less fulsome in his praise of the Countess of Mar, whom he described as a Jezebel.

The deposed queen spent the next ten months in the custody of Sir William Douglas; King James VI remained at Stirling in the care of his guardians; and Bothwell fled to Denmark where he died in prison in 1578. Within a year of Mary's surrender at Carberry, a civil war between those who fought in the name of the queen and those who fought in the name of her son, King James VI, had broken out between the opposing factions. Argyll became the leader of the Queen's Party while his former friend, Moray, headed the King's Party. There would be five years of fighting before the adversaries came to terms with one another in February 1573 with the signing of the Pacification of Perth.

In 1568, Mary was able to escape from Lochleven, but the Battle of Langside, near Glasgow, fought on 13 May 1568, was won decisively by her political opponents and she was forced into exile, landing in England at Workington. De Silva, the Spanish ambassador, wrote to Philip II, identifying the difficulty that now faced Elizabeth I. To treat Mary as a sovereign would offend the Scots but to keep a queen in custody would be a challenge to the concept of monarchy. There was no suggestion that Elizabeth might grant her cousin any freedom without raising everyone's suspicions.[10] Mary would remain in England as a prisoner for the next nineteen years.

In captivity, aside from writing innumerable letters, many of them in complex ciphers, trying to secure her freedom, the queen's French upbringing offered some solace. Her education fostered a love of books as well as embroidery. They both proved to be diversions for a woman often kept in close confinement. During her time in Scotland, Mary amassed a library of 243 books, including the subjects of moral philosophy, astronomy and cosmography as well as languages including French, Spanish and Italian. Many of the books were written in Latin, which she continued to study in the company of her tutor, George Buchanan. The collection also contained histories, poetry and romances. During the summer of 1566, when she feared that she might die during childbirth, Mary left all her Greek and Latin texts to the University of St Andrews to form the basis of a library. The rest of her collection she bequeathed to Mary Beaton. They were all left behind, in Edinburgh Castle, when she fled in 1568. The following year they were delivered into the care of Moray who personally destroyed six overtly Catholic texts.[11] Mary rebuilt her collection during her captivity to the extent that when she was moved from house to house, her custodians complained about the books which also had to be transported wherever she went. Today the most famous of these is the illustrated Book of Hours she carried to her execution on 8 February 1587 in the great hall at Fotheringhay Castle. During the course of her imprisonment, Mary's devotions offered not only a source of comfort but turned her into a Catholic martyr. It is perhaps not surprising that the book of prayers became a relic.

Chapter Four

The Making of a King

James Stewart, 1st Earl of Moray, James VI's uncle, returned to Scotland from Dieppe[1] on 11 August aboard an English vessel arranged by Elizabeth I's minister, William Cecil. Having visited Mary in her prison he assumed the role of regent for his nephew on 22 August 1567. Scotland was well used to the concept of government by a regent, supported by a privy council, during royal minority. Moray was the fifth of eight regents appointed during the reigns of James V, Mary, Queen of Scots and James VI. The sixteenth century began with the regency of Margaret Tudor in 1513 during the minority of James V, progressed via the Duke of Albany who was regent from 1515 until 1524, before the minority government of Mary, Queen of Scots that began in December 1542, shortly after her birth. Now, it became Moray's task, as it had been his predecessors, to protect his sovereign and their kingdom until James VI came of age to rule for himself.

The earl was qualified for the task in the eyes of those opposed to Mary, being Protestant and having acted as his half-sister's adviser. Moray's perceived reluctance to take on the regency was another aspect in his favour so far as many of the nobility of Scotland was concerned. William Cecil, Elizabeth I's minister, welcomed a reformer who would adopt a policy of friendship between the two nations, even if both of them were required to placate Elizabeth who was alarmed at the prospect of a reigning queen being deposed by her own people. The difference between Moray and the earlier regents was that Mary's supporters, led by the Earls of Argyll, Huntly and Arran refused to recognise Moray's authority or the right of James to wear his mother's crown while she lived. The Hamilton family's support for the queen was another factor in Moray's selection as it would have been impossible for Châtellerault or any of his sons to claim the role of regent as immediate heirs to the throne.

In England there was the additional difficulty of hosting the Catholic claimant to the English throne. Elizabeth I could neither free her cousin nor send her to France or to Spain because of Mary's value as a pawn in European Counter Reformation politics and, for similar reasons, nor could the English make war on Mary's behalf on the Presbyterian Scots. In September 1568, Moray eased Elizabeth's dilemma by presenting the York Conference, arranged to discuss the terms of an Anglo-Scottish treaty, with the so-called Casket Letters. The contents of the documents, which included sonnets and love letters said to be written by Mary to Bothwell before Darnley's death, helped to place the blame for her husband's murder on the queen's shoulders and justify her deposition, irrelevant of whether they were forged or not. The letters also formed the evidence which was used by James' teachers to accuse his mother of murdering his father and to validate her overthrow. It was essential that the boy grew up in the hands of his mother's enemies believing in his own right to rule in Mary's stead. George Buchanan, James' tutor, even went so far as to implicate the king's nurse, Margaret Beaton, in the conspiracy as a go-between between Mary and Bothwell.[2]

Moray's agenda in Scotland was to create political stability. He needed to unite the different factions within the so-called King's Party and to vanquish the men of the Queen's Party who continued to support Mary's right to rule. One of the first things he did, on the advice of John Knox, was to pardon prisoners captured at the Battle of Langside rather than execute them for treason. Even so, the first years of James' reign were punctuated by a series of bloody episodes, beginning in June 1568 when Moray took an army to subdue Mary's supporters. His orders included the burning of Rutherglen Castle near Glasgow which belonged to the Hamilton family.

At Stirling, surrounded by high walls, the thirteen-month-old monarch's nursery household continued largely unchanged while the Marian civil war, that followed Mary's abdication and flight, was conducted around him. James' staff included Helen Little and Lady Rires, seven rockers, two ladies who may have been responsible for the care of his clothing and nappies,[3] a laundress named Margaret Balcomie who once washed the linen for Mary, Queen of Scots at Linlithgow,[4] and a pastry chef, as well as more menial servants who cooked and cleaned for the household. James' wet nurse, Helen Little, was helped by her daughter, Sarah (or Nanis) Gray, and two servants,

Helen Blyth and Gilbert Ramsey. Another of Helen's daughter's, Grissel, is thought to have looked after the king's clothes and was described, in 1579, as a seamstress.[5] Also among the household were a group of viola players who would be associated with the king's musical education but who, for the time being, provided entertainment. The four Hudson brothers came to Scotland with Lord Darnley but by 1568 James, Robert, Thomas and William Hudson were given £50 a year for their livery and provided with their own table for dinner in the royal household.[6] The Hudsons remained part of the king's household throughout his minority and continued to serve him when he became an adult. By 1589, only three of the brothers were in the king's domestic service. James Hudson appears as the king's buyer in London,[7] Robert was treasurer of the Chapel Royal and Thomas, who was part of the Castalian band of poets, appears to have had a hand in preparing court masques.[8]

James later accused Helen Little of drunkenness. The information was recorded by the king's French physician, Theodore de Mayerne, who became his doctor in 1611. De Mayerne blamed James' wet nurse for the king's inability to walk until the age of 5. He suggested that the king's early motor difficulties which continued into his adulthood stemmed from an inferior milk supply during his infancy. If this was the case, Helen Little was a poor choice as a wet nurse by Mary, Queen of Scots and both Lady Rires and the Countess of Mar failed in their task of caring for the king. It had been established since classical times that a wet nurse should be an experienced mother, be in good health, of placid temperament, be abstentious and in possession of upright personal habits. Doctors were convinced that there was a connection between the personality of the nurse and the quality of milk produced. It was also claimed that the woman's characteristics would be transferred to the child through her milk. Soranus of Ephesus, who wrote a midwifery text in the second century AD, thought that alcohol destroyed both the body and the soul of the nurse as well as spoiling the milk she produced. James' physicians should have monitored Helen's diet to ensure that the food she ate was digestible and wholesome, so that her milk was of a superior quality. Similarly, in England the Ordinances for a Royal Birth, compiled by Lady Margaret Beaufort for the care of her own Tudor grandchildren, stipulated that the health of the wet nurse be monitored for as long as she was caring for a member of the royal family.[9] For the same reason a wet nurse would have been discouraged from eating foods that contained garlic, onion or too much spice. It seems unlikely that Little would have been tolerated if she was a habitual drunk; the only caveat being the fear of unsettling the baby's health by a change of milk supply and the fear that the infant might die as a result. Whatever the cause, James suffered with pain in his legs throughout his life and struggled with a clumsy gait. In August 1584 the French ambassador, Fontenay, visited the Scottish court and sent two long letters to Mary, Queen of Scots. In them he described the king as 'ungainly, his steps erratic and vagabond'.[10] It has been suggested that rather than Helen Little being at fault, James may have suffered from rickets, porphyria or even a neuromuscular disorder.[11] His son, Charles, was also slow to walk suggesting that the developmental delay may have been an inherited condition.

The personal consequences of Mary's deposition were far reaching. There was no maternal oversight of James' household and his upbringing, even though she remained in correspondence with the Countess of Mar and, on occasion, with the earl. From her confinement in England, she sent James letters and gifts. It is said that she sent him an alphabet and a pony for his second birthday. The letters that Mary sent were never delivered because they were addressed to a prince rather than a king. By the time he was 4, the Scottish Parliament ordained that there was to be no correspondence between the pair, except through the filter of the privy council. Elizabeth I took an interest in her cousin's son, but her chief concern was that he was raised a Protestant and that the influence of France in Scotland remained negligible. Shortly before Mary's forced abdication in July 1567, Elizabeth wrote to her ambassador in Scotland, Sir Nicholas Throckmorton, requiring him to 'deal with the lords having charge of the young prince for the committing of him unto our realm'.[12] She suggested that the baby would 'enjoy surety and quietness'[13] in England. Later still, it was suggested that Margaret Douglas, Countess of Lennox might care for her grandson if he was transferred to England but the Scots did not want to lose control over James, and Elizabeth, while perceiving the potential benefits of guardianship of the Stuart Crown, also recognised the danger of welcoming into her realm a male heir to her own throne.

At first the royal household was composed largely of women. Many of them were of noble rank. The girls who rocked James' cradle included Christiane Stewart, the daughter of Lord Coldingham. She was one of the king's kinswomen as the granddaughter of James V and his mistress Elizabeth Carmichael. Her father, John Stewart, was among the group who sailed to France with Mary, Queen of Scots in 1548. Moray was careful to ensure that the women, and by association their families, accepted him as regent. On one occasion he presented the countess with £500 Scottish pounds to give to the rockers.[14] By the time the king was about 2 years old he would have been weaned. Little and her assistants chewed the food to feed to James. It was also their task to toilet train the king, play with him, watch that he did not injure himself and care for his basic requirements. As well as looking after the physical needs of the king, it was the household's task to ensure that as he grew, he knew his letters, his prayers and manners. Even though he was still in long skirts it was time for James to begin his lessons. Alphabets often took the form of horn books, a wooden board mounted with a piece of paper and then covered by a thin piece of cattle horn, containing twenty-four rather than twenty-six letters because 'u' and 'v' were the same as were 'i' and 'j'. The latter was often used as the capital form of its companion while 'u' appeared in the middle of words and 'v' was written at their beginning. The teaching aid might also contain numbers and even the Lord's Prayer.

There was an expectation that James would look and behave like a king at all times when he made rare public appearances but it was also the responsibility of James' governess and nurses to discipline him. Although he was a king, it was expected that he would respect his guardians and teachers. The humanist scholar Erasmus published a book on the education of children in 1530, in seventeen sections, addressed to the son of Adolph, Prince of Veere, entitled *On Civility in Children.* The text describes the importance of behaving in a civilised manner and covered everything from the correct way of blowing your nose to how to behave at table. Unfortunately, James does not appear to have acquired the courtly behaviour which 11-year-old Henry of Burgundy was expected to conduct himself, or even those manners set out in a medieval book on the subject by Robert Grosseteste and reproduced by Lydgate as *Table Manners for Children.* Fontenay commented that James was 'uncivil and in speaking, eating, clothes, games and conversation in the company of women'.[15] Much later, Sir Anthony Weldon, the attributed author of *The Court and Character of King James I*, described the king's personal habits, which included his habit of leaning on other men's shoulders because of his physical weakness and 'his fingers ever in that walk fiddling about his codpiece'[16] when he ruled England as well as Scotland. Weldon was not an unbiased commentator. He was dismissed from his court post as Clerk of the Green Cloth by James in 1617, having written an abusive pamphlet about the Scots. The attack on the king, which included the suggestion of James' homosexuality, was not published until 1650. The character assassination of the king, which summed him up as 'the wisest fool in Christendom', included the suggestion that 'he never washed his hands'.[17] Handwashing was an important part of etiquette both before and after meals. In a world where people were judged by their politeness and manners, the suggestion that James lacked personal social niceties was an indictment on the Stuart's political acumen, and, by association, all the Stuart kings that followed, as it inferred he was not fit to rule. The saying 'manners makes the man' was an apt one for life during the sixteenth and seventeenth centuries.

Erasmus, a Catholic reformer, who was concerned that children grew up 'neither fearing God, neither regarding either manners or obedience'[18] would have at least approved of the importance placed upon James' religious education from infancy onwards. The whole of the king's household at Stirling was managed on a day-to-day basis by John Cunningham who was master of the household. One of his responsibilities was to ensure that everyone assembled for daily worship. They were guided in their prayers by John Dunkeson who, as the king's chaplain, was responsible for 'godly and honourable conversation' within the household as well as prayers and preaching.[19] It was essential, according to Moray, who habitually listened to Bible verse while he dined, that no 'ungodly and light behaviour be given by any person' for fear that 'imitation may do hurt to his Highness's tenderness'.[20] The king was not the head of the Church in Scotland in the same way that his English cousins were heads of the Church in England, but his guardians were determined that he should be thoroughly grounded in Presbyterian tenets. The Scottish Kirk, thanks to men like John Knox, the Protestant Lords of the Congregation and the Reformation Parliament of 1560, not only ended Scotland's relationship with the Catholic Church but ensured its independence from the Crown. However, no one wanted the renewed possibility of religious discord between a monarch and his or her people. James would one day govern Scotland and Parliament passed an article in December 1567 which insisted that in future:

> all kings, princes and magistrates which hereafter in any time to come shall happen to reign and bear rule over the realm, at their first entry, before they be crowned and inaugurated, shall make their faithful liege and promise to the kirk of God, that they shall maintain, defend and by all lawful means set forward the true religion of Jesus Christ publicly professed and established within this realm, even as they are obliged and morally bound in the law of God, as well in Deuteronomy as in the eleventh chapter of the second book of Kings; and as they crave obedience of their subjects, so the bond and contract to be mutual and reciprocal in all times coming between the prince and God and his faithful people according to the word of God.[21]

At the same time the General Assembly of Scottish ministers asserted that the king should be a defender of the Kirk and a 'comfortable instrument of God'.[22] It meant that ideology and theology were central to James' education from his earliest days. The king was expected to learn Biblical knowledge, and apply established doctrinal and moral values to his daily life. Obedience to his elders was a part of that learning process. Essentially, it was the nursery staff's task, overseen by the Countess of Mar, to mould the king to function successfully in Scotland's Presbyterian society. On a theological level it was also a matter of urgency that he learned to read as soon as possible. Personal study of the Bible was fundamental to godly belief, and personal salvation, which, in turn, would help James rule his people wisely.

James VI' bedchamber at Stirling might have been fit for a Protestant king but it was a gloomy place for a young child. His bed was draped with black damask and even his pillows were fringed with black. Perhaps to assist the king in understanding the nature of monarchy, and to remind him of his illustrious lineage, James' bedchamber contained a painting of James V. It was a visible reminder of the child's descent from the Tudors and his claim to the contested throne in England as well as providing a role model. James V was barely out of babyhood when his own father, James IV, was killed during the Battle of Flodden in 1513.

In May 1568, the regent wrote to Mar asking him to remove everyone from Stirling who was not part of Erskine's own family or essential to the care of the king. Moray knew that whoever controlled James would have the upper hand in the civil war. For the King's Party, James was the means by which Mary's overthrow could be justified and the regency legitimised. During his early years, the king was often depicted as a godly infant pleading for justice for his murdered father. Darnley's parents even went so far as to commission a painting depicting James VI dressed in royal robes kneeling beside his father's tomb. The Earl of Lennox and his Countess kneel behind their grandson, while Darnley's younger brother, Charles, is at the back of the family group. Insets illustrating Henry's murder and Mary's surrender at Carberry as well as a series of explanatory inscriptions drive home the message of the legitimacy of Mary's removal and her son's ascent to the throne. James' authority as rightful monarch, which he was too young to wield, was manifested in the ceremonial attached to his coronation and his appearance at the opening of parliament.

In order to reduce the risk of abduction it was essential that the king travelled infrequently from Stirling's imposing fortress and that his household remained as small as possible. It was convenient for leaders of the King's Party that James could be kept isolated. Without him they would not have enjoyed a right to rule. Moray, whose leadership required him to steer his way through a quagmire of shifting factions and double dealing, stated that James' steward was to provide only for those men and women identified on the household roll. Outside the castle, the Scottish nobility continued to vie for power. By June 1569, George Gordon, 5th Earl of Huntly, an ally of the Earl of Argyll, submitted hostages to the regent in a show of good faith and surrendered royal ordinance kept at Huntly Castle. The queen's supporters continued to dominate the north of Scotland as well as holding strategic fortifications including Dumbarton Castle, and thanks to a change of loyalty by its captain, Sir William Kircaldy of Grange, Edinburgh Castle. Queen Elizabeth I wrote to Mar and his countess in January 1568 commending their care of the boy she described as 'the Prince, our godson'[23] and assuring James' governor that she intended to act in a manner 'to the sureity and benefit of the child, to the continuance of the Earl's government as to us thought metest'.[24] The queen concluded that James' security was essential and that in the event of him being in danger, the English could be relied upon to support the royal household and its governor. She was not the only one concerned with the arrangement's Mar made to keep his ward safe. In 1570, Mary, Queen of Scots sent a letter to the earl, 'desiring him to keep her son the Prince from the hands of her enemies'.[25] Mary's letter was hardly needed. The twists and turns of the Marian war meant that James was more closely guarded than ever by the end of January 1570.

On 23 January 1570, the first of James VI's regents was assassinated. Moray was travelling from Stirling to Edinburgh via Linlithgow. A gunman, James Hamilton of Bothwellhaugh, was waiting for Mary's half-brother there, shooting him in the stomach before fleeing. The regent was carried to Linlithgow Palace where he died, becoming the first recorded head of state to be assassinated by a firearm. His funeral, which was led by John Knox, attracted several thousand mourners. Later he came to be called the 'Good Regent' because he recognised the authority of the Kirk and due to his own religious practices. James was later less glowing in his description of the man who 'unnaturally rebelled and procured the ruin of his owne sovran and sister'. [26] In the aftermath of Moray's murder, Mar tightened the security at Stirling still further and wrote to Elizabeth I asking for her support in the face of the new danger his young ward faced. In 1572, Queen Elizabeth wrote of 'the universal good report we hear of your carefulness and circumspection',[27] to describe the countess' care of the king during his infancy.

It was five months before another regent was appointed. During that time the King's Party were leaderless and Scotland war-torn. The privy council assumed responsibility for both governing and the care of the king until a new regent could be appointed. In March 1570, when James was 4 years old, they appointed George Buchanan, who was Principal of St Leonard's College, St Andrews, to direct the king's education. He was a graduate of both St Andrews and the Sorbonne and was widely regarded as the leading humanist academic in Britain at the time. He would inspire both awe and fear in the king. In later life, James told one of his courtiers that he reminded him of the Scottish academic, and the king trembled at the man's approach. As well as being a harsh task master, Buchanan did not believe in sparing the rod even if his pupil was a king.

Most boys began their formal education at about the age of 6 or 7 years, at the same time that they were deemed old enough to leave the care of their mothers and nurses. The Education Act of 1496 made it compulsory for the eldest sons of Scottish landowners, aged 8 or 9 years, to study law, the arts and Latin for a minimum of three years. The aim of the act was to ensure that regional justice and local government was administered effectively. Protestant reformers and humanists sought to extend Scotland's education system to include other tiers of society as a way of ensuring godliness and morality.

James was still somewhat young to begin his formal education when Buchanan was appointed but his council knew that he needed to be prepared to rule his realm. In addition, while Mar was Protestant, the countess' beliefs were more suspect, as was her friendship with the king's mother, and the council may have been concerned about the extent of her influence. Annabell Murray was a stern foster mother who occasionally terrified the little boy in her charge but the king viewed her as a substitute for his own mother. In about 1572, the king wrote a letter to her in which he referred to her as Lady 'Minny' which means 'mother'. By providing James with tutors and moving him into a more masculine environment, the influence of Annabell would be reduced and his shaping as Scotland's king could begin in earnest.

The countess was not the only suspect noble woman resident in the castle. Jane Stewart, Countess of Argyll, James' aunt, had been raised at court and was close to her half-sister, Mary, Queen of Scots. Jane, who fled from her husband never to return in 1567, despite the joint efforts of John Knox and Mary, Queen of Scots[28] to bring the couple back together, was part of the Countess of Mar's household because she would not agree to the terms of Argyll's divorce settlement, believing that his offer of 10,000 merks was insufficient to keep her in comfort for the rest of her life.[29] The earl, who wanted an heir to inherit his titles and his estates, arranged for her to be outlawed at the Commissary Court of Edinburgh when she refused to return to him or agree to a divorce. Aside from being something of a scarlet woman in the eyes of the Kirk, Jane's loyalty to her sister was unshakable. She witnessed Rizzio's murder and is likely to have been with Mary, Queen of Scots when she gave birth to James. It was Jane who acted at Elizabeth I's proxy at his baptism and incurred the Kirk's anger for taking part in a Catholic rite. The countess was not a fit person to be so close to the king, whose character was beginning to take shape, any more than Lady Rires, or Reres, a former companion of both Mary and her mother Mary of Guise, who was part of James' household at Stirling from 1566. They could not be trusted not to provide a more sympathetic view of Mary than the one that the King's Party needed to maintain. Presbyterian Scotland could ill afford for James to have any empathy with his own mother. Nor did they wish to run the risk of the king turning papist when he grew up.

Buchanan, a Calvinist, was 64 years old when he assumed the responsibility for teaching James. He had a long association with the Stewart[30] family as well as a reputation as a scholar in Paris and Portugal. He was appointed by James V as tutor to one of his illegitimate sons as well as tutoring Mary, Queen of Scots in Latin and Calvinism when she returned from France. At that time, Buchanan described James' mother as having a 'surpassing loveliness of form…and fine qualities of mind'.[31] When the queen sent Elizabeth I a ring, it was with Latin verses composed with the help of Buchanan. However, the death of Darnley and Mary's subsequent marriage to Bothwell led to him revising his opinion of the queen, blaming her upbringing in France and her Catholicism on her vices. He claimed that 'the seeds of virtue'[32] were 'wizened by the allurements of luxury'[33] and that as a consequence 'a surface gloss of virtue'[34] hid the queen's corruption. It was he who prepared the indictment against James' mother and testified at Westminster about a poem, one of the Casket Letters, alleged to have been written by Mary to Bothwell when, he claimed, Darnley was still alive. In 1571 he published *A Detection of the Doings of Mary Queen of Scots* which explored the role of the queen in the murder of her husband, her adultery and illegal marriage to Bothwell. The Marian Party regarded him as the mouthpiece for the men who sought to demolish the queen's reputation. He was the ideal tutor to ensure that James learned to accept that his mother was a wicked woman and that her deposition was just. Buchanan emphasised his belief that James should be 'the most learned clerk in his dominions'.[35] He possessed no toleration for time wasting and frivolities such as dancing and music. He was aided by Peter Young, whose task it was to install a dislike of Catholicism in the king.[36] An assistant was essential since Buchanan's health was not always good and he was busy preparing works against the queen and her supporters, as well as writing a history of Scotland, *Rerum Scoticarum Historia*. In addition to the two scholars, Mar's brothers, David and Adam Erskine, the lay abbots of Dryburgh and Cambuskenneth, were responsible for his physical training as well as teaching him how to conduct himself as a monarch. Whatever the truth of the matter, and even if the king did have some motor difficulties, he was observed dancing, in 1579, by Henry Killigrew. James also learned how to play golf as is evidenced by ownership of two golfing gloves.[37] The inventory of James VI's library includes a gift of two golf clubs as well as bows, arrows and other archery equipment. As an adult, the king is known to have played tennis at Falkland Palace, a fact at odds with the idea of a shambolic and clumsy monarch. Henceforth, the Countess of Mar would no longer be responsible for her ward's education although it did not stop her intervening on his behalf on occasion. Once when Buchanan beat the boy for answering his tutor back, the countess reprimanded the tutor for laying hands on the king, who was the 'Lord's Anointed', to which Buchanan answered that if he whipped James' arse, she could kiss it.[38]

It was 11 July before James' grandfather, Matthew Stewart, Earl of Lennox, who also had a claim to the throne in the event of James' death, was appointed regent. In Scotland and in England there were concerns that the earl was intent only on continuing a feud with the Hamiltons and taking revenge for the death of Lord Darnley, rather than carrying the burden of government for his grandson. Lennox proved to be an unpopular choice with another faction because of the manner in which he sought the crown matrimonial for Darnley, which caused so many of Mary's problems. It did not help that Protestants viewed his religious beliefs with suspicion and everyone looked askance at the way his regency was backed by the English. Elizabeth I, who was persuaded of the benefits of Lennox's regency to England, did not trust him either and took the precaution of preventing James' paternal grandmother, Margaret Douglas, or his uncle, Charles Stewart, from returning to Scotland to join Lennox. Unsurprisingly, it was not long before Mary, Queen of Scots' supporters, led by Huntly, Argyll and Châtellerault, began to gather an army to provide an alternative to the new regency. Men who had supported the King's Party while Moray was regent changed sides because they did not feel able to serve the king's grandfather.

In October, Lennox confirmed Mar in his position as governor, adding that given his experience in raising kings 'there is no meter personage to commit the custody and education of his majesty unto, nor no more proper place for His Highness residence than within his Highness' castle of Stirling'.[39] The king's grandfather laid out ordinances for James' safety, which included prohibitions on moving the boy from the castle or permitting armed men to enter it unless they were pledged to James or to Lennox. He went on to list how many servants recognised visitors might bring with them. An earl might bring a maximum of three servants into the castle while a baron could only bring one man with him.[40] He also issued orders that his grandson was not to leave the safety of Stirling's fortifications. Like Moray before him, Lennox knew the value of his ward.

On 28 August 1571, James fulfilled his first public duty as king at the opening of parliament which was held in Stirling. He was dressed in a royal robe and addressed the lords stating that 'because my age will not suffer me to exercise my charge myself, by reason of my youth, I have given power to my grandsire as regent and tutor to me, and you to assist him therein, as you will answer to God and me hereafter'.[41] The lesson for James was that he was the rightful king of Scotland. His education at Buchanan's hands required him to develop an early understanding of his status and the obligations that went with it. It was a lesson he learned readily enough. On one occasion when he was told that a king should not be angry, he retorted that the royal arms contained a lion rather than a sheep. Despite the dour environment in which he was nurtured, James developed a dry sense of humour that he would retain throughout his life. It was not the lesson that Buchanan wished to teach. The tutor's *De jure regni* is known to have been circulated in manuscript form by 1570. In it he explored the relationship that should exist between a monarch and his people. It laid down the proposition that subjects were within their rights to depose an unworthy sovereign.

While Buchanan rehearsed the theory that he would teach his pupil in the coming years, the people of Scotland continued to wage war on one another. In Edinburgh, the keeper of Edinburgh Castle, William Kirkaldy of Grange, changed sides and fired on Lennox's men, forcing the regent to retreat to Stirling Castle. It meant that James' capital would be at the centre of a three-year siege while the garrison of Edinburgh Castle fought for the rights of Mary, Queen of Scots. George Gordon and Claud Hamilton, one of the 3rd Earl of Arran's younger brothers, another of Châtellerault's sons, pursued Lennox back to Stirling where Parliament was meeting on 3 September. When they arrived, dawn had not quite broken. It is unclear whether they intended to kidnap James or harm the regent. In the melee that followed, the Earl of Morton's home was set on fire and two of his men killed. The arrival of the Earl of Mar with a body of men from the castle forced the attackers to retreat but by then Lennox had already surrendered. In the chaos that followed the skirmish, he was shot in the back and his captor, David Spence of Wormeston, having been injured, was dragged from his horse and killed despite Lennox's demands that Spence, who treated the regent with honour, be spared. Lennox returned to the castle and was carried to his chamber where he died later the same day. He became the second of James' regents to be assassinated in less than two years, but on this occasion the king heard the warfare in the town and saw his bleeding grandfather carried from the courtyard to his deathbed.

Fears concerning the king's safety would only grow with the passage of time and in the same way that he was supposed to learn godly behaviour from his household, James learned to be suspicious of the people who surrounded him. Shortly after Lennox's death, bars were placed over the windows of James' chambers to prevent any kidnap attempt, and if he ever left the castle he was surrounded by a heavily armed escort. The boy was a prisoner in his own castle. Weldon described him as having a 'naturally timorous'[42] temperament and evidenced it with the fact that James wore padded doublets as a means of safeguarding himself when he was England's king. If he did, then it is perhaps understandable. He saw his grandfather murdered in front of him, was nurtured by tales of his father's slaying and received intelligence about attempts on the life of his cousin Elizabeth I as well as details about the murders of Henri III of France in 1589 and his successor, Henri IV, in 1610.

Meanwhile, Parliament elected a new regent. The candidates included the Earls of Argyll, Mar and Morton. James Douglas, 4th Earl of Morton, one of the key conspirators in Rizzio's death and who was implicated in Darnley's murder was perhaps the most powerful of James' nobles during the regencies of Moray and of Lennox, but he did not gain control over the king or Scotland. The Earl of Mar replaced Lennox as regent in 1571. Unlike his predecessors Mar was 'given to quietness and peace'[43] and set about healing the rifts between the different groups. James' widowed grandmother Margaret, Countess of Lennox, Henry VIII's niece wrote on occasion to Mar reminding him of the 'natural love'[44] that she bore towards the king, as well as sending her grandson gifts. More important than James knowing that someone loved him, was that she sought financial advances against her husband's estates and payment of any outstanding debts that Lennox acquired during the course of his role as regent.

Mar's regency was a short-lived one. He became unwell and returned to Stirling where he died unexpectedly on 28 October 1572. Gossip hinted that he was the victim of poison, administered – it was added – by the man who replaced him as regent.

Chapter Five

Educating A Protestant Prince

James Douglas, 4th Earl of Morton, a candidate for the regency in 1571, was now appointed to the office. He was associated with Rizzio's murder as well as the Ainslie Tavern Bond, that commended Bothwell as a husband for Queen Mary. During the next six years, even his detractors acknowledged that Morton was able to bring peace to Scotland. The care of the king, his household and custodianship of Stirling Castle passed to Mar's brother, Sir Alexander Erskine of Gogar, because the new Earl of Mar, one of the king's classroom companions, was still a minor himself. Buchanan continued as royal tutor. The scholar was a personal friend of Morton, as indeed he was of both Moray and Lennox.[1]

After the fall of Edinburgh Castle in May 1573, Morton sent a casket to Stirling containing gold buttons with white and red enamelling, which once belonged to Mary, Queen of Scots, so that Annabell Murray could have them sewn onto the king's clothes. In May 1574, James received his first adult clothing made from red taffeta.[2] The breeching of the king meant that his governess, should, in theory, no longer have had an influence over James' household or education. However, Stirling remained the countess's home and Lady Minny was the closest person the king had to a mother. When Sir Henry Killigrew, a representative of Elizabeth I, visited James in 1574, he described the suspicion with which the king's tutor held James' female care givers and the tensions between the two groups. Buchanan, who was something of a misanthrope, told the English Ambassador that he was 'desirous to have him from the handling of womene by whome he is yet guyded and kept, saving when he goeth in his booke'.[3] Despite his views, Lady Mar did not intend to relinquish her oversight of the sovereign so easily. In 1575, when the theologian and scholar Andrew Melville visited the king, along with his nephew James Melville, he described the boy rehearsing rhetoric 'discourse walking up and down in the auld Lady Marrs hand, of knowledge and ignorance'.[4]

Killigrew described the demonstration that the king gave him of his education which included dancing gracefully, speaking French and reading 'a chapter of the Bible out of Latin into French, and out of French after into English'.[5] The king translated to and from Scots, French, English, Latin and Greek without difficulty by the time he left the schoolroom. On occasion his paternal grandmother, the Countess of Lennox, sent books from London to James including Ascham's *The Scholemaster*, first published in 1570. In it, Elizabeth I's former tutor provided an explanation of his favoured method of double translation of a Classical text into English and then back into Latin. The king's library also contained several dictionaries for him to perfect his understanding of the passages he translated. In addition, he was expected to exhibit neat handwriting, but unlike Elizabeth I who honed an elegant Italic script during her schooldays, James was required to write in a style known as Secretary hand, which remained in use from the medieval period until the seventeenth century. It lacked some of the flourish of Italic script but was more legible. James practised his penmanship of the alphabet and his signature on at least two occasions in one of his books.[6] The king's tutors provided him with an extremely challenging curriculum under a strict regime. James was expected to study in an atmosphere that has been likened to a 'hothouse'.[7]

Peter Young, Buchanan's assistant, was given the task of collecting a library for the king which revealed a traditional humanist education with a focus on classical languages and politics. Young, originally from Dundee, graduated from St Andrews University before studying under Theodore Beza in Geneva. The gentle tutor was tasked with instilling a dislike of Catholicism within his young charge but did not beat him with the gusto of Buchanan. Instead, Young used praise to encourage the king and when James left the schoolroom, he chose to keep his former tutor by his side. The catalogue made by Young (Additional MS. 34.275) is held by the British Museum and dates from between 1573 to 1583. One of the first texts that James was required to read was a version of *Aesop's Fables* translated into Latin. Its moral tales were ideal material for the instruction of the young king. He progressed to Cicero, Livy, Terrence, Ovid and Virgil. The catalogue reveals that many of the books were gifts. Even so, they largely reflect James' studies and his tutors' preoccupation with turning him into a godly monarch.

Helen Little, his former wet nurse, gave the king a child-sized book of psalms in English and on another occasion a work by the Huguenot poet Guillaume de Salluste Du Bartas on the Creation, called *La Semaine.* In return, James gifted her with a prayer book. He gave another one, his library contained several, to one of his former rockers, Jane Oliphant. While Jane's pedigree remains unclear, it is likely that she was related in some way to 4th Lord Oliphant, one of the signatories of the Ainslie Tavern Bond who found Bothwell innocent of Darnley's death and who was present at Bothwell's marriage to Mary. During the early days of the Marian War, the lord was a prominent member of the Queen's Party but by 1569 he was in the service of the king. The inventory reveals other women who had a limited presence in James' early life and education. Magdalen Livingston gave the king an illustrated copy of *The Books of the Maccabees*, part of the apocrypha which are not considered canonical by Protestant denominations. Magdalen's sister was one of Mary, Queen of Scots' four Marys and had been one of the queen's maids herself until 1567. Access to the royal household now came because she was part of the extended Erskine family, having married the 1st Earl of Mar's youngest brother in 1562. By the time she added to the king's library she was a widow, and an inventory of Stirling Castle made in 1585 identified Magdalen as having a chamber in the castle. Young's inventory lists several books given to James by Magdalen. Among their number is a Latin and French dictionary and an illustrated copy of Ovid's *Metamorphoses*, chronicling the world from its creation to the deification of Julius Caesar. Despite the books, she was perhaps another of the women that Buchanan regarded with suspicion. Mary Beaton, another of the four Marys, now Lady Boyne, gave the king Terence's plays in both Latin and French. It was to Lady Boyne, the most scholarly of the Four Marys, that Mary, Queen of Scots bequeathed her books in the event of her death during childbirth.

Young also recorded the king's daily routine. Unfortunately, no date is provided for the schedule of learning included in the manuscript. He described a typically humanist education which included Classical grammar, rhetoric, history and moral philosophy. James began his day with Latin followed by classical history and rhetoric. He also studied Plutarch and the

New Testament. Plutarch's *Parallel Lives* compared various Roman and Greek figures, providing examples of virtuous and flawed leadership, providing James with lessons on governance and kingship. For Buchanan the study of Greek and Roman literature was the only way that James would learn about a just monarchy. James' schooling has been described as a 'basic (if somewhat outdated) classical humanist education'.[8] The tutor was determined that his charge's schooling would be very different from the education which Mary, Queen of Scots received during her childhood at the French court. Aside from poor Latin, the tutor believed that it was as a direct consequence of her studies and upbringing that Mary sought to please others, rather than rule in a godly manner.[9] In 1574, the English envoy, Henry Killigrew, was able to report on the alacrity with which James was able to switch between languages without first studying the text. James would later joke, or possibly complain, that he wrote Latin before learning his native Scots' tongue.[10] Andrew Melville noted, with approval, the king's 'judgement' and 'memory' when it came to the learning of Latin.[11] After lunch the king was required to study mathematics, geography, cosmology and to compose essays. James' tutors encouraged him to view his reading critically and to argue with his masters and classmates about the contents of his reading material. It was a habit that stuck with him throughout his life. James may well have been one of the best educated princes of his time and retained his interest in learning and theology throughout his life.

In preparation for kingship, Buchanan's emphasis turned to politics. His *Baptistes* and the *Rerum Scoticarum Historia* sought to defend the removal of Mary, Queen of Scots. He dedicated the history to James, explaining that he had been prevented by ill health from fulfilling this aspect of the king's education as rigorously as he would have liked. The works were also a reminder to James about what happened to tyrannous kings. *Baptistes* featured arch-villain, King Herod as a warning about ungodly monarchs. Inevitably the curriculum Buchanan implemented in the classroom also focused on the Bible and Calvinist theologies. His tutors believed that the king's grasp of Latin and Greek grammar better aided his understanding of the scripture he studied and in turn this would help him to grow into the kind of Scottish ruler who would protect the Kirk. As early as 1524, Martin Luther described the importance of reading the New Testament in its original Greek. It was a model followed by all the early reformers as well as by humanists like Erasmus and Sir Thomas More, who believed reading the Bible in its original language gained a deeper understanding of it without the errors of translations. Both groups believed that clarity of knowledge would draw people closer to God as well as spurring the eradication of superstitious and corrupt practices.

There were also practical lessons on statecraft. In 1603, James told the Venetian ambassador that Buchanan had taught him about the city state's constitution.[12] In another instance, the tutor noticed that James was in the habit of signing documents containing requests without reading them and that he granted favours with too great a readiness. He submitted a request of his own, which James signed, and then Buchanan spent the following week telling everyone that he was the king of Scotland. When James challenged him on the matter, the tutor was able to provide a letter signed by the king confirming that he had handed his kingdom to Buchanan. James, uncowed by the severity of his master, picked only what he wanted to retain for his lessons. While he was able to exchange letters with Elizabeth I from 1585 onwards, which included a discussion about the meaning of kingship quoting Plutarch (no doubt read from a book that was once part of his mother's library) to support his argument, it did not mean that he agreed with Buchanan's view of how a godly king might behave.

It was not always easy for Young to source or finance the books that the king required for his education even though he was able to acquire more than 200 of Mary, Queen of Scots' books for James' library. Scotland was not a wealthy nation and the regent, Morton, was eager to refill the treasury as a way of strengthening his government. He forced the Countess of Mar, who held some of Mary, Queen of Scots' jewels, to return them, reformed the collection of taxes, and tried to reduce government spending. It was the latter that led to an exchange of letters between the Lord Chief Justice, Sir John Bellenden and Peter Young sometime between 1574 and 1575 on the subject of purchasing several texts, including Caesar's *Gallic Wars*, for the royal classroom.[13] The demand for books met with some exasperation on the part of the men who felt that the king already owned a sufficient collection.

The king's studies were not restricted to academic learning. He was, after all, a Renaissance monarch. Whatever Buchanan's personal views, princes and kings were required to be accomplished dancers and sportsmen. The king rode, hunted and demonstrated other knightly skills including the quintain, running at rings and shooting with a crossbow during the course of the English ambassador's visit in 1574. The previous year James' staff expanded to include a man to keep his horses. Later, the household at Stirling contained a keeper of the king's dogs and a falconer. On one occasion during his childhood, Robert Dudley, Earl of Leicester, sent James a pied horse.[14] Ownership of a stable of horses and of birds of prey were marks of wealth and power while the exchange of hawks, horses and hounds was part of European diplomacy. A picture of the king dating from about 1574 shows him dressed as a miniature adult holding a sparrowhawk on his gloved left fist. By the time he became king of England as well as Scotland, his library contained several books on the topic of hawking and hunting, reflecting his love of the chase. As an adult, James would, on occasion, miss church in favour of hunting, while Hawklaw hill, near the town of Cupar, was said to be the king's favourite place to go hawking while he was in residence at Falkland Palace.

Nor was James alone in his schoolroom. Like princes and princesses before him, he had companions who learned alongside him as well as serving him. As well as mimicking some aspects of the structure of a mature royal household, it was thought that the presence of other students would act as a spur to the king's own learning. Among their number was John, 2nd Earl of Mar, William Murray of Abercairney (who was Annabell Murray's nephew), and Walter Stewart. Between James and the new Earl of Mar there would be a lifelong friendship, despite occasional violent differences.

In 1576 Buchanan dedicated *De Jure Regni apud Scotos*, or *The Rights of the Crown of Scotland*, to the 13-year-old king. His dedication to *Baptistes* bluntly warned James from an 'undue desire of power' and stressed the importance of virtue:

> This little book must seem to a peculiar interest for yourself, inasmuch as it sets before you in the clearest manner what torments and miseries tyrants endure, even when they appear to be most prosperous. And this lesson I deem not merely beneficial, but absolutely necessary for you, so that you may early begin to detest what it must be your duty to avoid.[15]

Buchanan and Knox both believed that a monarch's subjects were free to rebel if the ruler was a tyrant or did not have the correct religious credentials. Buchanan's history was not an objective account of Scotland's past, or of the men and women he wrote about. The king's tutor went so far as to add that James was accountable to his people and that a monarch who failed in his responsibilities should be punished. Rather than ruling by divine right, James' tutors emphasised that a king ruled only within the law and was there to administer justice in accordance with it; to do otherwise was to become a tyrant. Buchanan used James' own family, in the form of James III and Mary, Queen of Scots (who both inherited the throne as children), to exemplify the failings that he should avoid. It was a lesson that the king rejected, preferring to see himself as above all other men in the model of an Old Testament king – albeit a Solomon or David rather than Herod. Buchanan's text was republished in English in 1642. By then, for many Puritans and supporters of Parliament, James' son, Charles I, was a personification of tyranny rather than a godly ruler.

Chapter Six

The 'Scotch Urchin'

By 1577, both Buchanan and Young featured on an English privy council list of influential men and were in receipt of English pensions.[1] However, James' grandfather was declared to have reached his majority aged just 12. It did not escape Morton's notice, the English government, or the rest of Scotland's nobility that James would soon want to rule for himself. Stirling was no longer a means of keeping the young monarch separate from his country's political turmoil. Morton's regency was increasingly unpopular, in part because of the amount of power that he centralised upon himself and his perceived self-enrichment at the expense of the Crown and his peers, but also because of his strengthening of the alliance between Scotland and England. James Melville described the regent as 'proud and disdainful … he was loved by none and envied and hated by many'.[2]

At the beginning of March 1578, the Earls of Atholl and Argyll, leaders of the anti-Morton faction, arrived at Stirling asking for an audience with the king. They informed him that they wished to summon a jury of their peers to judge a dispute between themselves and Morton. The regent also presented himself to James. He declared that the king must either punish the earls for the challenge to his authority or accept his resignation. The regent claimed his own infirmities and age as the reason for the latter, added that it was expected that the monarch, who was not even a teenager, would take up the burden of government. He suggested that rather than Stirling, James should reside in Edinburgh. The king retorted that he was too young for the responsibility but by the time Morton, who perhaps hoped for that response, returned to Edinburgh, James had changed his mind. Alexander Erskine, the king's guardian, was a political opponent of the regent. He recognised the opportunity Morton's gamble afforded. James now declared himself eager to rule. Like his grandfather before him, he was prepared to take his place as a political player and Morton was forced to step down. By

12 March 1578 the change of government was proclaimed in Edinburgh and the former regent retired, under duress, to Lochleven, where he tended his gardens. In England, Mary began to dream of freedom once again and Elizabeth I sent instructions to her ambassador to let Morton know of her support for him.

A new phase of James VI's education in Renaissance kingship was about to begin. Buchanan accepted a place on the privy council in his role of mentor. The king would learn from them by watching and listening how his realm was managed. However, James in his twelfth year, was about to learn at first hand one of Machiavelli's most important lessons – that self-interest is a driving force, even over family and friendship. John Erskine, 2nd Earl of Mar, known as Jock o'Sclaittis, was about seven years older than his friend and resented his uncle's authority at Stirling. Jock believed that as Earl of Mar, custody of Stirling and its occupants rightfully belonged to him rather than his uncle. Morton was able to persuade Mar that if he was returned to power, he would support the young earl's rightful claim to governorship of the castle and guardianship of the king. On 26 April, in events described by the English ambassador, Robert Bowes, Mar arose early and made to leave the castle as though he was going hunting. When his uncle gave him the key to the locked fortress, men loyal to Mar seized Erskine and pushed him out through the gates. During the scuffle that followed Alexander Erskine's eldest son, another of James' classmates, was killed. He was just 10-years-old. James, awoken to the sound of battle, was told wrongly that Erskine was dead.

Stirling's gates remained locked against Scotland's nobility while a parliament was called there, in which James was declared of age, Mar negotiated his position as the castle's custodian, and Morton took control of the government as First Lord of the Council. The Earls of Argyll and Atholl did not have a large enough army to emerge victorious against Morton and his supporters, so were forced to compromise. In England, Mary, Queen of Scots raised the possibility that James might be removed to France by the Duke of Guise, where she hoped he might be converted to Catholicism. In the bartering between the different factions that followed, overseen by chief negotiator Robert Bowes, it was agreed that James would remain at Stirling but that four members of the council should attend on the king at all times. Those nobles who opposed Morton declared this to be unreasonable because of the council's pro-Morton weighting. Instead, they countered, that James should be returned into the hands of Alexander Erskine of Gogar and that Edinburgh would be a better residence for the king in the future. Bowes suggested that both groups compromise by accepting a bigger anti-Morton faction onto the council but that James remain at Stirling. Atholl remained as James' lord chancellor. The path to conciliation was eventually smoothed by English coin. Even James' tutors were men who were paid to support the course of action most beneficial to the English government. George Buchanan received £100 but Peter Young declined £30.[3] Within a few months, the factionalism that divided his opponents allowed Morton to return to dominance, even though he was no longer formally recognised as regent. James was more a pawn in the negotiations that followed the coup than a king and the lesson cost him the life of a young friend.

Unsurprisingly, in the aftermath of the upheaval, James no longer trusted Morton. Matters were compounded when the Earl of Atholl, second only in seniority to Morton, died the following year, on 25 April 1579, after attending a feast at Stirling held by Mar to symbolise the reconciliation between the different factions. It did not take long for comparisons to be made with the demise of the 1st Earl of Mar and for rumours of poison to spread; a post mortem was subsequently demanded by the widowed Countess of Atholl. The story gained ground when a doctor was alleged to have tasted the contents of Atholl's stomach and almost died as a consequence. In theory, James achieved his majority at 12 years of age but his government was run by his privy council, which was led by Morton whose power was beginning to look unassailable.

During the summer of 1579, the former regent took the opportunity to attack the Hamilton clan after declaring the Pacification of Perth to be void for any man suspected of plotting the assassination of Moray. By then Châtellerault was dead and his son, the 3rd Earl of Arran, became insane in 1562. The 3rd earl's younger brother, John, the de facto head of the family, was forced into exile. The loss of the Hamiltons from Scotland's political landscape resulted in an unexpected void that allowed Morton's enemies to gain the upper hand once more. Until James married and fathered legitimate children, the Hamiltons claimed to be his heirs but their right to the succession now passed to the Lennox family. James' cousin, Esmé Stewart, Sier d'Aubigny, the son of Matthew Stewart's youngest brother, John, who had spent much of his life in France returned to Scotland. He was intent on benefiting from the political capital that unexpectedly fell his way. He arrived in Lieth in September 1579. Stewart almost immediately became 13-year-old James' favourite courtier, in part because he was a somewhat glamorous kinsman. The king's cousin was charming, witty and polished. He also treated the king with deference which was something new to him. The French ambassador in England, Castelnau, would write to his master Henri III, declaring of Esmé, he 'is so much beloved by the young king that he cannot live without him, caressing him with great affection from morning till night'.[4] It was not long before Esmé formed an alliance with the Earl of Argyll and other of Morton's enemies. The following month, James VI presided over his parliament and was declared able to rule in his own right. Bowes described D'Aubigny's movements in Scotland with growing alarm even though he said he favoured the Anglo-Scottish alliance. The power behind the throne was changing and the former regent's position weakened rapidly.

James' privy council was horrified by what was happening to his household. Esmé Stewart was the king's constant companion. The king showered his kinsman with gifts, including Dumbarton Castle. Even worse he was a French Catholic. Sir Henry Widdrington wrote to his masters in England that James had no eyes for anyone but his cousin. In England there was alarm that the Anglo-Scottish entente might be replaced by an accord with the French. Rumours began to spread that the relationship between the pair was more personal than kinship, even though the Sieur was married with four children. Esmé was quick to convert to Presbyterianism under the guidance of his young cousin when he realised one of the reasons for the hostility towards him, but the Kirk was not convinced by his change of faith.

In March 1580, James ensured that Robert Stewart resigned the earldom of Lennox which he presented to Esmé. By September, Esmé Stewart, Earl of Lennox was appointed as the king's lord chamberlain and first gentleman of the chamber. His duties included supervising the staff of the royal bedchamber, assisting the king to dress and undress and to ensure the monarch's safety. He also slept in the king's chamber. James moved from

Stirling to Holyrood House. Under Lennox's influence James' household took a more French form and its members were promoted based on their support of the newly elevated earl. Lennox, who recognised Mar's influence, ensured that the earl was isolated and forced to return to Stirling. In effect it was now Lennox, by the king's own agreement, who controlled who had access to James in his private quarters[5] and he was swift to appoint members of his own faction to various offices. Some of Morton's former allies, including William Ruthven, 1st Earl of Gowrie who was James' treasurer went over to the Earl of Lennox's side. Captain James Stewart, a son of Lord Ochiltree by his first wife, Agnes Cunningham, and one of Lennox's followers was selected as a gentleman of the bedchamber. A professional soldier, Stewart lacked the urbanity of Lennox but like his patron he was quick to find favour with the king and to take Elizabeth I's money to ensure Anglo-Scottish amity. Castelnau described him, in 1583, as 'very fickle' someone who 'only keeps on good terms with those whom he supposes to possess most power and favour'.[6] The Kirk's most influential man in the royal household, George Buchanan, was increasingly unwell and the men who James listened to now used soft words rather than beating him and overtly denying him power.

On 30 December Morton went hunting with the king but the next day Captain Stewart was able to publicly accuse him of murdering James' father during a privy council meeting. The former regent, who the king called 'father'[7] and promised to defend from his enemies, was arrested and imprisoned first in Edinburgh, then in Dumbarton Castle. James had learned the lesson of *De iure regni*, written by Buchanan, that dictated that a monarch must be master of both himself and his emotions rather than stoical acceptance of events; the king absorbed the importance of self-discipline for his own ends. David Calderwood, a Presbyterian cleric summarised how his supporters felt about the incarceration. 'It was a pitiful sight to many, to see him who had done so much for establishing of religion, and had hazarded his life, land and goods in setting up and maintaining the king's authority, to be overthrown.'[8] Andrew Melville, the radical Presbyterian academic who was elected Moderator of the General Assembly in 1578, wrote that the king was corrupted by Lennox and by James Stewart who became Earl of Arran in 1581. The 3rd Earl of Arran remained mentally ill, so it was easy enough to appoint Stewart as the earl's tutor with powers over the earldom before bestowing the title upon the favourite. James and his new advisers used the 1st Earl of Arran's disputed marriage to remove James Hamilton's title from him. Stewart's mother was the 1st Earl of Arran's child by his first wife, and the captain was able to claim that he was the king's nearest heir once he became earl. It was a lesson in the legal authority of kingship and one which James used to reward a man he liked. It must have been a pleasing sensation for the young king, who is often remembered for his close relationships with male favourites and for his generosity to them.

Morton was tried on 1 June 1581 and executed the following day, much to Elizabeth I's anger. The death of the former regent gave supporters of the Counter-Reformation hope that James might adopt his mother's beliefs. Mendoza, the Spanish ambassador, described it as 'a great beginning'.[9] Both the French and the Spanish recognised that an alliance with Scotland would be to the detriment of England. James was encouraged by his councillors to allow Philip to believe that he thought of him as a friend. He said that he wanted the Spanish to free his mother, but the king's advisors also recognised that nothing should get in the way of Elizabeth I declaring James to be her heir. More important than his mother, so far as James was concerned, was his own status as sovereign. When he pressed to be named heir to England's throne, Elizabeth is said to have dismissed him as the 'Scotch urchin', although there is no written evidence to confirm the episode.

According to Melville, it was Lennox and Arran who planted the idea of the monarch being the head of his or her nation's Church within the king's mind. The latter extolled the French system that made its king an absolute monarch. Patrick Adamson, Bishop of St Andrews preached that 'A Christian King should be the chief governor of the Kirk, and behoved to have Bishops under him, to hold all in order'.[10] At about the same time, James' view of his mother was seen to change. Buchanan had done his best to ensure the king hated Mary but Lennox encouraged him to see criticism of a monarch as an attack on royal authority. Rather than recognising that her son was creating a narrative of kingship, the captive queen hoped that she might enter into an association with James as joint sovereigns, facilitating her own freedom and return to power, and that he would adopt Catholicism. During her imprisonment, James' mother evolved, in the eyes of many people around

Europe, from a Jezebel who murdered her husband into a Catholic martyr who was the rightful heir to the English throne.

James had no memory of Mary despite the captive queen's attempts to remain an influence on her son's life. In 1580, James wrote to his mother in response to her complaint that he had turned away her secretary without receiving her letter or letting him give James a verbal message. The king emphasised that he knew the 'honour and duty'[11] that he owed Mary and thanked her for the gift of a ring she sent him. On another occasion she sent him a 'little ape'.[12] He always signed himself as king so that there would be no mistaking his status. Fontenay reported, without any justification, that James did love his mother. It is difficult to gauge the extent of his affection for Mary from the existing primary sources. Whether he was playing at being a dutiful son or whether he wanted to establish a better relationship with his mother is impossible to know. Soon after the arrival of Esmé Stewart in Scotland, Castelnau wrote to Henri III confirming that he had corresponded with Mary on the matter of supplying men and equipment to her and her son. He also raised the possibility with his master of James dying without an heir and the Hamiltons inheriting the Scottish throne.[13] When word of the proposed association between James and his mother became public in Scotland, a Catholic plot was suspected with the blame for the scheme placed on Lennox's shoulders, despite the earl's conversion, because of his links to Henri III (whose nephew James' was), with the Guises, and his perceived Catholicism. From her captivity in England, Mary, Queen of Scots hoped for exactly what the Scots feared. As well as looking with hostility upon closer ties with France, James' nobles quarrelled among themselves over precedence and the Kirk's distrust of Lennox and Arran turned into an episode that saw James stripped of much of his authority once more.

The Ruthven Raid of 23 August 1582 was planned by the Earls of Mar, Gowrie, Glencairn and a group known as the Lords Enterprisers who wished to remove the king from the influence of Lennox and Arran. They were supported in their desire to rid the king of his ungodly advisers by Andrew Melville, who favoured an ultra-Presbyterian form of government where the Kirk sat in supremacy over the Crown. He was elected moderator of the General Assembly in April and June of 1582. It was the intent of the raiders, with the support of the assembly, to limit James' power by providing a council to rule alongside him. The conspirators waited until Lennox and Arran were both absent. The king, who stayed at Ruthven in Perthshire at the invitation of Gowrie, was hunting near the castle on 22 August 1582 when armed men prevented him from departing. Lennox retreated to Dumbarton and Arran was captured. Once the king was in their custody at Stirling, the Lords Enterprisers presented him with a list of demands that included the removal of Lennox and tighter financial controls on the king. Gowrie, who was complicit in the murder of Rizzio and had been one of Mary, Queen of Scot's jailors, assumed the role of head of government. The 15-year-old monarch is said to have burst into tears when he realised the extent of the rebellion against him. For those seated opposite him, it was more a question of restoring balance to Scotland's political picture and remediating some of the Crown's financial problems. It did not help matters that Gowrie was personally liable for James' increasing debts. The king's history of lavish spending began with the gifts he gave to Esmé Stewart, which included lands confiscated from the Hamilton family and governorship of Dumbarton Castle. The conspirators took the precaution of making James issue a proclamation declaring that he acted freely before having him banish Lennox and acknowledge the freedom of the Kirk from a monarch's interference.

During the next ten months, James was kept captive while the Earl of Gowrie governed the country. Mar was unable to regain dominance over the king's household and appears not to have played an important part in the new regime. Lennox was sent into exile on 21 December and died in May the following year, without ever seeing James again. Scotland's Protestants were wrong in their assumption that Lennox's conversion was a political one only. When he was on his death bed, he refused to make a last confession or to receive the last rites according to the Catholic faith. The king never forgot Lennox. He even penned a poem about him while he was held in captivity, describing Esmé in terms of a phoenix while Melville thundered that the king was led into darkness by his former favourite.

James, held at Falkland Palace in May 1583, finally persuaded Sir James Melville of Halhill to help him. Melville served Mary, Queen of Scots during her time in France and afterwards, served James VI's regents in an ambassadorial capacity but resigned once the king was old enough to start governing his realm. He argued that the best way of dealing with the crisis would be for James to forgive the conspirators and move on, but the king was able to communicate with opponents of the Lords Enteprisers, including the Earls of Huntly and Argyll. An arrangement was made for him to escape at St Andrews on horseback under pretext of an invitation to dine with a kinsman, Robert Stewart, 1st Earl of March.[14] He evaded his captors in June 1583, shut himself up in the castle at St Andrews and made the decision to rid himself of courtiers who owed their loyalty to the Ruthven lords and declared that he would rule his own realm. James initially chose to pardon Gowrie, who begged forgiveness on his knees, until he knew his position was secure. The English ambassador, Bowes, reported that men who were dependent on Angus and Mar and thus sympathetic to an Anglo-Scottish entente were soon replaced, while the Earl of Arran took over much of the routine business of running the country.

Mar was forced into hiding in the west of Scotland in 1583. However, the king's desire for revenge, the lack of respect he experienced and his powerlessness was a dish he served cold. It was only when Gowrie and the Lords Enterprisers became involved in a new conspiracy in 1584, that included storming Stirling Castle, that Gowrie was arrested in Dundee where he had been since the previous year. Mar, who did not know that the conspirators' plans were thwarted, attacked Stirling on 18 April 1584 and seized the town. James raised an army of his own and attacked the rebels. When the garrison capitulated, the king hanged its captain as a warning to others. Mar, together with the Earl of Angus, sought shelter in England immediately afterwards, only returning to Scotland, and the king's favour, in 1585. Despite his involvement in the Ruthven Raid and its aftermath, James and Mar remained friends and the earl would serve his classroom companion throughout the king's life.

James was humiliated by his loss of power during his captivity and by the way in which the General Assembly of the Kirk described the abduction as a 'good and godly cause'.[15] His escape gave the 17-year-old king new confidence. He was determined that he would not be treated with so little respect in the future. Lennox and the Ruthven raiders taught him how to use cunning and duplicity to best advantage. He learned the value of patience and guile to achieve his own ends. They were traits that he continued to exhibit while his lords vied for authority and when foreign powers approached him. Now though, the new government declared James to be both the head of State and the Kirk. Being Scotland's monarch was something of a tightrope act, balancing different factions and religions to maintain some kind of equilibrium. The king, after his initial setbacks, learned much more quickly than his mother how to hold power, and a pension of £4000 a year from his cousin Elizabeth was more than enough to prevent him from forming an association with Mary. For James it proved that the policy of entertaining suggestions from all sides but committing himself to nothing was a sound one.

The power struggles of his youth taught him the importance of self-interest. From the deposed queen there was a heartfelt exclamation in a letter to Castelnau sent in March 1585, 'I am grieved to the heart by the crosses which I have to endure, but especially by the estrangement of my son from me, and his being set against me; praying God to let me die rather than learn for certain that such a thing can be'.[16] By the end of the same month Mary was forced to recognise that James had betrayed her interests and decided, without hope of enforcing her decision, to deprive him of the rights which he inherited through her. Despite the setback, the queen was unable to stop scheming either for her own freedom or for a throne to sit upon – whether it be Scotland's or England's. Buchanan may have taught James the theory about the usage and limitation of royal power but the Ruthven Raid was a practical lesson for James in how to appear as one thing while keeping his true thoughts to himself in order to achieve his own ends.

In November 1583, Lennox's son, Ludovick, who was aged 9 years, arrived in Scotland from France. It was not long before the boy was created 2nd Duke of Lennox and high chamberlain of Scotland. For Mary, Queen of Scots, it raised the possibility of a resurgence of French support but James was only interested in caring for his favourite's family. One of his first actions was to set about arranging advantageous marriages for Ludovick's sisters, Henrietta and Maria. Fontenay, writing to Mary, Queen of Scots about James claimed that his love for them and his favourites was a weakness because of the disapproval of his subjects. Whether the quality was a mark of 'limited political intuition'[17] or evidence of his better nature is a matter for debate. So far as his own mother was concerned, James was less forthcoming. Fontenay noted that the king asked no questions about the conditions in which Mary was kept or the way she was treated. Quite simply, the king grew up without any contact with his mother and he intended to be the only power in his realm. It was perhaps not surprising then that one of James' first acts as sovereign was to pass the so-called Black Acts of 1584 which affirmed the king's authority over the Kirk. He also published a volume of his own work entitled *Essays of a prentise in the divine art of poesie* which prohibited his subjects from writing anything that promoted rebellion.

Although he was forced to repeal the Black Acts, 1584 was only the beginning of James combining his authority as a king with his love of learning for the better instruction of his people, the most famous of which was *Daemonologie*, published in 1597, on the subject of black magic and demons. Grounded in his own involvement with the 1590 North Berwick witch trials, James went on to endorse the discovery and punishment of witches. While the king promoted his own work, he set about suppressing Buchanan's writing as well as discrediting his history. In the same year as the Black Acts, Parliament passed an Act 'for the punishment of the authors of the slanderous and untrue calumnies spoken against the King's majesty, his Council and proceedings, or to the dishonour and prejudice of his Highness, his parents, progenitors, crown and estate'.[18] The lessons of James' childhood, that his mother was a wicked woman and that a monarch might be lawfully deposed, were finally, and forcefully, spurned. Buchanan was to be rejected as the puppet of the King's Party and the regents associated with it. Nonetheless, the tutor's views would return to haunt the Stuart kings of England and Scotland during the seventeenth century.

Elizabeth I, who was the king's godmother, began writing to James in 1585. Before that date, communication was conducted through ambassadors. The queen did not address him as a godson but as a brother monarch and while the action was a move to strengthen the relationship between England and Scotland, the letters provided another element of James' education, if only in the form of a further lesson in prevarication from the wily queen who excelled at not committing herself to one side or another. Somewhat ironically, in one of her first letters, she warned James 'I...hope you will remember that who seeketh two strings to one bow, they may shoot strong but never straight'.[19] She was also able to influence the format of James' household as well as Scottish politics because the king and his protectors were reliant upon financial help from England as well as not wishing to jeopardise the possibility of inheriting Elizabeth's throne. It was in Scotland's best interests to promote a friendly relationship with its neighbour, even if politicians did sometimes hint that ties with France might be re-established if necessary. It is perhaps not surprising that James began to address the aging queen as 'madam and mother' on occasion.[20]

Chapter Seven

The Value of a Son

At the same time that James began to rule for himself he began to patronise a group of court poets. He also found time to write and translate verse himself. It was a model that echoed both George Buchanan's and Mary, Queen of Scots' own interests. The king took, for his template, the French court and the Pléiade poets, who translated Classical works into their native language. He gathered a group of writers around him known as the Castalian Band. Their leader was Alexander Montgomerie, a Catholic from Ayrshire, and included among their number the Hudson brothers who had served James since he was a baby. The king translated Salluste Du Bartas' *Uranie* into Scots while Thomas Hudson, one of the viola players, translated *Judith.* They were a sound choice for James who wished to emphasise both his godly and academic credentials. Du Bartas was a Huguenot judge who served Henri IV of France and the subject of the king's poem was commitment to writing verse with a scriptural theme. When Du Bartas visited Scotland on a diplomatic mission in 1587 the king, who saw patronage as a way of augmenting his prestige, was generous in the gifts he gave him including 2000 gold coins, a knighthood as well as sending him back to France at his own expense. Among the manuscripts being circulated by the group was one by William Fowler, who at James' suggestion, translated Petrarch's *Triumphs* which explores the idea of redemption from sin and the triumph of virtue. In return, the king penned a sonnet to Fowler. The Scottish courtier, and double agent who was recruited by Sir Francis Walsingham to find evidence against Mary, Queen of Scots because of his association with Castelnau, claimed to have taught James the art of memory,[1] or *Ars Memoriae* which was a classical technique. Both Aristotle and Cicero wrote about the use of vivid visual images such as a familiar journey or a room to improve recall by making associations. The king was already trained in rhetoric which was seen as an aid to theological discussion and speech making so the skill was not unknown to him, but James wished to improve upon what he learned in the classroom. In 1591 his subjects were able to purchase *His Majesties Poeticall Exercises at Vacant Houres*. James, who grew up in an academic hothouse atmosphere at Stirling, had found a way to exercise and extend his royal authority through his writing. James' literary and political works helped him to construct his identity as ruler, to present his vision to the people he ruled and provide a pattern for his subjects to follow.

Scotland needed an heir and James' claim to the English throne would be more secure if he had sons of his own. During his infancy, soon after her incarceration in England, while she was still at Bolton Castle in 1568, his mother suggested that her son should marry one of the daughters of King Philip II of Spain. She wrote to her former schoolroom companion Elizabeth of France to suggest the union, in the hope that ties of friendship and marriage with both France and Spain might win her freedom. Failing that, she expressed a desire that James might be raised as a Catholic in Spain.[2] Marriage proposals for royal minors were part of European diplomacy and James' infancy and childhood was no exception. In 1583, Gowrie's regime suggested that the king, who was 16 years old, marry his cousin Elizabeth I who was 52. Some Scots favoured a continuation of the auld alliance with France and identified Catherine of Bourbon as a potential match, while a match with Lutheran Denmark ensured a Protestant bride and enhanced trade prospects. In 1585 James sent Peter Young, who he trusted, to negotiate with Frederick II of Denmark about the possibility of a marriage between the king's eldest daughter, Elizabeth, and James. However, the princess was betrothed to the Duke of Brunswick and Young suggested that Elizabeth's younger sister, Anna was very pretty and would make a suitable alternative as a way of bolstering a Protestant alliance. Both countries were wary of committing themselves and the Scots could not afford to alienate the English, who were wary about any treaties that James might make, so the plan did not progress further at that time.

On 8 February 1587, the Queen of Scots, who had been convicted of treason against her cousin three months earlier, was finally executed. Shortly before her death, Mary carried out, in so far as she could, her threat to disinherit James by leaving her claim to the English throne to Philip II of Spain. In a letter written to Berardino de Mendoza, the Spanish ambassador in London, Mary wrote, 'I have said that I consider him, should my son not return into the bosom of the church, as being a prince the most worthy to govern and protect this island. I have written to the same purpose to his holiness'.[3] In other correspondence, written to the Duke of Guise, Mary described James as 'unfortunate and deluded'.[4] James had already agreed with the English that he would make no reprisals for his mother's beheading, on the understanding that her death would not damage his own expectations of inheriting Elizabeth I's throne. Despite this, Elizabeth I never conceded that James was her heir apparent for fear that it would make him the centre of plots to deprive her of it while she lived.

James finally married Anna, or Anne, of Denmark, in Oslo, on 23 November 1589. He returned to Scotland the following May when his bride was crowned. James appointed Annabell Murray as one of her ladies but Anne dismissed the countess from her service in 1590 after the elderly woman was heard saying that she wished the king might have made a match with France. Despite rumours to the contrary, the queen did not become pregnant with her first child for almost four years, causing some speculation about the relationship between the couple. As Anne approached her first confinement, James requested that she should leave Holyrood House for Stirling where she stayed at Lady Mar's lodgings, now known as Mar's Wark, close to the Holy Rude Church where James was crowned, rather than stay in Edinburgh.[5] Henry Frederick Stuart was born on 19 February 1594. The arrival of an heir strengthened James' dynastic position in both Scotland and England but he recognised that his own birth led to Mary, Queen of Scots being toppled from her throne.

Henry was transferred soon after his birth, together with his wet nurse Margaret Masterton, to the Prince's Tower in Stirling Castle. James followed the custom of granting custody of the infant to the Earl of Mar and his mother, the redoubtable Lady Minny. The decisions that James took about where Henry should live and who should look after him caused an argument with Anne. The queen, who enjoyed a secure and happy childhood in Denmark, wanted to keep her son close to her but James had no intention of Henry being used for political leverage against him. Instead, the king drafted the ordinance for the Nursing and Keeping of Prince Henry[6] which included not giving the baby to anyone unless the order came directly from

James' own mouth. It was a wise decision. The first plot to kidnap the boy surfaced less that a fortnight later when a group of Catholic earls conspired to seize the baby. The General Assembly and Elizabeth I demanded that the conspirators be punished, but this was complicated by Anne of Denmark's involvement with the men behind the scheme, because of her determination to gain control of Henry. James was resolved that Henry and his household, which now included his wet nurse, four rockers, a doctor and an apothecary, would stay at Stirling during his childhood. Anne did not understand the complicated loyalties of Scottish politics and could not, the king decided, be trusted.

The Chapel Royal was demolished and replaced on James' orders with a modern Renaissance building worthy of a Protestant dynasty. The baby was baptised there on 30 August 1594. The king's accounts show gifts of fabric for clothing to the king's own childhood nurse, Helen Little, and her two daughters to attend the ceremony and celebrations that followed it. There was a similar gift for Annabell Murray.[7] The infant's father was less concerned about offending either his nobles or his wife than risking Elizabeth I's displeasure. He asked her to be Henry's godmother and she obliged in the proxy form of the Earl of Sussex, who presented the boy with a royal gift of gold cups. It was a welcome addition as the treasury was stretched by the festivities which included a masque, a model ship with thirty-six cannon that fired and sugar subtilities shaped like fish.[8] Unfortunately, Andrew Melville penned a celebratory poem entitled *On the Birth of the Scoto-Britannic Prince* which waxed lyrical about the union of Scotland and England under one king. Melville was celebrating a Protestant prince to lead like-minded rulers against the papacy and the Hapsburgs, but Elizabeth I was furious at the reference even though her cousin's succession, as the closest male descendent from Henry VII, seemed increasingly likely.

In March 1595, Margaret Masterton, the wet nurse selected because of her connections to the Erskines, became unwell and lost her milk, causing the queen to renew her attempts to gain custody of her son. Robert Bowes wrote to Robert Cecil explaining the nurse's milk dried and that the prince was unsettled by his change in nurse, a woman from Stirling, found at short notice by the Mars. Alarmed about the risks to Henry's health, Anne demanded that the boy be moved to Edinburgh so that she might oversee her son's care. On 1 April, the ambassador reported the growing family crisis, 'her Majesty rides to Stirling, to the dislike of all who would have taken the Prince out of Mar's hands'.[9] Anne resented the earl's role in her son's life and was already becoming embroiled in court politics in a bid, if not to gain custody of her son, to have him closer to her. When James refused, the queen asked that if Henry was to remain at Stirling that both the castle and the prince should be transferred into her possession. Anne persevered, despite her husband's determination to adhere to Scotland's traditions of raising the heir to the throne in the keeping of the Earl of Mar at Stirling. She was still arguing her case in May. Reports to England from Bowes speculated about the troubles that might arise from it between Mar and the chancellor, Maitland, or between Mar and the queen. The breach between the royal couple split the court. Sir John Maitland, the chancellor, was loud in his support for the queen[10] but the king was adamant that for the good of the Stuart dynasty, Henry remain behind the fortifications at Stirling. Not only did James not allow Anne to oversee her son's nursery, or to keep him close at hand, he also limited the number of times she was able to visit him. The king, whose childhood has been described as lacking in love and close family ties, chose his foster family at the expense of his relationship with Anne because he believed that Henry, who was a threat to his own throne in the same way he had been used against his mother, would be safer at Stirling. By July 1595, Anne was distraught and there was a scuffle beneath the walls of Stirling Castle between the two opposing factions.

Mar's credentials as guardian to the royal heir, so far as the General Assembly of the Kirk was concerned, were impeccable apart from the matter of his wife. In December 1592, the earl, who was a widower, married Marie, the daughter of Esmé Stewart, 1st Duke of Lennox, and one of Queen Anne's ladies-in-waiting. The union pleased the king but was opposed by many of James' nobility because of Mar's hereditary responsibilities since Marie was a Catholic. The king sought to make a match for the girl in 1584, before she and her sister arrived in Scotland from France, when she was just 7 years old. At that time, James arranged for her eldest sister, Henrietta, to marry George Gordon, 5th Earl of Huntly, who helped rescue the king from the Ruthven raiders. The Kirk pressed Mar to provide instruction for his wife so that she might become Protestant, thus removing the perceived threat to the boy's upbringing. James concurred and ordered that Marie should be coached in Calvinism so that she might make a profession of faith. Mar arranged for Patrick Simson, the minister at Stirling, to teach his young wife. So thorough was her conversion that by 1639 she was a supporter of the Solemn League and Covenant, an agreement between Scotland's Presbyterian covenanters and the English Parliament for the preservation of the reformed churches and removal of Catholicism from their shores.

Despite the rift in their marriage, when Anne became ill James visited her at Holyrood and the couple were reconciled, although they would never be so close as they were in the first days of their marriage. By December, Anne was pregnant once more. Elizabeth Stuart, named after Elizabeth I, was born on 19 August 1596 at Dunfermline, which was part of the queen's dower. When Henry was born two years previously, bonfires burned in the streets but celebrations were more muted with the arrival of a girl, and besides which James found himself in financial difficulties so could not afford the fanfare associated with his son's arrival. Her baptism took place on 28 November at Linlithgow. By then the weather was far too inclement for many guests to make the journey and even if they did, they were instructed to bring their own dinner with them. It was perhaps for that reason that Elizabeth I, who was the new princess' godmother, chose not to send a proxy, or even a gift. Nor did James' Presbyterian ministers send their congratulations to their monarch on the birth of a daughter. It was symptomatic of the growing difficulties that existed between the Kirk and Crown. Some of the hostilities arose from a request to the General Assembly for financial support for the Crown.

Princess Elizabeth was placed in the care of Alexander Livingston, the keeper of Linlithgow Palace, and his wife Eleanor, or Helen, Hay. Livingston had accompanied James' favourite, Esmé Stewart, into exile and it was he who carried Lennox's last letter to the king from France. He was subsequently commissioned with the task of accompanying Lennox's children back to Scotland. He had also raised a force to help the king in the aftermath of the Ruthven Raid. Livingston was a man the king could trust and the queen regarded Eleanor as a friend. Rather than wages, James, who continued to struggle to meet the costs of a growing family who each required their own household, gifted the couple lands and titles. Among their number was the appointment as baillie of all the king's lands in the county of Linlithgow. At first the staff consisted of a wet nurse and two of Helen's female relations – Elizabeth Hay and Alison Hay, Lady Dunkerrant. Alison fulfilled the post of nurse while Elizabeth looked after the princess's wardrobe and kept a record of accounts. Even as an adult, the princess would remain close to the women who cared for her during her early years. Among the expenses listed for Elizabeth was fabric for her gowns, ribbon and four dolls, described as babies, for her to play with.

Eleanor Hay was a Catholic, although her husband was Protestant, and this caused dissension with the privy council who wished to ensure that the royal family were raised according to Presbyterian rites, rather than risk one of James' children being sympathetic to Catholicism. In 1594, Eleanor was summoned to appear before the Presbytery of Glasgow to answer charges of papistry, and in 1596 she was called again to explain 'why the sentence of excommunication should not be pronounced against her'.[11] Orders were given for the lady to take lessons from Patrick Simpson, who so successfully converted the Earl of Mar's wife from Catholicism. Eleanor proved more intransigent although in December she agreed to attend sermons in the church at Linlithgow and to read the Bible every day. Despite the Kirk's fears, Eleanor proved an attentive and caring governess. She and her husband became substitute parents to Elizabeth who was raised in the company of the Livingston's five children at Linlithgow and on occasion at the Livingston's home at Falkirk.

The Kirk was alarmed about the beliefs of Elizabeth and Henry's guardians, James' financial reforms, his desire to control the Church through the appointment of bishops to impose a hierarchy, and his perceived leniency towards his Catholic nobility who he used to check the power of his Protestant lords. On 17 December, the king was harangued at the Edinburgh tollbooth during a disturbance instigated by the city's preachers. Furious, he left Holyrood for Linlithgow, the home of his infant daughter, threatening to move his government from the city. The Reverend David Black of St Andrews regarded the whole of the nobility as lacking moral and religious fibre and, in 1596, accused the queen of being a papist. He was correct in his accusations. Anne, raised a Lutheran, was guided by her friend, Henrietta Stewart, the Countess of Huntly. In Linlithgow, the following May, Eleanor Hay was excommunicated because of her refusal to abjure her faith.

Elizabeth's sister, Margaret, was born on 24 December 1598 at Dalkieth and placed in the hands of her wet nurse, Helena Chichton. Eleanor's Catholicism did not prevent the king placing the newest addition of his family with the Livingstons. Margaret's arrival saw new appointments to the household. At least two more rockers, Christian Scimgeour and Marian Hepburn, were appointed. Eleanor was assisted in her duties of caring for two princesses by Margaret Stewart, Lady Ochiltree, who was present at the birth of Elizabeth's younger sister. She was another of Anne of Denmark's friends as well as being a member of her household. Despite the agitation of the Kirk, the two princesses remained in Eleanor's care. In May 1599 the king paid a tailor, Peter Saunderson, for clothing for his two daughters to be worn at the baptism of Elizabeth's younger sister, Margaret, and in June payment was made for furniture for use by the king's 'dearest daughter' Elizabeth.[12] The baptism at Holyrood was an opportunity for the toddler to spend time with her family and for her father's subjects and visitors to see the little girls for themselves. It was the responsibility of Lady Livingston and Lady Ochiltree that the two princesses were treated with deference in public and that Elizabeth, young as she was, knew her manners. In March 1600 the king recognised the Livingstons' contribution to his daughters' education with the grant of a charter to Falkirk. That same year Livingston was elevated to the peerage.

Anne of Denmark was rather less satisfied, even though it was much easier for her to visit Linlithgow than Stirling. She wanted an opportunity to raise her daughters herself. In March 1600 Margaret, who was sickly from birth, became ill. Her death the same month galvanised the queen. At the end of the year, she set about creating a nursery at Dunfermline. It was her intention to gain custody of Elizabeth and her household, possibly as a preliminary to requesting guardianship of Henry from Mar. However, James preferred for his daughter to remain at Linlithgow. Anne, thwarted once more, and having converted to Catholicism found no support from the Kirk. Instead, in May 1602, some of the General Assembly's number suggested that the little girl, who was of an age to be learning her prayers and attending to stories from the Bible as well as attending church services, be moved to the care of Jean Fleming, Countess of Cassilis, the widow of John Maitland the former lord chancellor and current wife of John Kennedy, 5th Earl of Cassilis. The countess was described as 'a lady without all religion'.[13]

At home in Linlithgow, Elizabeth was raised to be an asset to her parents. It was Eleanor's job to oversee the princess' religious and moral education and to ensure that she was well versed in the social graces so that she might deport herself as a king's daughter. Conduct books dating from slightly later in the seventeenth century, provided instruction in manners, etiquette and moral behaviour. From a young age, girls, whatever their rank, were required to be obedient and respectful. The conduct books and earlier works like that of the Spanish humanist Juan Luis Vives, emphasise the need for girls to be virtuous and to learn domestic skills including needlework and household management. The dolls, described as babies, purchased by the king for his daughter, reflect that Elizabeth's role was to grow up, make a marriage that was beneficial to James, and have children of her own. Eleanor and the women in Elizabeth's household taught the child how to behave modestly, which meant not talking or laughing too much and even how to walk in the clothes that turned her from a baby into a miniature adult. When Elizabeth left Eleanor's care to make the journey to London in 1603, she demonstrated at both York and Leicester during public receptions that she knew how to conduct herself as a princess of Scotland.

The king's own carefully planned education did little to shape his beliefs in the direction that Buchanan intended but now James was determined that his heir would understand the duty of kingship as he himself recognised it. To that end, he wrote *The True Law of Free Monarchies* and *Basilicon Doron*, written in the form of a letter to his heir, in which he set out the divine right of kings as an instruction manual in the duties of monarchy. James, who valued the virtues of a humanist education, decided that rather than his son's schoolmaster providing training for kingship, it was James' own duty to train his lawful successor. The books provided a theological justification of absolute monarchy and were printed in 1598 and 1599 respectively for other people to read, besides Henry, so that they might also understand the role of a king. At first only seven copies of the book were printed. One of them found its way to Sir Robert Cecil in England, while Adam Newton, who was appointed at Henry's tutor received another. James argued, using his knowledge of the Bible, that a king was ordained by God and that only

God could unmake a monarch. James took the opportunity to criticise the influence of the Kirk and its assumption of a more democratic form of government, which at the time of writing was not only trying to interfere with the way in which the king ruled his country but with whom he chose to lodge his children. He also contended that there was a duty for a crowned head to fulfil, with honour, the office that they were given and which was willingly promised at the time when a sovereign was crowned. Above all kings had responsibilities to God. He provided biblical quotations to support the argument, contrary to everything that Buchanan believed, that kings were more important than their subjects and it was this that give them the prerogative to impose new laws. James' only concession was to add the caveat that tradition was an important barometer of what was acceptable or not and that God would punish wicked kings and that monarchy obliged kings to be more careful about committing sins because they were the role models for their people. A monarch would be judged not only for his own faults but for the errors of his people. But for James the law of nature meant that Henry, as heir to the throne, would learn how to be a father and leader to his people. James maintained that the most important way of guarding against evil and behaving in a regal fashion was regular reading of the Bible. A godly education based in scripture was essential if Henry was to fulfil his father's, and God's, requirements. Inevitably, radicals like Andrew Melville, who favoured a Calvinist theocracy, objected to the king's new book even though the work focused on study of the scripture and the necessity of being a good Christian. Unsurprisingly, in 1603, when Pope Clement VIII offered to provide James VI with finance to support his claim to the English throne in return for sending Henry to Rome to be educated, the king refused.

Basilicon Doron, translated as *Royal Gift*, instructed Henry that Parliament was to be used as a court for the passing of new laws. The focus on law and justice formed the second part of the book and considered the practical methods by which a state was governed. The king was careful to note that the book was not designed to be used as a manual for ruling all kingdoms – just for Scotland because of the particular nature of the realm. At about the same time that James wrote the manuscript, he took to describing himself as a Solomon or a David. The third and final section of the book, which included advice on marriage and adultery, provided Henry with information about the codes of conduct to which a monarch should adhere. It covered everything from personal grooming to the need for self-control. Later, when James corresponded with his heir, he referred to *Basilicon Doran* expecting Henry to understand references to it from a very young age. Suffice to say Elizabeth's education was not considered in so much detail while she was still in the care of Lady Livingston. Her duty was to be an enhancement to the Stuart name as befitted her future role as a wife and mother, married for the best interests of her father, or even her brother.

Chapter Eight

Sparks of Majesty

When Henry was in his sixth year, James decided that it was time for him to leave the care of women. Adam Newton, a noted linguist who taught Greek, Latin and French, was already in position as the prince's tutor. More important, perhaps, was the fact that Newton was also the first professor of law appointed at the University of Edinburgh in 1595. It is thought likely that James' own former tutor, Peter Young, recommended Newton to him, knowing of the king's views about the importance of monarchs understanding law and the legal system so that they might rule more effectively. The tutor, who was a Presbyterian, knew that his position relied upon his respecting royal supremacy rather than expressing more radical views supported by ultra-Presbyterians. This understanding turned him into a staunch supporter of the king[1] whose dislike of the views of men like Buchanan was well known.

Newton was assisted by men such as Walter Quin, an Irish poet, who were also invited to Stirling to teach Henry. The poet wrote in Latin, English, French and Italian and it was his task to teach the prince both 'poesie', as poetry was known, and languages. Quin met James in 1595 and presented him with a poem on the subject of the English throne the following year and in 1600 he published a work in the king's honour. The Irish poet was also a client of Elizabeth I's favourite, Robert Devereux, 2nd Earl of Essex who, with one eye on the future, was seeking to win James' favour before he ascended England's throne.

The king was determined that Henry should be provided with a household that mirrored that of a monarch so that he was prepared for its ordering and management when he became an adult. One of Annabell Murray's nephews, David Murray of Gorthy, served the prince as first gentleman of the bedchamber. Mar's cousin was both a soldier and a poet. Robert Douglas, whose father was executed for his part in the Ruthven Raid and whose maternal grandfather was master of James VI's household before his execution for treason in 1585, became Henry's stable master. Also among the household was David Foulis, another supporter of the Earl of Essex. The prince was well provided with companions including Mar's sons and daughters. In reality many of the men and women, or their families, who served Henry at Stirling had agendas of their own. It was the prince's task, as he grew up, to distinguish where to bestow his support for his own interests. For Henry, politicking needed to come as naturally as breathing. By the time he entered adolescence the prince had decided that his now active royal court would be a focus of culture and the patronage of learning as well as a centre for Protestantism. For now, access to Henry's childhood household held the promise of future preferment and influence.

The prince's education began, much as his father's and Tudor cousins had done, with Latin grammar and rhetoric before advancing to modern languages. Newton seems not to have applied the double translation method favoured by Buchanan although Henry was required to write essays in the form of letters, in Latin, in a range of styles using Classical authors, provided as models by Newton, to annotate and then imitate. It was compulsory that James' heir, and his younger siblings, send annual New Year letters covering their academic progress, written in the different languages they studied, to their father. To begin with Henry's letters were poorly penned, in an Italic hand, but on one occasion, the letter sent to the king on 1 January 1603–1604, was carefully copied rather than being an original work. James recognised that his son's tutors sought to create a good impression of Henry's progress and replied:

> My Sonne, I am glad that by your letter I may perceive that you make some progress in learning, although I suspect you have rather written than drafted it, for I long to receive a letter from you that may be wholly yours, as well matter as form, as well formed by your mind as drawn by your fingers, for you may remember that in my Book to you I warned you to beware with that kind of wit that may fly out at the end of your fingers, not that I commend not a fair hand writing.[2]

James went on to advise Henry, who would celebrate his seventh birthday on 19 February, to 'trust a little more to your own strength, and away with childish bashfulness'.[3] It was essential in the king's view for a monarch to think independently from his advisors and to be able to argue his case coherently.

The Earl of Mar and Sir David Murray were charged with overseeing Henry's exercise, martial skills, riding and other courtly activities, such as dancing, that were demanded of royalty. The king's accounts for April 1600 list the purchase of two crossbows, a quiver, a gilt winding key and twelve arrows.[4] Like James before him, Henry's education would equip him with a love of the chase but the king also intended for his son's education to have a more martial flavour. James sent Sir Richard Preston, who was a professional soldier, to teach his son the use of arms.[5] Henry would learn to handle a pike and a gun as well as a sword and dagger. As he advanced in years, the prince preferred athletic and soldierly activities to his schoolbooks. He also received golf lessons. James purchased four tennis rackets as well as two golf clubs for his son in September 1600.[6] On one occasion, when Henry was older, the prince did not realise that Newton was standing nearby chatting with another of his schoolmasters as he prepared to strike the ball. Someone called a warning to Henry that Newton would be struck to which the prince responded, 'had I done so I had but paid my debts'[7] demonstrating that the schoolmaster did not always spare the rod to encourage his pupil in his lessons.

Scottish politics remained volatile. The youngest of James and Anne's sons was born four months after the conclusion of the Gowrie Conspiracy which saw an attempt by Alexander Ruthven and his brother to kidnap the king from under the noses of his gentlemen. There are other theories about the circumstances that led to the death of the two men, during an unscheduled visit to Gowrie House on 5 August 1600, including a royal cover up by James who was intent on destroying the family. Whatever the truth of the matter, the king used the episode to bolster his authority and to emphasise that he ruled by divine right. He ordered a public thanksgiving for his safe deliverance, while in Dunfermline preparations were underway for another royal lying-in. Janet Kinloch, the midwife, was summoned and orders given to John Murray to carry the news of the outcome to the king. Prince Charles, a sickly infant, was born on 19 November 1600 and was hastily baptised for fear that he would not survive. A second christening was performed on 23 December at Holyrood with more pomp, at which time he was invested with the titles Duke of Albany, Marquess of Ormonde and Earl of Ross. Anne did not attend – women recovering from childbirth remained in their chambers – but Marie Stewart, the Countess of Mar and her sister, Henrietta, the Countess of Huntly, were both in attendance. The day after Charles' birth the Ruthven family's estates were confiscated by Act of Parliament and the family's titles voided. It meant, quite conveniently, that a debt of £80,000 owing to the family by James was excused.

Like his brothers and sisters before him, Charles was provided with a wet nurse and rockers, one of whom, Marian Hepburn, received a pension of £166 13s 4d in 1602 and an annuity of £15 in 1605.[8] The baby's household was entrusted into the care of Alexander Seton, Lord Fyvie, but there is no known ordinance laid down for the boy's household. Dunfermline was part of Anne of Denmark's dowry and Alexander was appointed the castle's constable in 1596. Charles was in Fyvie's charge but he was not made responsible for the boy's education until the prince was in his third year. When the privy council issued their instruction, James VI of Scotland was also James I of England and the king was making arrangements for the care of his children, whom he planned should remain in Scotland while he and Anne of Denmark went south. In the event, it was only Charles who stayed.

Fyvie's wife, Lillias, died in 1601, leaving four children. Her daughter Anne was in her eighth year at the time of Charles' birth while another daughter, Margaret, was about the same age as the prince. Seton, who needed a male heir, took as his second wife, Grissel Leslie, five months after he was widowed. Their daughter, Lilias, was born in 1602. Charles was not without companions at Dunfermline to entertain him, encourage him to talk and to walk, as well as to share his games. Records of a pension granted to Margaret Stewart, Lady Ochiltree for her 'carefull and dutiful attendance upon the late Queen and their royal children' show that rather than either of Fyvie's wives, it was Margaret who was appointed as the prince's lady governess.[9] The nursery at Dunfermline began to evolve as Charles left infancy. John Murray was appointed as the boy's valet[10] in the same way that David Murray of Gorthy filled the post for Henry. Jean Drummond, later Countess of Roxburghe following her marriage to John Ker, Earl of Roxburghe in 1614, is known to have cared for Charles from February 1602. It is likely that her assistance was required when Charles was joined in his nursery by a short-lived brother, Robert. Lady Ochiltree is described as caring for the baby 'til the hour of his decease'.[11] The selection of Lady Ochiltree as governess for James' younger sons was one designed to find acceptance with the Kirk. Her first husband, Andrew Stewart, was a staunch Protestant who died in 1578. His sister, another Margaret, became John Knox's second wife. By the time she took responsibility for Charles, Lady Ochiltree was married to Uchtred Macdowell of Gathland who was implicated in the Ruthven Raid but who was pardoned, in 1584, for his part in it.

By contrast Fyvie, who was a favourite of both the king and the queen, was suspected of being a Papist, having been educated in Rome by his father who was a supporter of Mary, Queen of Scots. More importantly, he was a learned man who would be well suited to overseeing the education of a prince. He spoke Italian fluently, having completed his education with a doctorate from the University of Bologna where he was known for his learning of philosophy. It was also reported that he excelled at mathematics. At the time of his appointment as Charles' guardian, he was Lord President of the Court in Session, a post he held until 1604 when he became lord chancellor of Scotland. Like Prince Henry, James intended that his younger son would benefit from an education provided by someone who understood the law.

Thomas Murray was appointed to be Prince Charles' principal tutor at about the same time. The king offered the tutor £200 a year for life to teach his son. Like Newton, Murray was a religious conformist and the Murrays of Tullibardine, to whom Thomas was related, were loyal servants of the Crown. In addition, Murray had written poetry recognising the king's authority over the Kirk and had translated James' own poem, *Lepanto*, celebrating the defeat of the Turks in the 1571 battle, into Latin. Poetry, patronage and career progression were things that went hand in hand in the courts of Renaissance princes, even the schoolrooms of younger sons. The king's poem was also a reminder of the extent of James' own scholarly interests since it included reference to poetry from Italy and Spain as well as to works by Homer and Virgil. The verses were even translated into French by Du Bartas, who was much admired by the king. James' work would be reprinted as *His Majesties Lepanto, or Heroicall Song* following Elizabeth I's death in the same way that *Basilicon Doron*, written as an instruction manual for Prince Henry, was republished and purchased by the king's new English subjects either as a memento of the occasion or by men and women who were anxious to find out more about their sovereign.

More practically, for the moment, Lady Ochiltree took delivery of a walking aid described as an oak stool with wheels to help the little boy.[12] Like his father, Charles' motor development occurred later than usual. He did not walk unaided until he was 6 years old and at 4 years had not yet learned to talk. He may have suffered from macroglossia, or having a tongue that was too large for his mouth. It must have seemed unlikely on occasion that Charles would reach an age where he wore breeches rather than long skirts and even if he did, society was not kind to people with deformities and disabilities. Robert Cecil, 1st Earl of Salisbury and now James I of England's new chief minister, was nicknamed 'pygmy' by Elizabeth I because of his height and the fact that scoliosis left him with a hunched back. James preferred to call his minister, 'my little beagle' which at least suggested loyalty. Henry Howard, 1st Earl of Northampton, another of the men who courted the king before Elizabeth I's death, rapidly became a favourite but in about 1605 was accused by James of making 'cruel and malicious speeches against Baby Charles and his honest father'.[13] Both Cecil and James tried to protect their own children from the stigma of disability that haunted them both. Cecil paid for his daughter, Francis, to have an operation in an attempt to correct her twisted spine while James turned to alternative cures for Charles' tangled speech and weak legs once it was clear that the little boy was well enough to join the rest of the family in England.

Chapter Nine

Princes and Princesses of Both Scotland and England

The Earl of Mar travelled south with King James in 1603 leaving Prince Henry at Stirling under the watchful gaze of his countess and younger brother. It was originally intended that James' children would remain in Scotland until they were older but at the beginning May the queen, who was four months pregnant, took the opportunity to try and gain access to her son. She was under instructions to follow the king south within twenty days of his own departure but she saw a chance, in her husband's absence, to finally gain control of her eldest son. She travelled to Stirling with Jean Drummond and demanded that she be permitted to leave with Henry. However, the Countess of Mar refused to allow it. It is not clear whether this was one of the last acts of Annabell Murray before her death or whether she was already dead and it was Marie Stewart who refused to deliver Anne's son into her hands without the king's warrant. What is certain is that the queen miscarried shortly after her arrival at Stirling and refused to leave there without Henry.

With the queen incapacitated, the Erskines were able to present the problem of guardianship of the prince to James, whose authority was essential if Henry was to leave Mar's care. While they waited, Lord Fyvie, the most important of James' judges, along with members of Scotland's privy council, arrived at Stirling to persuade Anne to begin her journey to England, but with no success. If anything, it made her angrier. James sent Mar back to Scotland and together with the king's lord chancellor, the Earl of Montrose, the earl tried again to persuade the queen of the importance of departing for England as originally planned, as well as explaining to her the importance of presenting his new subjects with a united front. The king could not take possession of his new throne with his queen causing a crisis back in Scotland.

Finally, at the end of May, the Duke of Lennox was sent from London with a warrant to receive Henry from the Earl of Mar and to give him to the queen. Anne's antipathy to Mar had grown with each passing year she was denied access to her son. She wrote to James demanding public reparation for the dishonour done to her and punishment for Mar and his servants. James advised Anne that she would be better making friends with the earl. On 27 May, Anne left Stirling with Henry for Edinburgh. The prince, who spent the first ten years of his life in the care of the Erskines, was to leave his foster family but was accompanied by other members of his household including David Murray and Adam Newton, who remained central to the prince's education as well as providing stability in his life.

Letters began to flow south, giving James updates regarding the health of Baby Charles, as the king called his youngest son, soon after he departed for London. In one of the first letters Fyvie sent, on 29 April 1603, the prince, described as 'that precious jewell',[1] seemed to be in better health than previously but it remained evident that the prince was not as strong as might be expected of a child of his age. Charles' care and education remained in the hands of the women of his household which was managed by Lord Fyvie. Even so, that same year, Walter Quin compiled *Corona Virtutum principe dignarum ex varijs Philosophorum, Historicorum, Oratorum, et Poetarum*, or *A Crown of Virtues Worthy of a Prince from Various Philosophers, Historians, Orators and Poets* drawn from various classical works for use by the young prince on James' orders. The king intended for his younger son to receive the same thorough grounding in the classics and the princely virtues as Henry as soon as he was of an age to begin formal studies.

Almost as soon as Anne and Henry arrived in Edinburgh, Princess Elizabeth was placed in a coach with her guardians and departed from her home at Linlithgow. She travelled south with her mother and elder brother on 1 June 1603. For Elizabeth, who had led a sheltered life, the throng must have been alarming, as was the information that once they arrived in England she would be in the care of a new governess. A warrant was issued discharging the Livingstons for their 'dewtiful caire and service'[2] on 5 July after the princess arrived in Windsor. When Elizabeth was told the news, although she was not to be separated from Lady Livingston until she reached London, she burst into tears at the thought of losing her beloved foster parents. Eleanor, still troubled by the Kirk's denunciation of her, said her farewells both to the princess and to her own daughter, Anna, who kept a record, in the Scots language, of Elizabeth's belongings, the gifts she was given and the expenses that she accrued. The document, in Italic script, demonstrates that she shared Elizabeth's handwriting lessons. It also references gifts purchased for the tutor and for her dancing master. The girls were probably also accompanied by her former governess' niece, Anna Hay, a daughter of the Earl of Erroll, who was about 11 years old at the time. The cousins were assigned to Anne of Denmark's household on arrival in England but Anna Livingston remained with Elizabeth. It was an opportunity for them to complete their education and make good matches that would benefit their families. Anna Hay married George Seton, 3rd Earl of Winton when she was 17 years old, while her cousin married Alexander Seton, whose father was the grand master of James VI's household at Prince Henry's baptism in 1594. Anna's connection to both the queen's and Elizabeth's households, as well as friendship with Jean Drummond, helped smooth the way for her husband to become the Earl of Eglinton. Her correspondence reflects the time she shared with the princess in the schoolroom at Linlithgow demonstrating both that she played the virginals and, unlike her mother, had been raised as a Protestant. A relation, a minister, said of her 'although bred at Court, yet proved a subdued and eminent Christian, and an encourager of piety and truth'.[3]

Several English ladies travelled to Berwick at their own expense to attend the new queen in the hope of advancement. Among their number was Anne Harington and her daughter Lucy, the Countess of Bedford. However, it was Francis Howard, Lady Kildare who was appointed as Elizabeth's governess as well as becoming a lady of Queen Anne's privy chamber. She carried a letter from the king recommending her services. She had been a member of Elizabeth I's household and was a near relation to the late queen through her descent from the Carey family. Her mother, Catherine Carey, was part of Elizabeth's household at Hatfield before she became queen. Francis' uncle, Robert Carey, was careful to ensure that he was the one who carried the news of the queen's death to James before anyone else. It was late in the evening on 26 March 1603, two days after he set off, that Carey arrived in Holyrood to inform the king, who had retired for the night, of the news. Lady

Kildare's appointment was part of the Carey family's reward for its foresight in serving the interests of James VI during the queen's last years. Robert was forced to wait longer for his own preferment, even suffering demotion from appointment as a gentleman of the bedchamber to a gentleman of the privy chamber beforehand.

It was Lady Kildare's responsibility to accompany Elizabeth on the journey to London, to ride with her and to accommodate her needs, travelling only a moderate distance each day, while Anne of Denmark and Prince Henry travelled ahead. The princess caught up with her family on 15 June when she arrived at York, where she was expected to take her place on the public stage as the city greeted its new royal family. As well as being provided with lavish entertainment and a feast, Elizabeth was given a purse of gold angels. The little girl was expected to conduct herself with decorum and to give thanks for the gift. It was Lady Kildare's responsibility to ensure that Elizabeth was suitably attired and spoke without hesitation or lack of manners. They travelled onwards, with Elizabeth falling further behind her mother as she became more exhausted by the demands of the journey. On 21 June the princess arrived in Nottingham where it was decided that she would remain for a few days while the queen and the rest of the royal entourage continued their journey.

Prince Henry and his mother made a detour to visit the Earl of Huntingdon so it was Elizabeth who was given a formal reception at Leicester on 22 June. From there she travelled to Anne Harington's house at Coombe Abbey near Coventry and met with the Countess of Warwick and her niece Lady Anne Clifford, who was 13 years old, and the daughter of George Clifford, 3rd Earl of Cumberland. Anne, under the tutelage of the poet Samuel Daniel, was taught music and dancing but was forbidden by the earl from learning a foreign language. Raised largely by her mother, Margaret Russell, and her family, Anne did not see much of her father. She enjoyed an extensive education which was celebrated in the so-called Great Painting, a tryptic, made in 1646, depicting Anne as a girl of 15 surrounded by books. Margaret ensured that Anne, like Princess Elizabeth, received a humanist education which included a knowledge of medicine and alchemy which Margaret taught Anne herself. Both her parents were known for their Puritan beliefs so Anne was raised to be both pious and charitable. Hers was an education suitable for a noblewoman expected to marry and to run her own household. Anne also knew that any wedding would be made in the best interests of her family, rather than her being permitted to make a love match, even though her parents' marriage, made to consolidate titles and wealth, brought them only misery. It was generally accepted that love came after a marriage. Anne would meet the princess and her companions again at Windsor and at Anne of Denmark's court.

On 1 July, Elizabeth and her governesses, having made the remainder of the journey separately from the rest of the princess' family, made a grand entrance to Windsor in a litter. Her arrival was greeted by a fanfare of trumpets. Throughout her time on public view, Elizabeth demonstrated that she knew how to conduct herself as a princess should. As well as etiquette, good manners and deportment, Elizabeth was required to meet and thank many of her father's new subjects for their welcome and gifts, and leave them with a positive impression of the new ruling family. On the 3 July she watched as her brother, Henry, was knighted at Windsor and then looked on with Lady Anne Clifford, who later recorded the episode in her diary, while the king and the knights dined. That same day Elizabeth met the French ambassador, Christophe de Harlay, Comte de Beaumont who described her as 'very well bred and handsome enough, rather tall for her age, and her disposition very gentle'.[4] The ambassador had already sent his report about the character of Anne of Denmark. Some of James' English allies told him that she was both cruel and ambitious and that if her husband was to die that she hoped to rule through Henry.[5] The king was already discussing the possibility of a double marriage between the dauphin and his 6-year-old daughter and between his own heir and a daughter of Henri IV.

Three weeks later Elizabeth and Henry were sent to Oatlands, near Weybridge, in a shared household. The location was chosen to avoid the plague which was recorded in London soon after Elizabeth I's funeral and which spread quickly that summer. The siblings discovered an empathy with one another during the journey from Scotland and now the bond was strengthened still further. Henry and Elizabeth would share one another's company and tutors until James could find new guardians for his children. It was also an opportunity for the king to separate Anne of Denmark from his heir once more. Oatlands was a very different life from the quiet one which

Elizabeth had known in Scotland. The king appointed 70 servants to the nursery in the first instance, but by October the number had reached 141. In August the Venetian ambassador, Scaramelli, visited Henry who told the ambassador about his studies, dancing lessons, hunting and playing tennis. Another guest was the Earl of Nottingham, England's Lord High Admiral, who was Lady Kildare's father. It was the earl who introduced Henry to a love of ships and the navy.

For Elizabeth, Oatlands heralded a return to the classroom. Her accounts show the purchase of parchment, paper and ink as well as new apparel. The expensive fabrics were transformed into elaborate dresses, with slashed sleeves and large stiff ruffs. Dressed as a miniature adult, complete with a whalebone corset, the princess and her staff demonstrated an important message about the wealth and magnificence of the Stuart monarchy. The king had been a frequent visitor to Linlithgow where Elizabeth was raised with her foster-family amongst stories of her ancestors, but the Scots were less formal in their approach to kings and princes than their English counterparts and radical Presbyterians often treated their monarch with little respect. Now, more deference was paid to both Henry and Elizabeth, even if on occasion James might refer to them in public as 'my bairns'[6] and they needed to conduct themselves accordingly.

Francis Howard showed herself to be diligent in the care of her charge but in September her second husband, Henry Brooke, 11th Baron Cobham was implicated in the Main and Bye Plots. The first, allegedly led by Lord Cobham and funded by the Spanish, was a conspiracy to replace James I with his cousin, Arbella Stuart, who was to be married off to Thomas Grey, 15th Baron Grey of Wilton who, like the other plotters, loathed the number of Scots who followed James to England in search of office. The second was a plan, hatched by Catholic priests and Puritans, to kidnap the king in order to force him to dismiss the privy council, appoint the plotters in their stead, and accede to their demands for religious tolerance. It was only when details of the Bye Plot were revealed that the parallel Main Plot, and the involvement of Francis' husband, were exposed. All of Lady Kildare's attempts to ingratiate herself with the Stuarts and discredit her political rivals came to naught when she was dismissed from office because of her husband and brother-in-law's involvement with the scheme. Arbella Stuart wrote that the lady was 'as near a free a woman as may be and have a bad husband'.[7] Brooke was not executed despite being found guilty of treason and implicating Sir Walter Raleigh during the process. Francis' husband remained in the Tower until a short time before his death in 1618, by which time the countess was welcome back at court having come to an accommodation with James about her husband's residence, Cobham Hall in Kent, which the king leased to her for her lifetime together with a pension of £1500 a year.[8] For James though, it was a reminder of the dangers of conspiracy and in placing his two elder children in one household he increased the risk both to them and to him.

As the drama unfolded around them and plague, carried from London, made its presence felt, Elizabeth and Henry's household moved to Nonsuch where Lady Anne Clifford and her cousin, Frances Bouchier, visited them, staying about a week before Anne departed and Frances remained, becoming one of Elizabeth's companions.[9] Later the same year, by which time Anne Clifford had learned to play the bass viol, another of her cousins, Frances Russell, was granted a place in the princess' household. In September, Henry and Elizabeth moved to Winchester where their mother entertained the prince with a masque. Ann Livinston's accounts for the period show that a servant was paid to carry dresses from there to Nonsuch on the princess' behalf. The entertainment caused some damage to the queen's reputation because it was considered too childish for more sophisticated tastes. The French ambassador described it as 'rustic'[10] while Arbella Stuart, the king's cousin, who was present was equally unimpressed but described the children's games that were played at the time.

On 19 October 1603, Lord and Lady Harington were appointed to care for Elizabeth. The Kirk would have approved their selection, as both were known to be devout Protestants. John Harington, having completed his education at the Inner Temple, was in the service of the Dudley and Sidney families whom he was related to through his mother, Lucy Sidney. In 1586 he had accompanied the princess's grandmother, Mary, Queen of Scots, on her journey to Fotheringhay and in April 1603 he had entertained King James on his journey south. When the king injured himself falling from his horse, Harington provided his own coach for James to continue his journey. In July he was created Baron Harington of Exton at the king's coronation. His son, another John, was already part of Prince Henry's household and was being educated alongside him while the Harington's daughter, Lucy, Countess of Bedford was part of Anne of Denmark's household. The countess's own education reflected Harington's view that women should receive an education that mirrored those of their male counterparts. She could speak French, Spanish and Italian, was an important patron of musicians and of writers including Ben Jonson, the metaphysical poet John Donne and Michael Drayton. She was also a patron of the lexicographer John Florio, who was Henry Wriothesley's tutor as well as William Herbert, 3rd Earl of Pembroke's schoolmaster. She was known to be a skilled courtier, and one of Anne of Denmark's favourite ladies. Despite the extravagance of her life style, Lucy was also a devout Calvinist. This did not, it is rumoured, prevent her from taking part in some of the court masques bare breasted. As well as her literary patronage and court life, she was also known for her love of gardens and garden design. She was ideally placed to help in the education of the king's daughter as well as to ensure the continued good fortune of her extended family. In time, the countess and the princess, who was fifteen years younger than Lucy, would become close friends as their adult correspondence shows.

Elizabeth, having said goodbye to her beloved elder brother in December, journeyed to Exton and then to the Haringtons' home at Coombe Abbey in Warwickshire, while Henry and his household moved to Hampton Court. The princess did not travel alone. Alison Hay, Lady Dunkerrant, remained by her side. The princess' household was composed of three ladies-in-waiting including Anna Livingston, a doctor, a personal French maid, a seamstress, a dancing instructor who was appointed in 1604, French and Italian teachers, several grooms and a music teacher. One of the things she would miss about Oatlands was riding the parkland with her brother.

The music teacher, Dr John Bull, had formerly been the organist at the Chapel Royal. His skill with the keyboard saw him gain a professorship of music at Gresham College, London as well as European recognition for his skills. He was paid £40 each year to teach Elizabeth and her brother, Henry, but he found time to compose pieces for both the organ and the virginals. The princess' household was also home to a tuner and a man who played while Elizabeth danced. The dancing master, Francis Cardell, was the son of Queen Elizabeth I's dancing master who joined the court of Anne of Denmark. In

January 1604, Elizabeth wrote to Robert Cecil asking that Cardell might be appointed to her household as her dancing under his instruction pleased both her parents.[11] As well as teaching Elizabeth to dance, he was also employed as a lutenist. Sadly, the master died the following year and it was Frances' father, Thomas, who served Elizabeth until her marriage, in 1613, and her departure from England. The appointments, and the way in which the young princess was dressed and even how her hair was done, served to strengthen the likeness between James' daughter and her godmother, Elizabeth I. Her writing master, Jean de Beau-Chesne, even taught the princess to write a signature that was almost identical to the old queen's. At first it was a way for the Stuarts to emphasise their shared bloodline with the Tudors and their right to the crown. It was also a way of projecting royal authority. As she grew up, Elizabeth's popularity with her English subjects grew, not least because they believed that as well as the name, the princess inherited Elizabeth Tudor's virtues and religious beliefs.

Harington's niece Anne Sutton, the daughter of 5th Baron Dudley, joined the household to act as companion to Elizabeth during her studies as did Elizabeth Dudley, Frances Bourchier (who was a daughter of the 3rd Earl of Bath), and Philadelphia Carey, a daughter of Robert Carey. Anne, known as Dudley, rather than Sutton, was pleased to find a home with the princess. Her father, Edward, abandoned his wife and children to live with his mistress in 1592 when she was still a toddler.

Elizabeth missed her beloved elder brother. It was to Henry that she wrote her first letter when she was 7 years old. The correspondence between the two would continue throughout the princess' childhood. Like Henry, Elizabeth was required to write to her father to demonstrate the skills she acquired in the classroom. She wrote in Italian, French and English as well as demonstrating a grasp of an Italic hand. Elizabeth would grow up to write hundreds of letters, many of them in cipher, to lobby on behalf of her husband, promoting the cause of her children and of her English nieces and nephews.

Henry, together with his parents, travelled to Hampton Court in December 1603. As with Henry's sister, Elizabeth, James wished to ensure that his son would appear as a Renaissance prince at court. Amongst the early appointments to be made was of Alfonso Ferrabosco II, who was made a groom of the privy chamber with the responsibility of teaching Henry the 'art of music'.[12] Henry was required not only to dance but to play the viol. It was a popular instrument as it was relatively easy to learn as well as being associated with refined tastes.

Besides acquiring more courtly polish, the prince learned first-hand the business of managing a kingdom and demonstrated his dancing skills during the festivities. In January 1604, he sat next to his father at the Hampton Court Conference which sought to address England's religious divisions. James made some concessions to his Puritan subjects and authorised a new translation of the Bible, but rejected significant changes to religious rites. The king's Catholic subjects were disappointed in their hope for freedom to worship how they chose. At the end of four days, James' desire to shape religious policy, which was about containing the power of the Church, and exploring his vision of Christian harmony had exposed tensions within his new realm.

Henry usually remained with his household at Nonsuch in Surrey. Henry VIII built it to compete with French Renaissance palaces and it was where Edward VI spent much time as a child. Its custodian, John Lumley, had attended the previous three coronations and was a judge at Mary, Queen of Scots' trial. More importantly he was one of the foremost book collectors of his age and amassed a large library at the palace which now provided Henry's tutors with the resources they needed for the prince's education. Newton's salary was now £250 per annum. As well as languages and the usual necessities of a humanist education, the king wished for his son to become proficient in law. Sir John Harington of Exton recommended godly preachers for Henry's chapel and the prince was soon immersed in Calvinist theology. One of the appointments, George Hakewill, spent time at the University of Heidelberg where he developed pronounced Calvinist views. He was also a noted orator and disputant. Like James, Henry was expected to interrogate his reading and then discuss its contents with his masters and companions.

Nonsuch became a *Courtly College*.[13] Young men and boys from leading families were invited to learn alongside him with their own tutors. Among their number was John Harington of Exton, the son of Elizabeth's guardian, William Sidney the eldest son of Sir Robert Sidney who later became Earl of Leicester, and Robert Cecil's son, William. Robert Cecil, like King James, wanted to ensure that the heir to the throne grew up alongside the boys and young men who would one day act as his own advisers. A noble education bore many similarities to a princely one. Like Henry, Sidney's education began at the age of 6 but in the company of his siblings, even though Henry's father was prepared to pay £20 a year for a tutor for his heir alone.[14] In time, the aim was that the prince's boyhood companions, who also learned to wield pikes, use crossbows, fire pistols, ride and to hunt, would form his adult household and government. As well as lessons and outdoor pursuits there were also entertainments that are known to have included playing shuffleboard, but he is just as likely to have played ninepins, bowls and pell-mell which was similar to croquet and played on grass.

James determined that Henry should continue to learn practical statecraft by governing his own household from a young age, with the assistance of his senior staff as well as accompanying him on official visits and sitting next to him during meetings. It was not always as straightforward as might have been assumed. On one occasion the eldest son of the Earl of Leicester, William Sidney, who was 15 years old, stabbed his school master, Mr Bird[15] when, it is thought, the tutor attempted to whip the boy. It seemed likely, in the immediate aftermath, that Bird would not survive the attack. King James intervened and dismissed the youth from his son's court.

On 22 March 1604, the prince was in London, at St Paul's Wharf, to receive a gift from the Earl of Nottingham – a 25-foot-long sailing vessel named the *Disdain* which had battlements like the *Ark Royal*.[16] It fuelled a lifelong passion for ships and exploration. The boat was built by Phineas Pett who was the master shipwright at Chatham. The following month the king granted Pett a shilling per day as the prince's servant and captain of the *Disdain*. For Phineas it meant royal favour and on the death of his brother, Joseph, in 1605 promotion to the post of Master Shipwright at Deptford. It was from Pett that Henry learned the basics of vessel construction, rigging and ship design. In 1607, the shipwright presented Henry with a 'curious model'[17] covered in carvings and paintings, possibly of the *Ark Royal*. A conversation on shipbuilding followed. In 1608, Henry visited Pett at Woolwich and was shown around the dockyard there, during which he viewed the keel of the new and largest ship in the navy, and was provided with a tour of the *Ann Royal*. In 1610, it was Princess Elizabeth who came to Woolwich to see the dockyard for herself, having already met with Pett at St James's and knowing of her brother's friendship with the shipbuilder. By 1610, and the launching of the *Prince Royal*, a three-decker designed by Sir Walter Raleigh, Henry's interest in ships and shipbuilding was undiminished. The prince summoned Pett more frequently to answer his questions and explain maritime matters as his schooling came to an end.

By April 1604, Prince Charles' health was good enough for him to make the journey to London. On 14 April, Dr Henry Atkins was sent to Scotland with an apothecary, Edward Phillips, to attend the prince and Lord Fyvie was given funds to transport his charge south. Atkins wrote to Robert Cecil on 3 July from Dunfermline to say that Charles 'is beginning to walk alone, which he never did before'.[18] In August, the party escorting the prince began its journey south which was recorded by George Seton. Charles' escort was no less splendid than the rest of the royal family's when they made their progress from Scotland to London. At Leicester, where Charles spent a day and a night on 15 August, at the home of Sir William Skipwith, seven hogsheads of beer were required to supply his entourage.[19]

In February 1605, Alexander Seton's guardianship of Prince Charles came to a conclusion and he returned to Scotland to continue in his role as chancellor. The same document also confirmed the good health of the boy, although Robert Carey recorded that no one else in England wanted custody of the prince because of his reputation for sickliness. Carey's wife, Elizabeth who was mistress of the sweet coffers[20] to Queen Anne, was appointed to care for Charles, who was created Duke of York in January 1605. Carey recognised that many people thought that the new duke was too sickly to thrive. He wrote that his enemies were glad of his new role caring for the prince because if the boy died, the Careys would lose favour at court. Elizabeth Carey's views are not recorded. She was already mother to three children and was determined that the little boy would prosper in her care – even if it meant disagreeing with the king.

Chapter Ten

Henry Frederick: the Rising Sun of England

By 1605 the *Courtly College* was re-established. The Irish poet, Walter Quin, journeyed south and took his place in the household as the prince's assistant tutor with a salary of £50 each year. Newton liaised closely with Robert Cecil who helped to shape the prince's household. Together they wished to form Henry into a champion of Protestantism. Thomas Chaloner the Younger, who was known for his interest in alchemy, chemistry and natural history, was appointed to the role of governor in August 1605. The prince's new governor was part of Robert Cecil's faction, as well as a boyhood companion of the minister, and well trusted. Thomas also hastened to Holyrood as soon as Elizabeth I died. Having been sent to Scotland by Burghley during the 1590s, he maintained a secret correspondence with James thereafter and now cashed in on his forward-thinking, although it has also been suggested that the appointment was made to recompense Chaloner for his financial losses when James I made alum production, which Henry's new guardian introduced to Britain, a monopoly of the Crown and Chaloner was forced to lease his workings to him.

Chaloner, educated initially at St Paul's, went on to study at Oxford but did not take his degree, preferring instead to travel. He accompanied Robert Dudley, Earl of Leicester to the Low Countries on campaign in 1585 as a volunteer. As well as mathematics and navigation, Chaloner had a particular interest in alum which was used as a mordant for fixing colours in woollen cloth. Whilst visiting Italy, Chaloner visited alum mines and recognised the shale deposits in which the alum was found as similar to the geology of his Guisborough estates. As well as a fixative, alum was also used for the curing of leather and in medicines. Together with his cousin and foreign workers, who came from Italy and Germany, he developed a process for its extraction and use. In 1584 he published a booklet about the medicinal properties of saltpetre. Chaloner's links included friendship with John Dee and the Dutch inventor Cornelius Drebbel, as well as connections to Venice and Florence. The prince's household expanded to include Thomas Fleetwood, whose daughter was married to one of Chaloner's sons. One of Fleetwood's sisters was married to Henry's cofferer, David Foulis.

Men with expertise were called upon to assist the prince with his studies as the need arose. Elizabeth's guardian, John Harington of Exton, acted as a tutor for the prince on occasion. It was he who introduced the prince to the works of Tacitus. Henry also received some tuition from John Harington of Exton's cousin, John Harington of Kelston, a former courtier, soldier in the service of Elizabeth I and inventor of a flushing toilet. It was this Harington, who spent part of James' reign in prison for the debts of his cousin, Sir Griffin Markham. In 1607 he sent the prince a letter and a poem about Bishop Gardiner. During an interview with the king, Harington discussed philosophy, Aristotle, witchcraft and the health benefits, or otherwise, of tobacco. That same year, Harington translated from Italian to English the *Health Regimen of the School of Salernum*. The medieval guide to good health may have been used as part of Henry's education. By 1608, Harington was corresponding with Prince Henry on the matter of medieval kings, treason and the Wars of the Roses. He sent the prince, at Henry's own request, in 1608, a version of the *Orlando Furioso,* or the *Life of Ariosto*, which Harington originally translated in 1591. The introduction to the work contained a defence of poetry fitting King James' narrative of the Stuarts as poet-kings. For Harington, the work in both 1591 and 1608 was a method of seeking office, but for the prince it was another lesson in literary criticism as well as an entertaining chivalric romance about knights, ladies, battles and vengeance. Elizabeth I was shocked at the content of some of the verses but no doubt a teenage boy was less concerned about any dangers to his morals than the aging queen might have been about the modesty of her maids of honour.

Thomas Harriot, the astronomer, explorer and mathematician, and a colleague of Sir Walter Raleigh, who was in correspondence with Kepler taught Henry about navigation and the use of telescopes. Henry, who was curious about the world around him soon added telescopes and automata displaying moving stars and planets to his collection. As well as Harriot, Henry was able to learn about the universe, as it was understood in the seventeenth century, from Thomas Lydiat who began his career as a theologian but, by

1603, studied mathematics and cosmography. Henry paid him £40 a year and granted him use of his library. For the prince, and the men who taught him, the study of the universe was more than about an understanding of emerging scientific ideas, it was for a better consideration of God's ordering of His creation. Mapping the stars also allowed navigators to sail the seas with greater accuracy and led the prince back to exploration, cartography, shipbuilding and the martial world of a Protestant prince.

It was not enough for a prince to be scholarly. He was required to know how to behave in courtly settings and show himself to best advantage to his subjects and visiting foreign dignitaries. Henry is known to have taken part in Anne of Denmark's court masques. On one occasion, in 1611, he played the part of Oberon the fairy king. It was a reminder, not only about Henry's gracefulness and his ability to remember lines, but an aide-memoire that Henry aspired to be a virtuous and heroic ruler. The masques at court were often allegorical tales or linked the Stuarts to Britain's mythological past and Anne of Denmark wished to emphasise that she was the mother of a new line of monarchs. Henry was educated, and presented at court, as Henry Tudor once taught his own eldest son Arthur, to be 'founder of a new generation of ideals, ambitions and military policy'.[1] In 1610, when Henry was 14 years old, he was invested as Prince of Wales and among the celebrations was a masque created by Ben Jonson which identified the prince as the 'Rising Sun of England'. As well as the performance there were fireworks, a mock naval battle and a joust. Henry was denied the opportunity of making a grand entry to London by horse because of the prohibitive costs that a procession would occasion. Instead, he arrived with the royal fleet. For Anne of Denmark the celebrations at court were an opportunity not only to celebrate Henry but to try and extend her political reach as his mother now that he was leaving the schoolroom. Her masque, *Tethy's Festival*, was written by Samuel Daniel, Anne Clifford's former tutor. It was the first occasion that Prince Charles', as Zephyrus the west wind, took part in a court entertainment accompanied by twelve little girls who played nymphs. Elizabeth also took to the stage in a costume designed by Inigo Jones. Both Henry and his sister understood that behind the drama and elaborate costumes, the Stuarts were intent on impressing foreign ambassadors, reinforcing their divine right to rule and conveying subtle political messages to their subjects. Performance and politics went hand in hand.[2]

Tilting, swordsmanship, shooting and sports were equally important skills in a prince's repertoire. Although the use of longbows in seventeenth-century warfare was declining with the rise of the musket, it remained law that all boys between the ages of 7 and 17 should practice shooting, although it is questionable how rigorously the law was applied. In a letter that Henry wrote to his friend John Harington, he described how he was much improved at tennis and also at handling his pike.[3] When his uncle, Christian IV of Denmark, visited England in the summer of 1606, Henry took part in the jousting that was part of the celebrations. In 1608, Sir Henry Lee, who was Queen Elizabeth's tournament champion, presented the prince with a set of jousting armour, made at Greenwich and costing £200. The hardened and tempered carbon steel was richly decorated and was at the forefront of military technology. Henry was not only taking part in court spectacles, he was also learning about war and becoming used to wearing twenty-five kilograms of armour. In 1610, a tilt was held at Whitehall on 3 June to celebrate the creation of Henry as Prince of Wales. Several of his companions, including Robert Sidney, were made Knights of the Bath at the same time. Among the men who took part in the tilting was Theophilus Howard, heir to the Earl of Suffolk, who was something of a favourite with the king and queen. Theophilus and his younger brothers were among the young men who shared Prince Henry's education and leisure time. The earl, their father, had cause during the summer of 1607, along with his brother-in-law, Lord Salisbury, to write to Adam Newton, who was Henry's tutor, to remind him that 'swimming is a dangerous thing, that the comparison holds not between our boyes and sonnes of Kings'.[4] James might have sympathised with his son's passion for hunting, tennis or even swimming but Henry's pre-occupation with chivalric ideals, exploration and all things military ran counter to James who increasingly viewed himself as *Rex Pacificus*. He aspired not only to bringing peace between his own three kingdoms but across Europe.

Henry's tutors ensured that the Prince Henry corresponded with a network of foreign notables and English travellers abroad, honing his skills in using correspondence as a diplomatic tool and enabling him to find out more about the geography, history and culture of the people that wrote to him. At the beginning of the seventeenth century, it was becoming usual for the sons of noble families to study at either Oxford or Cambridge and then take a trip, that became known as the Grand Tour, which saw them venture to France, Italy and Greece to see for themselves the buildings and places that they read about in their school books. It was effectively a hands-on view of the classical antiquity that Renaissance scholars valued. Sir Francis Bacon stated that 'he that travelleth into a country before he hath some entrance into the language, goeth to school, and not to travel'.[5] While it was not possible for Henry to undertake this journey for himself, the prince's companion, John Harington, went on a tour of Europe in the autumn of 1604 with his tutor. He sent letters in French and Latin to Henry describing the places he visited. In 1608 he was sent by his father to study at Sidney College, Cambridge, which Sir John helped to found on behalf of the Countess of Sussex, before being sent to Italy and Venice where the English ambassador, Henry Wotton, described him as Henry's 'right eye'.[6] As well as completing John's education with an early version of the grand tour of Europe, the correspondence between the two companions gave the prince an insight into the politics, geography and traditions of the places that Harington visited. William Cecil, the son of Robert, made his own version of the journey in the company of his tutor and also sent letters back to the prince, although not as frequently as he sent missives to the Earl of Salisbury. It is only possible to imagine that discussion that took place between the young men and the prince when they returned to Henry's court.

The French ambassador, writing in October 1606, reported that the prince spent two hours a day studying but that he employed the rest of his time at various sports including throwing the bar and vaulting. It was significantly less time than his father or his Tudor predecessors spent in the schoolroom and he failed to complete a number of tasks set for him by Newton. He should have gifted his father verses translated from English into Latin based on poetry by Guy du Faur during the New Year celebrations of 1606, but Henry abandoned the task midway through, not it seems because he was unable to do it but because he was insufficiently interested.[7] James only had himself to blame. *Basilicon Doron* counselled against a king being overly scholarly. It was essential that monarchs were men of the world. Henry preferred athletic and military activities to Latin. He would rather tackle one of Harriot's mathematical problems or issue a challenge to find the trajectory of a cannon ball to allow gunners to aim better, than to translate works from one language to another.

The lure of seafaring, exploration and making war on the Catholic Hapsburgs, who claimed all of the New World for themselves, drew Henry into the orbit of Sir Walter Raleigh, much to the irritation of the king. The prince first met the Tudor adventurer when he was 9 years old and had already begun to plan the expansion of the navy. Raleigh shared his knowledge of ships, naval strategy and science with the prince as well as his writings. *The History of the World* was initially dedicated to James' heir who visited the Tower where Raleigh was imprisoned since his trial for treason in 1603. Harriot also visited the explorer. He had previously travelled to Virginia with Raleigh during the 1580s and created a phonetic alphabet to represent the Algonquin language and learned the uses to which the indigenous population put plants. It is perhaps not surprising that so many of Henry's household became investors in the Virginia Company, which was founded in 1606. The 13-year-old prince even sent his gunner, Robert Tindall, on the first expeditions to act as his eyes and ears. Tindall created the earliest map of Chesapeake Bay as well as identifying Cape Henry, named in honour of the prince's involvement with the initiative. It meant that the Courtly College was one of the first places in England to learn of the new land and its potential for colonisation. Together with Raleigh, Henry became immersed in the Thornton voyage of 1608 which saw Captain Robert Thornton commissioned to explore along the Amazon for the elusive mines of El Dorado and find a good location for Tuscany to locate a garrisoned settlement in order to exploit Brazil's forests. Raleigh and Henry thought discovery of the fabled gold would encourage James to release the explorer from the Tower. The sighting of Amazon warriors only served to whet their appetite. Prince Henry, aside from wishing to be fabulously wealthy, was concerned about exploration as a means to expand English influence.

Henry's interest led Chaloner to reveal to the prince his correspondence with one of his own former pupils, Sir Robert Dudley, the explorer who took an expedition to the West Indies in 1594 and ventured up the Amazon himself. The natural son of Elizabeth I's favourite, the Earl of Leicester left England for Tuscany amid much scandal in 1605 and was outlawed by James when he failed to return to England. Dudley soon began to send drawings for ships of his own design to Henry because he thought they would please the prince and might help smooth a possible return to England. Henry was also friend of Sir Thomas Roe, the navigator, and sent Roe on a mission to the West Indies in 1610 which saw him venture up the River Amazon into the interior of Guiana in search of the fabled El Dorado on the prince's behalf. He was also a patron of the North West Passage Company and the colonisation of North America.

Dudley's patron, the Grand Duke of Tuscany, encouraged Robert to foster good relations with the prince's household, believing that it would assist in the diplomacy between the two states just as, in Venice, the English ambassador, Henry Wotton, also nurtured his links with the prince and his household. The Venetians took care to include the Prince of Wales in their official correspondence with England from the time James became king. On one occasion in 1603, a letter arrived from the Doge which James described as 'bigger than the prince'.[8] Wotton was in the habit of sending gifts to Henry and on one occasion facilitated a shipment of twenty paintings from Venice for the prince. Henry's household also fostered links with Lotti, the Tuscan agent in London. The Florentine's aim was for a wedding between a Medici bride and Henry Stuart while the Venetians were hoping for a political alliance against Spanish interests. In March 1610, Chaloner, Prince Henry's chamberlain rather than his governor, arranged for the Tuscan envoy to London to forward copies of several books and paintings from the Medici Collection to Henry at St James's Palace for Henry to study. Negotiations commenced for Henry to marry Cosimo II's sister, Caterina. Henry, interested in art and the cultural heritage of Florence, recognised that the books and paintings that he requested were part of the negotiations. Eventually, the grand duke sent more than a dozen bronzes including the statuette entitled *Pacing Horse* by Pietro Tacco.[9]

By the time he left the schoolroom Henry had amassed a library at St James's Palace. In 1609, John, 1st Baron Lumley, left the prince his library of some 3000 works. Among the collection were books and manuscripts from the library of Thomas Cramner, Henry VIII's reforming Archbishop of Canterbury, including a New Testament in Latin and Greek edited by Erasmus. There were also commentaries on St Paul's epistles and works by

Thomas Netter, written in the fifteenth century to condemn the heresies of the early English reformer, John Wycliffe. Lumley also amassed extensive historical, philosophical and other works described as the liberal arts which encompassed grammar, logic, rhetoric, mathematics, geometry, music and astronomy. Henry, and later Charles, studied Euclid's *Elementa* in Greek as well as Cicero's speeches and Thomas Linacre's *Rudimenta grammatices.* They might also have dipped into medical text books, including the work of Galen, and studied Classical law in Gratianus' *Decretum*. The Prince of Wales extended the collection with the addition of a further 1000 books, reflecting his interest in the natural world, astronomy and all things military. Among the books purchased for Henry was *Opera Mathematica* by François Vieta, whose work on algebra, equations and trigonometry was as cutting edge as Kepler's work on astronomy and mathematics.

The library was managed by the mathematician Edward Wright, described in his time as a natural philosopher, who was appointed to teach Henry mathematics in 1608. In 1586, sailing under the name Edward Careless, Wright was Captain of the *Hope* under the command of Sir Francis Drake. In 1589 he was part of the Earl of Cumberland's privateering expedition to the Azores. As a result of the voyage and his interest in cartography, he wrote *Certaine Errors in Navigation.* In it he addressed errors in Mercator's mathematics and presented a solution to the problem of sailing the shortest route between two places without being able to determine longitude, by a process known as great circle sailing. This method of navigation involves following a route that describes an arc along a circle that divides a globe into two equal halves. All lines of latitude are great circles which makes sailing a north-south voyage a straightforward matter. The problem for navigators making a longitudinal, east-west journey was that the further away that two points are from the Equator, the smaller the circles become so that the globe is not divided equally. Great circle sailing relies on the mathematics of circles bisecting the earth equally. In order to achieve a great circle and the shortest distance, navigators needed to make a series of calculations taking account of prevailing winds and tides and adjusting position accordingly, without the benefit of a coastline to take an accurate reading. Wright recognised that an exaggeration of scale was needed when measuring along the meridian lines, to ensure that the scale on a map or chart would be the same in all directions. The solution was published in tabular form. When *Certain Errors* was republished in 1610, Wright dedicated it to his pupil.

Henry's interest in navigation led Wright to make the prince a model astrolabe and pantagraph as well as adding a number of maps to the prince's library including a theoretical sea chart of the Northwest passage between the Atlantic and the Pacific oceans that had been sought since Christopher Columbus' voyage of 1492. Martin Frobisher made the first English attempt in 1576, while Henry Hudson sought the route in 1610 on behalf of the Virginia and British East India companies. His ship, the *Discovery*, became trapped in sea ice during the winter months and when the ice began to break up the following spring, his crew cast him adrift rather than continue the search for the passage. He was never seen again.

In 1609, when Henry was 15 years old, he presented the king with an oration in the style of Cicero as a New Year's gift rather than a letter. He mimicked Cicero's own style in order to demonstrate his engagement with *Basilicon Doron* and to express his gratitude in the care that his father had taken in selecting a liberal humanist education as his preparation for life as a prince. Most importantly, perhaps, he recognised the need for eloquence when persuading his subjects and Parliament to cooperate.

Henry's household evolved, with the guidance of James and the Earl of Salisbury, into a court that mirrored his father's. Newton became Henry's private secretary while Chaloner changed from governor to lord chamberlain. David Murray, who had slept on a truckle bed in Henry's chamber since the prince was an infant at Stirling, became the keeper of the privy purse. The three men represented continuity, and in their own ways, remained father figures to the Prince of Wales. Sir Charles Cornwallis was now appointed treasurer while Sir John Holles, known for his Puritan principles, became comptroller of the household. The prince was swift to demonstrate an attention to detail for the regulation of his staff. He also set about enhancing his image as a Renaissance prince. Salomon de Caus, who was Henry's former drawing master, and the Florentine, Costantini de Servi were summoned to redesign the gardens and picture gallery at Richmond Palace. Michael Drayton and Samuel Daniel wrote plays and masques while Inigo Jones designed sets and costumes. The prince emphasised his godly Protestantism by employing twenty-four chaplains[10] and demonstrated his interest in the sciences, cosmology and navigation through his patronage of men like Edward Wright and Thomas Lydiat.

Henry's circle expanded to include the mentorship of the nation's political and intellectual elite, many of whose sons had shared his education and were among the companions destined to become his advisers. Among this number were Robert Cecil, Earl of Salisbury, the king's chief adviser, who helped to found the Courtly College and who was a friend of Adam Newton. It was through the increasingly exhausted minister that all council business passed and it was to him that the prince turned for political information and to better understand the workings of government. Other members of his father's court recognised that Henry represented the future and were also eager to share their knowledge with him in the hope of future office, wealth and preferment. It was under the influence of men like William Herbert, 3rd Earl of Pembroke, who was tutored by Samuel Daniel, and Thomas Howard, 14th Earl of Arundel, that Henry developed his understanding of art, literature and patronage. Henry's court took on the lustre of a Renaissance prince. He collected Dutch and Italian art and sculpture as well as buying whole collections of coins and medals, many of which still remain in the Royal Collection. Herbert was a poet and a patron of poets and writers. Shakespeare's First Folio was dedicated to Herbert and his brother, Philip. He was a patron of Inigo Jones, Ben Jonson, George Herbert and a friend of John Donne. He has been described as an '*uomo universale*'[11] of the period. Not only was he a patron of the arts he was also chancellor of Oxford University, a politician, industrialist, and one of the men who invested in exploration and colonisation of North America. Herbert's appearance on the tournament field fulfilled Henry's desire to be surrounded by a chivalric court. Despite his support of the theatre, the earl was an important protector for Puritan writers. The family had long held Calvinist views which resonated with Henry's own beliefs. William Herbert's uncle was Sir Philip Sidney, who in the prince's mind was the epitome of a Protestant hero. Even more important than anything else was that Pembroke was one of the leaders of the anti-Spanish faction. Pembroke and his supporters favoured Protestant marriages for James' children but would consider a French match to counterbalance the growing power of Spain in Europe.

It was not always important to know who was delivering a lesson in kingship. In 1611, shortly after the king elevated his most recent favourite, Robert Carr, to the peerage, creating him Viscount Rochester, Prince Henry received an anonymous tract entitled, *An Instruction to Princes to know how to Govern state well* warning him of the risks associated with relying on flatterers and favourites. Like Machiavelli, the anonymous writer suggested that such men could be found everywhere, were wrapped up in their own affairs and to rely on such people would only conclude with a ruler being despised. Henry, like his Tudor predecessors, would have been familiar with the tract's reference to Machiavelli's work, *The Prince*, which also warned of allowing men from speaking too freely to a monarch. A 'wise ruler will follow another way, and choose shrewd men for his service, permitting them alone to speak frankly, but only when he asks them and not otherwise'.[12] Henry's reaction to Robert Carr was an increase in his own political involvement in the political life of his father's realm and court. Everyone was welcome at St James's apart from Viscount Rochester. The prince was increasingly perceived as being willing to challenge his father. He was also much more popular than James. The latter wanted peace but his son was a much more radical supporter of Protestantism and the men he gathered around him saw themselves as grooming a successor for Elizabeth I to defend Protestant Europe from the Hapsburgs.

But fate had other plans when Henry became ill after swimming in the Thames. On 24 October 1619 the prince played tennis but looked pale and unwell. The following day he took to his bed. By 5 November, it was clear that the prince, who was ill with typhoid, would not survive and on 7 November he died. He was just 18 years old. Phineas Pett, the Master Shipwright, recorded the grief at St James's Palace 'where I found a house turned into the very map of true sorrow … the most renowned Prince of the world, our royal and most loving master, departed this life, not only to the loss and utter undoing of his poor servants, but the general loss of all Christendom of the protestant religion'.[13] Shock radiated from St James's across the realms which Henry had been prepared to rule over.

In Henry's place there remained Charles who seemed so unhealthy as to be unlikely to live to adulthood, let alone marry and father children of his own. Suddenly England, which had enjoyed almost a decade of knowing that there was a Stuart heir with the makings of a potentially great monarch, faced an uncertain future. If the king were to die unexpectedly while his remaining son, Charles, was still a minor there would be a regency. If James and Charles were both to die, it would be the king's sole surviving child, Elizabeth, who would become queen. In addition to raising the possibility of another queen upon the throne, it also thrust the spectre, once more, of a foreign succession into people's minds.

Chapter Eleven

Elizabeth: The Winter Queen

James I believed that while his sons required a classical education, there was not the same need for his daughter to learn Latin or Greek. Like many people of the time, the king believed that women were intellectually, emotionally and physically inferior to men. Society believed that suffering during childbirth was a universal female punishment for Eve listening to the snake in the Garden of Eden. Women were expected to be silent and virtuous. When she married, Elizabeth would be subject to her husband, until then she was subject to her father or, in the event of his death, her brothers. James was able to justify this view by natural and divine order. He took the view that women were 'all naturally addicted to vanity, where it [education] did one good, it did harm to twenty'.[1] His daughter circumvented the prohibition of being taught Latin by suggesting to her elder brother that she would help him improve his Italian if he helped teach her the language.[2] What was essential, in the king's view, was that Elizabeth's guardians, Harington and his wife, safeguard Elizabeth's virtue and ensure that she was raised as a godly Protestant. It is not surprising that portraits of the princess created during her childhood often emphasise meekness. Days in Harington's household began and ended with prayer and meals, included a reading from scripture, providing Elizabeth with practical routines and lessons in piety.

Elizabeth already knew her prayers and her letters, how to look and behave like a member of the royal family on public occasions and had impressed her father's new subjects and visiting ambassadors with her behaviour and graceful dancing. At 10 years old she was painted by Robert Peake, adorned with a rope of diamonds that once belonged to her godmother and holding a prayer book highlighting the importance of virtue. Coombe Abbey, a former Cistercian abbey, was surrounded by gardens and parkland. Harington also provided the princess with plants from around the known world. As well as providing opportunities for botany lessons it was a real-world demonstration of the wonder of God's creation. Similarly, when Elizabeth was given the chance to see the night skies through a telescope, it was not to provide lessons in astronomy but to recognise the extent of God's handiwork.

Like her father and brother, Elizabeth learned to ride and enjoyed hunting. Her stable consisted of twenty horses.[3] As well as providing the princess with exercise, and food for the table, hunting and the ownership of both horses and dogs was a symbol of Elizabeth's nobility and wealth. A work by Paul van Somer, painted in 1617, depicts the princess' mother, Anne of Denmark, in hunting costume posing with her hounds and her horse while Prince Henry was portrayed hunting at Coombe Abbey with his friend John Harington, by Robert Peake the Elder in 1603. Hunting was a royal pastime and the Stuarts loved their dogs, which were often depicted alongside them in portraits. In 1642, Elizabeth chose to be painted by Gerard van Honthorst, her children's art master, with one of her dogs. The latter could be interpreted as a symbol of her fidelity to her dead husband and to her Protestant faith.

It soon became apparent to John Harington, who was an indulgent guardian, that the upkeep of the stables, the cost of her household and with a procession of pets that included monkeys, parrots and dogs, that the £1500 per year allocated for the princess' expenses were not sufficient. King James was prevailed upon to make an additional allowance of £1000 per year but Harington, who was scrupulously honest, was soon out of pocket. Harington's own adult daughters, Lucy and Frances, were well educated and the princess' governor provided his ward with a liberal education. The king stipulated that Elizabeth was to learn scripture and have a general understanding of history. The princess also learned to draw and to understand the different orders of architecture that existed because Harington considered this to be something that a princess ought to understand. Elizabeth's dancing and music lessons continued throughout her childhood. Theodore Diodati, the son of a prominent Calvinist theologian and trained physician, was part of the Harington household, having originally been employed as tutor to Prince Henry's companion, John. It is likely that he taught Elizabeth and her companions both Italian and French. Elizabeth owned a version of the New Testament in French as well as several other texts in the language. As his pupils left childhood, Diodati began to make the transition to doctor having originally studied medicine at Leiden. His own son would be a friend of John Milton, whose writing was characterised by his Puritan beliefs that individuals should be permitted to read scripture without the interference of a Church hierarchy.

In April 1605 Queen Anne gave birth to a daughter, Mary, at Greenwich. Despite the fact that the infant was female, there was much celebrating in England. The baptism, conducted by the Archbishop of Canterbury, was held in the chapel at Greenwich. The last royal baptism in England had been for Edward VI in 1537, and on the occasion of so much rejoicing, the king did not ask guests to bring their own meals to the celebrations that followed the christening. The baby was provided with her own household, under the charge of Sir Thomas Knyvett and his wife, Elizabeth, at their home at Stanwell, Middlesex, rather than joining her elder sister's household at Coombe. It would be a fleeting appointment for her guardians as Mary succumbed to a fever before she was 2 years old, on 16 September 1607. For the king and queen, it was the second loss within a few short months, Anne having given birth to a short-lived daughter, Sophia, in June 1606. James gave orders for a tomb to be erected at Westminster Abbey shaped like a baby sleeping in its cradle for the last of his and Anne's nine children.

Knyvett is better remembered for his part in foiling the Gunpowder Plot when he searched the cellars beneath the Houses of Parliament early in the morning of 5 November. Catholic plotters, dissatisfied with their new king and his failure to grant them freedom to worship how they wished, planned to blow up Westminster Palace along with Parliament, James and his heir. The conspirators decided that the murdered king would be replaced by his eldest daughter, rather than 5-year-old Charles. They thought that Coombe Abbey would be more easily accessible than the younger prince's home in London. Robert Catesby, one of the plotters, suggested a hunting party near the Harington home would be the best cover for seizing the princess. Sir Everard Digby arranged for a chase to meet at Dunchurch, in Warwickshire. It was hoped that Harington and the rest of his household would join the gathering, leaving Coombe vulnerable to attack. The problem for the plotters was that their plan did not remain secret. John Harington heard rumours several days before the planned abduction. When he received a message from a neighbour informing him of the theft of several horses by men believed to be Catholics, Harington wrote to London for instruction.

Meanwhile another messenger arrived with news of the thwarted attack on Parliament. Harington did not wait for a response to his letter. Instead, he moved Elizabeth to safety inside Coventry's walls. Once the conspirators were rounded up, the princess, shaken by the episode but unharmed, was able to return home where she wrote to her brother, Henry, expressing her gratitude to God for the family's deliverance from danger. When it was explained to her that the plotters intended to crown her, she told her guardian 'What a queen should I have been by these means'.[4]

Elizabeth remained safely at Coombe Abbey in the years that followed. Lord Harington obeyed James' strictures about teaching the princess Latin but she was able to study history, geography, sciences, art, music and modern languages. Harington also built her an aviary that contained an assortment of birds. It was near to a group of 'little wooden buildings in the different orders of architecture'[5] and a 'Fairy-farm' stocked with miniature cattle from Shetland and the Isle of Man.[6] As well as providing entertainment in what Elizabeth described as her 'territories', they combined to create interactive lessons for the princess.

There were occasional trips to London to be enjoyed. In 1606 the Haringtons travelled to court with their ward and her companions when Elizabeth's uncle, Christian IV of Denmark, visited England. The princess stayed at Greenwich and was able to see both her brothers. The visit began with a shower of presents for the children but quickly descended into drunkenness, which included the King of Denmark becoming so intoxicated that he had to be carried away from the festivities covered in 'wine, cream, jelly, beverage, cakes, spice, and other good matters'.[7] It could be described as an education of sorts for the gently reared Elizabeth. Harington wrote that he was 'well-nigh overwhelmed with carousel and sports of all kinds'.[8] His cousin, somewhat confusingly also named John Harington, wrote that he 'never did see such a lack of good order, discretion and sobriety'[9] and commiserated with Elizabeth's guardian 'who doth much to fatigue himself with the royal charge of the princess Elizabeth: and, midst all the foolery of these times, hath much labour to preserve his own wisdom and sobriety'.[10]

The princess returned to court for the Christmas of 1607 and met the French ambassador once again, who described the 11-year-old as 'handsome, graceful, well-nourished and speaks French very well, much better than her brother'.[11] On 14 January 1609, Elizabeth was deemed old enough to attend a ballet and in the company of Lady Harington entertained the wife of the Flemish ambassador. It was a practical lesson in what might be expected of a consort. She also attended a masque written by Ben Jonson when John Harington, Henry's companion, was married to Elizabeth Ratcliffe. When Elizabeth was 13 years old the Haringtons moved to their home in Kew so that their ward could attend court where she completed her education. She was also provided with apartments at Hampton Court and at Whitehall. Elizabeth attended masques, banquets and tournaments but still found time to buy books from Matthew Lownes including, in 1612, a copy of Foxes Book of Martyrs.[12] Music and dancing were an important part of court life, having both political and social nuances, and James wanted his children to be proficient in both. At one feast, held by her brother, Elizabeth was still awake at 3:00 am. At Kew, lessons continued. Lord Harington, generally an indulgent guardian, complained that Henry's desire to ride with his sister interrupted her studies. Although, it is also apparent from their letters and the correspondence of ambassadors that the pair shared tutors on occasion.

When she was 14 years old, Elizabeth received her first marriage proposal, from the king of Sweden's heir, Gustavus Adolphus. The marriage to the king of Sweden's heir, Gustavus Adolphus, would have been a good one except for the fact that the queen objected to a union made for her daughter with Denmark's enemy. Among other candidates for her hand was Prince Maurice of Nassau who was dismissed as being too lowly for a princess' hand. Besides which, James saw the marriage of his children as an opportunity not only to benefit the nation but to enhance his reputation as a European peacemaker, uniting Protestant princes and arriving at an accord with Catholic kings. As the number of Elizabeth's potential suitors grew, her mother entered into negotiations with the Spanish ambassador. At first the Duke of Savoy was mooted as a possible husband but when Philip III's wife died, the Spanish king entertained thoughts of taking Elizabeth Stuart as his own wife. Denied a role in her children's early lives, the queen was determined to play a part in her daughter's nuptials. She suggested that if Philip III married Elizabeth that the princess would be prepared to convert to Catholicism. When the plan became public, Elizabeth, supported by her brother, declared that she would never change her religion. Soon afterwards, James I's hopes that she might marry into the French royal family also fell through. If she was not to marry a Catholic king, then Elizabeth should marry a Protestant prince while Henry wed a Catholic to achieve James' ambitions.

Frederick V, Elector Palatine, a Calvinist, was the same age as Elizabeth. Despite the difference in their ranks, the prince was related to many of Europe's ruling families and was the grandson of William the Silent of Orange. At first the young couple exchanged letters, a standard tool for both royal diplomacy and developing a personal relationship before meeting. If Elizabeth married the elector, James would not need to provide her with a significant dowry. Even better, Prince Henry was delighted by the idea of the match. Frederick's tutor, Daniel Tilenus, was one of the men who taught that it was the duty of Protestant princes to support one another. The union between the Palatine and England would solidify the position of Protestant Europe. Frederick arrived in England on 18 October 1612. His education ensured that he was charming, spoke French fluently, which was the couple's shared language, having enjoyed numerous visits to the court of Henry IV during his childhood, and knew about the importance of courtship. He even took the trouble to learn the latest dance steps before his arrival. It did not take long for her proposed spouse to win Elizabeth's affections, even though the queen took to calling her 'Goodwife Palsgrave' because she thought the match was beneath a royal line. It must have seemed to Frederick that everyone liked him apart from Anne of Denmark. And, when Henry fell ill with typhoid, it was to Frederick that Elizabeth turned.

The death of Henry, whose last clear words were to ask for his sister, increased the expectations of the anti-Catholic faction that it would be Elizabeth who restored Britain to its status as a dominant Protestant power, as it had been under her namesake. Until Charles, who was 12 years old, married and produced legitimate heirs, the princess was second in line to the throne. Charles remained small for his age and was prone to ill health. Was it advisable, under the circumstances for the princess to leave the country? Could a more worthy husband be found for the girl who might bring three kingdoms as her dowry? But by then, Elizabeth was in love with Frederick and James did not look for a better born husband for his daughter, or prohibit her departure, as he might have done. The pair were betrothed on 27 December 1612 and married on 14 February 1613

When Elizabeth left England for the Palatinate, at the end of April 1613, she sailed aboard the *Prince Royal* which was captained by Phineas Pett. Her former guardians, the Haringtons, accompanied the princess to Germany at their own expense. John Harington died at Worms during the journey home. His remains were returned to Exton for burial but the cost of caring for his royal charge had ruined him. Harington's eldest son, John, died less than a year after his father. Elizabeth's governess, Anne, was forced to sell off much of her husband's estates to pay his debts which stood at somewhere between £30,000–£40,000.[13] Harington had accounted honestly for his care of Elizabeth but by 1612 he petitioned for the right to coin brass farthings for three years in an attempt to recoup his expenses.

In Heidelberg it swiftly became apparent that none of Elizabeth's tutors had taught her the importance of living within her means. Her account book from her childhood, kept by Anna Livingston, included payments for tooth picks and the cost of livery for footmen but she was never forced to live within a budget. The princess was permitted to buy whatever she wished as a child whether it was pearls, books, or to pay children to dress like shepherdesses at her miniature farm. Now, as the mistress of her own home, Salomon de Caus was summoned to create a new garden with fountains, statues and greenhouses. In between pursuing her love of hunting, of ballets and other diversions, the 16-year-old gave away her jewels and ran up debts. It fell to the master of Frederick's household, Hans, Count Schomberg, to try and bring about reforms which included a memorandum of advice for the Electress about the best way to manage her allowance. There was another document about managing staff. Elizabeth came to rely upon the count in all matters. He fell in love with Anne Dudley who accompanied the princess to the Palatine as her lady-in-waiting. It was a match that Elizabeth encouraged but her friend died in childbirth in 1615. Schomberg died the following year. Lady Harington returned to Heidelberg in 1616, drawn not only by the salary and the king's command but by her affection for her former charge.

By then it was also apparent that no one had thought to teach Elizabeth about the facts of life; her education had focused on chastity and virtue rather than the mechanics of reproduction. The princess gave birth to her first child, Frederick Henry, on 2 January 1614 having stoutly denied, throughout the previous autumn and winter, the possibility that she might be pregnant. The

Stuart line was secure once more but, in 1618, Frederick was offered the kingdom of Bohemia. He was crowned in November 1619 and forced to flee with his family a year later, following his defeat at the Battle of White Mountain. Elizabeth, given the name the Winter Queen by her husband's enemies, became an exile in the Netherlands, doing all that she could to win support first for Frederick and then for his heir. When Frederick died in 1632, she was the mother of fourteen children, ten of whom survived infancy and early childhood.

James I's grandchildren were raised in the royal nursery at Leiden, the Prinsenhof, under the guardianship of the de Plessens, a French couple, with instructions that they should adhere strictly to Calvinist beliefs as described by the Heidelberg Catechism of 1563, specifically designed for use in schools, which took the form of a series of questions and answers. The Prinsenhof was three hours from Elizabeth's home in The Hague. An assortment of German and English teachers provided the growing family with a comprehensive education that included Classical and modern languages, mathematics, astronomy, rhetoric, logic, philosophy and the sciences. They also studied art, under the tuition of Gerard van Honthorst, music and singing. The boys were sent to Leiden University to complete their education before learning to soldier on the battlefields of Europe's Thirty Years War. Rupert of the Rhine, Elizabeth's fourth child, who spoke Czech by the age of 3 years, was at the Siege of Rheinsberg in Westphalia by the time he was 14 years old. His mentor was Frederick Henry of Orange-Nassau who was recognised as an effective general and political leader. Rupert, his younger brother, Maurice, and their eldest surviving brother, Charles Louis, who became heir to the Palatinate following the death of Henry Frederick in an accident in 1629, spent much of the 1630s in England at the court of their uncle, Charles I who offered them a home after the death of Frederick V. Elizabeth's younger sons, Philip and Edward, were educated at the French court at the request of their brother Charles Louis who hoped to be restored to the Palatinate with the support of the French when it became clear that his uncle was unable to provide him with either funds or men.

Elizabeth ensured that her daughters received a classical education of the kind enjoyed by their brothers. James I's eldest granddaughter, Elizabeth, born in 1618, corresponded with Descartes who dedicated his *Principles of*

Philosophy to her. Her brothers and sisters called her 'La Greque' because of her grasp of the language. Elizabeth's sister, Louise Hollande, born in 1622, was a talented portrait artist who rejected her Calvinist upbringing to become a Catholic nun. Like the rest of her siblings Sophia, the youngest of Elizabeth and Frederick's daughters, received an excellent education. She spoke five languages, wrote her memoirs and was a friend of Leibniz, who has been described as one of the 'great thinkers of the seventeenth and eighteenth centuries'.[14] Evidently, James I's daughter regretted that her schooling was not more akin to that of her brother, Henry, and ensured that her own daughters received a much more thorough education. From their schoolroom, Elizabeth's daughters graduated to her court at the Hague where they would acquire the polish necessary for the granddaughters of a king and hopefully secure suitable husbands, even though they were without dowries and Elizabeth Stuart was a queen without a kingdom.

Mary, Queen of Scots, aged about 7 years, François Clouet. (*Public domain via Everett V. Meeks, B.A. 1901, Fund, Yale University Art Gallery, accession no. 2009.46.1*)

Mary, Queen of Scots, with her son, James, Style of sixteenth-century British Painter (nineteenth-century). (*Public domain via Metropolitan Museum of Art, New York, accession no 17.190.2*)

James Stuart (1566–1625), later King James I of England. (*Rijksmuseum, Amsterdam object no. SK-A-4390*)

George Buchanan, print made by Jacobus Houbraken, 1742. (*Public domain via Yale Center for British Art; Yale University Art Gallery Collection, B1998.14.568*)

Falkland Palace. (*Photograph: Kyle Hewgill*)

The courtyard and drinking fountain at Linlithgow Palace. (*Photograph: Kyle Hewgill*)

Linlithgow Palace. (*Photograph: Julia A. Hickey*)

Stirling Castle. (*Photograph: Julia A. Hickey*)

Chapel Royal, Stirling Castle. (*Photograph: Julia A. Hickey*)

Aberdour Castle, home of the Earl of Morton. (*Photograph: Julia A. Hickey*)

James VI, king of Scotland, 1603. (*Public domain via Harris Brisbane Dick Fund, 1917, Metropolitan Museum of Art, object no 17.3.756.1779*)

Anne of Denmark from the studio of Nicholas Hilliard, c.1605. (*Public domain via Yale Center for British Art, Paul Mellon Collection, B1974.2.50*)

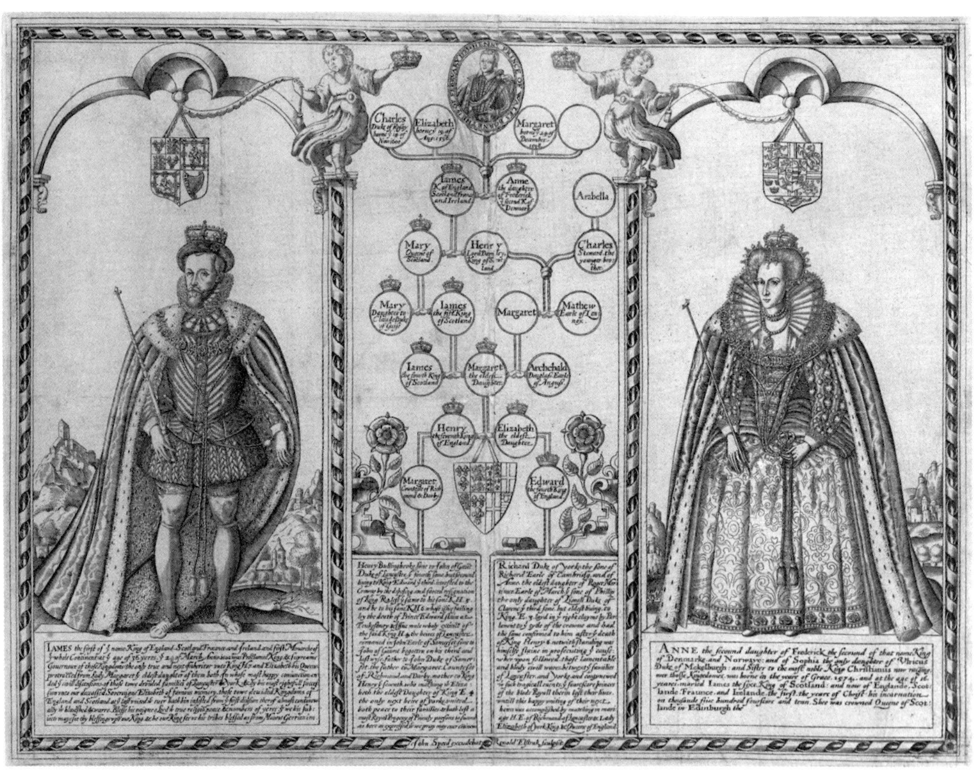

James I and Anne of Denmark, engraved by Renold Elstack, 1651. (*Public domain via Metropolitan Museum of Art, New York, object number 28.7.13*)

Calendar House. (*Photograph: Julia A. Hickey*)

Dunfermline Palace. (*Photograph: Julia A. Hickey*)

Henry Frederick (1594–1612), Prince of Wales, with Sir John Harington (1592–1614), in the hunting field, by Robert Peake the Elder, 1603. (*Public domain via Joseph Pulizer Bequest, 1944, Metropolitan Museum of Art, New York, object no 44.27*)

Princess Elizabeth (1596–1662), later Queen of Bohemia, by Robert Peake the Elder, *c*.1606. (*Public domain via Metropolitan Museum of Art, New York, object no. 51.194.1*)

Anne of Denmark and Charles I as a child (1611–1612). (*Rijksmuseum, Amsterdam, object no. RP-P-1907-2289*)

Charles Stuart (1600–1649), Prince of Wales, later King Charles I of England, attributed to Peter Oliver. (*Rijksmuseum, Amsterdam, object no. SK-A-4350*)

Memorial to Sir Thomas Chaloner, attributed to Daniel Lysons. (*Public domain via Yale Center for British Art, Paul Mellon Collection, accession no B1977.14.20284*)

John Harington, by Crispin van de Passe, 1620. (*Rijksmuseum, Amsterdam, object no. RP-P1910-423*)

Anne Harington depicted on the Kelway monument at St Peter's and St Paul's Exton. (*Jules & Jenny from Lincoln, UK, CC BY 2.0 via Wikimedia Commons*)

Coombe Abbey. (*Photograph: Julia A. Hickey*)

His Majesty James I, king of England, and his royal progeny, together with the family of the king of Bohemia. (*Rijksmuseum, Amsterdam, object no. RP-P-OB-33443*)

Portrait of Frederick V of Bohemia, Queen Elizabeth and their children. (*Rijksmuseum, Amsterdam, object no. RP-P-1939-384*)

Charles I and Henrietta Maria, by Wenceslaus Hollar. (*Public domain via Metropolitan Museum of Art, New York, object no 52.614.1a.b*)

Henrietta Maria when pregnant, by Anthony van Dyck, 1636. (*Public domain via bequest of Mrs Charles Wrightsman in honour of Annette de la Renta, 2019, Metropolitan Museum of Art, New York, object no 2019.141.10*)

James Stuart, Duke of York. (*Scan by NYPL, Public domain, via Wikimedia Commons*)

Children of King Charles I, by Richard Cooper. (*Rijksmuseum, Amsterdam, object no. RP-P-OB-19.223*)

Double portrait of William II, Prince of Orange (1626–1650) and Princess Mary Stuart (1631–1660), later Princess Royal, by Anthony van Dyck, 1641. (*Rijksmuseum, Amsterdam, object no. Sk-A-102*)

William Cavendish, Duke of Newcastle. (*Public domain via Yale Center for British Art; Yale University Art Gallery Collection, B1998.14.645*)

Henriette-Anne d'Angleterre, Duchesse d'Orléans, by Claude Mellan. (*Public domain via Harris Brisbane Dick Fund, 1953, Metropolitan Museum, New York, object no. 53.601.312*)

Katherine, Countess of Chesterfield, and Lucy, Countess of Huntingdon, by Anthony van Dyck, *c.*1636–40. (*Public domain via Yale Center for British Art, accession number B1981.25.252*)

Katherine Stanhope, Countess of Chesterfield. (*Rijksmuseum, Amsterdam, object no. RP-P-OB-55.730*)

Algernon Percy (1602–1668), 10th Earl of Northumberland after Van Dyck, Henry Bone. (*Public domain via Metropolitan Museum of Art, New York, object no. 95.14.47*)

Last moments of King Charles I, depicting the last meeting with Princess Elizabeth and Henry, Duke of Gloucester, 1836. (*Rijksmuseum, Amsterdam, object no. RP-P-1910-3669*)

St James Palace. (*Photograph: Adam Hewgill*)

Hampton Court. (*Photograph: Kyle Hewgill*)

Portrait of King Charles II of England, 1653, Philippe de Champaigne. (*Public domain via The Elisabeth Severance Prentiss Collection, The Cleveland Museum of Art, The Elisabeth Severance Prentiss Collection, object no. 1959.38*)

Portrait of Sophia, Princess Palatine, by Gerrit van Honthorst, 1641. (*Public domain via bequest of Mr and Mrs William A. Fisher, Detroit Institute of Arts, accession number 72.860*)

Chapter Twelve

Charles: A Subject and a Sovereign Are Clean Different Things

In January 1605 Charles was made a Knight of the Bath and Duke of York. That same year the prince wrote his first New Year report to the king which he signed 'York'. He also wrote to his brother, who he clearly hero-worshipped. This letter was written by someone else and signed by him. In it he thanks Henry for the letter he received and then says 'I will give anything I have to you, both horses and my books, and my pieces, and my cross bows, or anything that you would have. Good brother, love me, and I shall ever love and serve you'.[1] Henry was not always so generous to his younger brother in return even if Charles wanted to dress like him and do everything that his elder brother did.

Elizabeth Carey cared for Charles until he was almost 11 years old while Robert Carey filled the role of governor of the prince's household at Whitehall Palace. They both supported Puritan ideals. Their own sons were tutored by the theologian Henry Burton who would have his ears cut off in 1637 for attacking the views of the Archbishop of Canterbury, William Laud. He served in both Henry and Charles' households reflecting the king's desire that his son's should be raised as godly princes. It was no difficulty for Elizabeth Carey to ensure that Charles was provided with religious instruction based on scripture reading and that the routines of the house reflected pious practices of the time.

Charles' residence in London meant that both his parents spent more time with their youngest son than they did with either of his surviving siblings. Anne doted on him and the sentiment was returned. Elizabeth proved a kindly governess; protecting her charge from King James' attempts to improve his youngest son's speech by having the string under his tongue, the lingual frenulum, cut. Instead, she used different tactics to encourage the prince to talk and overcome his stammer, including singing lessons. When the king ordered a pair of reinforced iron boots to be made for his son by Edward Stuteville, a London bonesetter, to strengthen Charles' ankles and joints, she refused to let James carry out his intentions. Robert Carey's memoirs record that his wife went into battle on her charge's behalf and eventually the king was forced to give up. Instead, Carey took the boy riding every day. The prince turned into a skilled horseman who was his brother's equal. Charles learned to shoot both with a bow and arrow and with pistols. There were also dancing lessons. By 1610, his legs were sufficiently strong, and he was sufficiently well taught, to dance the part of Zephyrus at the masque to celebrate Henry's investiture as the Prince of Wales.

Thomas Murray remained key to Charles' schooling and imbued a love of learning in the prince but not an independence of interest that characterised Prince's Henry's approach to study or strength of will that marked the start of his adult life. Instead, he set out to please his father. By 1607, Nicolo Molin, the Venetian Ambassador, reported that Charles learned 'far quicker'[2] and more 'earnestly'[3] than his elder brother. During his early childhood he wrote to his brother and to his father in English, and although he learned French it was not with the same aptitude as his sister or even his older sibling. In February 1610, James was required to translate a question put to Charles by the ambassador. The year previously he began to study Latin using the same books as Henry. Murray stocked his pupil's library so that Charles could study the works of Horace, Ovid, Seneca and Virgil which were the staples of a humanist education. The tutor also introduced his own nephew, William Murray, who was the same age as Charles, to the prince's household early in his mastership. The son of a Dysart minister would become the prince's closest childhood companion while one of Thomas' own daughters would marry one of Prince Henry's tutors. Carey's son, Thomas, was another of Charles' companions.

Charles was also required to play tennis and to tilt just as his brother and father were tutored in the skills which identified them as princes. In common with his siblings, Charles learned to ride and to hunt. By 1609 he was able to write to his brother commenting on how much he enjoyed Henry's company and the opportunity of hunting with him. All three of James' children spent the summer of 1608 at Nonsuch. As well as getting to know Henry and Elizabeth it was also a chance for Charles to meet the men who surrounded Henry and for them to influence his taste in art and literature. Henry and Charles both shared an appetite for art.

In 1611, when Charles left the Careys' care, being sufficiently healthy to leave his nursery for an all-male household, the prince wrote to his father that his course of study was completed. Instead, the 11-year-old proposed that he should 'attend always upon Your Majesty, so that I could learn to obey and serve Your Majesty in all things'.[4] Rather than expressing irritation, James merely insisted that his younger son should stick to his lessons. Elizabeth Carey returned to her former employment as one of Anne of Denmark's ladies-in-wating, with an annual pension of £400 a year, while Robert became part of the prince's household, which like his brother's before him, mirrored the court of an adult. Prince Henry did not much like Carey so did not want him to hold any post in his brother's household but the queen intervened on his behalf and Carey remained by Charles' side as the chief gentleman of the bedchamber. New tutors were appointed to join Thomas Murray. In 1612, Jehan de Beauchesne, who taught Elizabeth to write in an Italic hand, was appointed to the prince's household. The French Huguenot wrote a manual on handwriting entitled *A Booke containing divers sortes of hands* in 1570 and began his career in royal service working as a scribe for the Keeper of the Records at the Tower of London. Having travelled to Italy where he studied under other calligraphers, he produced a second handwriting manual in 1580 and a third one in 1595 dedicated to the daughters of the Earl of Shrewsbury. In 1613, the writing master was granted a yearly pension of £50 for teaching Charles.

1613 was a momentous year for the Stuarts. Prince Henry became unwell while Frederick of the Palatine was courting Elizabeth. On 24 October 1612 he played tennis with a member of Frederick's household but looked pale and ill. The following day, Sunday, he took to his bed. By the 5 November, it was clear that the prince would not survive and on 7 November he died. Charles, just 12 years old and now his father's heir, acted as chief mourner at Henry's funeral at Westminster on 7 December. The men who prepared Henry for the Crown would no longer reap the benefits of patronage while the men who formed Charles' household were promoted. Pett, the shipbuilder, described himself as 'burying all my hopes of my future preferments'.[5] Some of them, like Walter Quin, found employment with Charles. Like his brother before him, the younger prince was required to be proficient in Classical and modern languages and to be able to write poetry. It was essential for an erudite Renaissance prince to create fluent and imaginative stanza that echoed his Classical training. For James it also reflected the face that kingly government went together with public scholarship. In all, only five men made the transition from one household to the other.[6] Edmund Verney, who was later killed while holding the Royal Standard at the Battle of Edgehill, became a gentleman of the privy chamber. In addition to his own chaplain, clerics from Henry's household joined Charles' retinue including George Hakewill and Richard Milbourne. From them, if he had not already done so earlier in his schooling, Charles adopted the Calvinist belief in predestination which placed salvation of the elect in the hands of God alone.

Charles, not naturally athletic, was a more devoted scholar than his brother. The Spanish ambassador described the prince as a 'sweet, gentle child'[7] who was more comfortable in his library than at court. Like Henry, he received a humanist education of a king prescribed by George Buchanan, and followed the mantra set out by *Basilicon Doron*, which was now rededicated to the king's new heir. As well as grammar, Classical and modern languages, rhetoric and theology the prince read widely and was encouraged to interrogate the volumes he encountered by debate with his companions and masters. But now, Charles was required to take the place of Henry, who had been popular with his father's subjects for his militaristic interests and who had been viewed across Protestant Europe as a warrior in the making. Henry's younger brother committed himself to a regime of physical exercise, which included horse riding and running around the grounds of St James's Palace to improve his physique and stamina. The Venetian ambassador reported that, within a year of starting his new programme, Charles was able to outrun the servants and companions who accompanied him. He mastered the use of the crossbow and the pike in an attempt to develop his physique and took part in tilts to emphasise that he could fill the void left by his brother. But nothing could change the fact that Charles was a slender youth who grew to only five feet four inches tall.

Militaristic traditions and physical violence were not things which came naturally to Charles as they did to Henry. It was Anne of Denmark who encouraged him in his interest in the Order of the Garter and who gave him books on the subject, as well as other associated chivalric topics. Her thoughtful and sensitive son cherished the manly virtues and heroism aspired to by the Order. The prince had been installed as one of the Order's members when he was 10 years old but the ideals and convictions of the garter knights were close to his heart throughout his life. In 1638, when his own son was elected to the Order, Charles wrote about the 'joyful and pregnant hopes of your manly virtues in which we are assured you will increase to your own honour, both in prowess, wisdom, justice and all princely endowments'.[8] The emphasis that Charles placed on warrior culture had less to do with joining in the Thirty Years War on the side of Protestant Europe, as his contemporaries hoped, and more to do with ideas of loyalty and courage. Combat was replaced by the religious aspect of being a knight. It was Charles, when he became king, who required members of the Order to parade in cloaks bearing the cross of St George. Moral virtue, spirituality and defending true religion were more appealing to the new heir than thundering down the lists trying to knock an opponent from their horse. Of the fifty books at Whitehall, which formed Charles' personal library, two-thirds were related to the Order of the Garter and many of them were from his mother.[9] Charles wore his garter medal throughout his life and went to his death with the blue sash of the Order around his neck.

The prince who once, aged 6 years, appeared before the Venetian ambassador while shouldering a harquebus, did, however, turn his attention to weapons and to the events of the war that was simmering in Europe. Soon after Prince Henry's death, Sir Edward Cecil, a professional soldier in the Dutch army, offered to provide the new heir to the throne with models of the instruments and engines of warfare which were essential to a seventeenth-century army. They finally arrived in 1616 and the prince was taught about their use by the men who delivered them. In 1620, when Elizabeth wrote to Charles begging for help, her brother offered her money from his own revenues and proposed to lead a military expedition on her behalf, demonstrating both valour and the militaristic vigour that he was so often regarded as lacking. In the event, James put a halt to his son's enthusiasm.

As well as the burdens of new responsibility, Charles inherited his brother's collection of artworks, medals and books. It was another passion he shared with Henry. Abraham van der Doort accompanied the collection becoming a groom of the chamber. Charles kept him in his service after he became king, and he became the keeper of Charles I's cabinet room and compiled an inventory of the king's collection. He was also responsible for caring for the collection, becoming the first Surveyor of the King's Pictures. The artist, who came from a family of craftsmen, designed medal and coin designs for Charles, and the Royal Mint, as he did for Henry.

Charles, like his brother before him, was required to present a final exercise to his father to mark the end of his formal studies. Rather than an oration, Charles chose to edit a collection of James I's previously unpublished poetry. Before it was completed, the work was presented to the king for correction. Although Charles did speak in public, in March 1621 on behalf of his father to a parliamentary committee against monopolies, he confessed to William Laud in 1624 that he lacked confidence and that he would not make a lawyer because 'I cannot…defend a bad, nor yield a good cause'.[10] His lack of rhetorical skill and his inability to argue a case left him at a disadvantage, as did his tendency to trust those nearest him. Perhaps because of Henry's popularity and his often-vocal disagreement with the king, James did not follow exactly the same model of preparation for kingship with his younger son as he had with his older. There would be no alternative royal court for Charles to learn how to rule or to forge his own diplomatic ties. It would be four years until James' remaining son was installed as Prince of Wales. Instead, Charles was required to join his father more often at state functions. James understood that monarchs needed to serve an apprenticeship before they ascended the throne. In 1614, the king took Charles to the state opening of parliament. By 1617, James trusted him sufficiently to sit on the privy council while James was making a visit to Scotland. It was also a way of the prince displaying the fruits of his education to his future subjects and demonstrating that he, like his father, would rule because he understood the principles of divine right. The Venetian ambassador was less impressed. Henry grew up to be independent but all that Charles still wished, was to please his father.

The 14-year-old prince grew to resent the king's new favourite, George Villiers, known as Steenie because of his resemblance to St Stephen. Villiers was given money, titles and honours. There was no one closer to James than the young man he called his 'only sweet child'.[11] There were some disastrous exchanges between the pair, including when Charles turned a fountain on Villiers at Greenwich, soaking him in the process, and rousing his father's fury. James always sided with Villiers, on one occasion boxing his son's ears. By June 1618, however, Villiers, who recognised that Charles was the future, established himself as the prince's mentor and role model and the prince grasped the importance, in another lesson taught by Thomas Murray, who made the transition from tutor to secretary, of getting along with the man who possessed his father's ear. It meant that the prince, whose desire to please his father contained a strong element of fear, played second fiddle to the commoner and was grateful for Villiers' patronage, describing him as being like a brother.

Charles inherited other mentors from Henry to whom he could turn for advice. The Earls of Arundel, Pembroke, Salisbury and Montgomery were all patrons of the arts and leaders of the political world. Perhaps more importantly for the prince, aside from their relationship with his beloved brother, was that they were all Knights of the Garter.[12] When Charles became king, the Earl of Arundel and the other nobles associated with the Order would be counsellors he felt he could trust and who were, in his mind, within the natural order of men that a king should turn. As well as his nobility, Charles was provided with a model and further written instruction by his father. James spent his life trying to reconcile the complex religious beliefs of his subjects. In 1620, after Anne of Denmark's death and a health scare of his own in 1619, the king distilled his understanding into a *Meditation upon the 27th, 28th and 29th Verses of the 27th Chapter of Saint Matthew*. James provided his son with a pattern for kingship by drawing parallels between the thorns used to crown Christ on his way to Calvary and the cares placed on the shoulders' of a monarch. James' policy on religion was based on a Calvinist consensus and sought to suppress extremism, whether it was Catholic or Puritan. It was for this reason that he favoured giving bishops authority since it removed power from radical Presbyterian or Puritan church elders.

It was increasingly urgent that Charles marry and produce legitimate heirs. A proposed Catholic match with Spain, dating from before Elizabeth's marriage to Frederick, led to discord within Charles' household. This was caused, in part, by the Spanish invasion of the Palatine in August 1620.

James' subjects, and Parliament, wanted war rather than conciliation and they wanted the Prince of Wales to marry a Protestant. The king was infuriated by their interference in royal prerogative and saw the union as a way of restoring his daughter and son-in-law to the Palatine. Spanish diplomats were under instructions to keep negotiations going for as long as possible in order to keep the English out of the war in Europe. One of Charles' chaplains, Hakewell, wrote a book decrying the possibility and presented it to the prince, resulting in his dismissal. Murray, Charles' former tutor, found himself under house arrest before being discharged from his post when it was discovered that he knew about the book and was also opposed to the union with Spain. Buckingham vacillated between calling for war and his view, which coincided with the king's own, that a Spanish match would be beneficial. Inevitably, Charles agreed with his father and best friend. It did not help that two of the men who had been at the prince's side throughout his childhood and whose advice he valued were no longer welcome at court to provide a more balanced argument. Meanwhile, Puritan writers declared that Elizabeth was a Protestant heroine and Henry became a model of Protestant virtue. Charles, who was dutiful to his father's wishes, was viewed as a disappointment.

Tired of waiting for a betrothal, in February 1623 Charles and the Duke of Buckingham left England, with James' agreement, calling themselves Jack and Tom Smith, disguised in large hats and false beards, to negotiate for the prince's hand to the infanta of Spain themselves. It was an extreme response but one which reflected that Charles, who usually preferred routine, could make unexpected decisions if guided by people he trusted, on this occasion thinking that he would be able to cut through diplomatic negotiations. Aside from being unprepared for ordinary life, such as using suspiciously large denominations (at one point before they left England, they gave a ferryman a 20-shilling piece), Baby Charles and Steenie were unaware that the infanta, Maria Anna, had no wish to marry a Protestant and that Philip IV, the infanta's brother, would not agree a union unless the anti-Catholic laws in England were repealed. By the time the prince arrived in Paris, his disguise bulked up by a periwig, to visit the Louvre and see the royal family there dine, James I had second thoughts. He feared that Charles might be taken hostage and then forced to accept whatever terms the Spanish chose to impose upon him before permitting him to return home. He ordered Carey, who was 63 years old at the time, to pursue his son with the royal fleet, an appropriate retinue and gifts for the Spanish.

For Charles there was the adventure of the kind of travel that was usually reserved for the sons of nobility rather than heirs to a throne, and the chance to see places that he could only otherwise have read about. He travelled through France and down the Iberian Peninsula. The arrival in Madrid of the Prince of Wales and his small escort was contrary to all the complicated rules of the Spanish court. The English ambassador, John Digby, 1st Earl of Bristol, was horrified and hastily wrote a letter home designed to distance himself from the fact that he expected the prince's undertaking to fail. Unexpectedly though, Charles and the 17-year-old king of Spain, Philip IV, became friends of a sort, both being interested in art and Philip being impressed by Charles' horsemanship and education. For James' heir it was a chance to experience a much more formal court than the one he knew at home. Spanish royalty were treated with respect that bordered upon religious devotion. It was divine kingship made real. For their part, the Spanish were shocked that the Duke of Buckingham treated the English prince with such informality. He was better dressed than Charles, sat in his presence and often wore his hat in the company of the young man who would become king after James' death.

Charles was initially so enthusiastic to marry that he agreed, in July 1623, to a secret treaty that granted tolerance to England's Catholic subjects, even though it would have been so unpopular that Parliament would never have agreed. In England, James made his privy council agree to the terms, even though the sought-after aid for Elizabeth and Frederick, and the return of the Palatinate, was not on the table for discussion. Nor was there any mention of a dowry for the infanta. Despite the assumption made by courts across Europe that Charles would convert to Catholicism and the efforts made by Philip IV to that effect, including the refusal to admit his chaplains into the royal palace, the prince refused to consider becoming a Catholic. The Spanish insisted that no marriage would go ahead until the secret treaty was put into effect. By the autumn the prince had come to see Spanish negotiations as a snare to keep him unmarried, although it was only when he was safely beyond Philip IV's borders that he sent a letter to Digby telling him not to proceed with a proxy marriage to the infanta. The ambassador did not yet know that he would be made into a scapegoat for the failure of the wedding plans. He was recalled to England and sent to live on his estates. When Charles offered to return him to favour if he took the blame for the episode, the earl angrily refused and found himself in the Tower, where he remained until 1628.

Before his departure, Philip IV gave the prince the *Pardo Venus* and a portrait of Emperor Charles V, both by Titian as parting gifts. Charles had already purchased works by Titian, Raphael and Veronese during his visit. His ambition was to make a collection that equalled that of any Renaissance ruler but especially that of Philip IV which was kept at the Escorial. Aside from relishing the art he saw during his travels, Charles recognised that magnificent art added to royal prestige. He forgot that for many of his subjects, the artists he hung on the walls of his palaces were associated with Catholic culture and therefore suspect. During the seven months that he was absent from England, the Prince of Wales received a practical education about Spain and its culture in the way that other noble grand tourists discovered about the countries they visited. He had also grown a real beard, in the style of the Spanish nobles that he met, and learned for himself that the diplomatic negotiations for Maria Anna's hand had been little more than a fabrication on the part of Spain. Charles no longer wanted to obey his father's wishes on the subject of peace in Europe. Instead, he was drawn to an alliance with France and war with Spain. In December 1624, it was agreed that James' heir would marry the youngest sister of King Louis XIII.

Chapter Thirteen

Family Man

When James I died on 27 March 1625, the Prince of Wales's household was dissolved. Carey wrote with regret of his dismissal but recognised that one of the new king's first acts was to reward him and Elizabeth for their service. Elevated to the peerage, they became the 1st Earl and Countess of Monmouth. Carey was given a place as a gentleman of the bedchamber as well as receiving an annual allowance of £500 and Kenilworth Castle, which the earl was to hold for life.

The new monarch married 15-year-old Henrietta Maria in 1625; the nuptials were held in Canterbury because there was plague in London. Quin, the poet, wrote a poem congratulating him on his marriage in four languages. He was subsequentially granted a pension of £100 per annum.[1] Before she left for England, Henrietta Maria wrote to Pope Urban VIII confirming that she intended to raise her children as Catholics. She might reasonably have supposed that Charles and his government would not interfere with her plan, given that the marriage treaty between England and France granted Henrietta the right to control the education of her children until they were 12 years old. Nor did she have any intention of allowing Charles to control appointments to her household. His refusal to agree to the employment of any of her French retinue, the couple's battle over the use of Catholic or Protestant rites for services and the presence of Catholic priests in the royal palaces would lead to arguments between the pair as well as increasing public distrust of the new queen.

Charles was crowned on 2 February 1626. For the time being, Elizabeth of Bohemia remained her brother's heir. She gave birth to her ninth child, a daughter named Henriette after her sister-in-law, that summer. There was no sign of Charles becoming a father, in part because Henrietta Maria, a devout young woman, was told by her priests, who were Oratorian Catholics, to abstain from sex on certain days of the week and for other more prolonged periods of time. While intercourse, for the purpose of begetting children, was part of marriage, her advisers argued that it hindered spiritual growth. From their perspective chastity was much more desirable. So great was Henrietta's determination to fulfil her perceived duty as a Catholic queen in a Protestant country that she refused not only to be crowned alongside her husband but even to attend the ceremony because it was both a Catholic feast day and the service would be a Protestant one. It did not bode well.

A month later, Lady Elizabeth Stewart, eldest daughter of Esmé Stewart, 3rd Duke of Lennox, and the king's ward, married Henry Howard, Lord Maltravers, the heir of the Earl of Arundel, without the king's consent. The king saw the union as an injury to his authority as Elizabeth's guardian and blamed the earl, who was part of the faction opposed to George Villiers, who became the Duke of Buckingham shortly after his return from Spain. In reality it is unlikely that Arundel knew about his son's union in advance but he was sent to the Tower while his son and daughter-in-law were closely questioned about the extent of his knowledge of their match. Not only was Elizabeth one of the king's cousins but the wedding was an infringement of the king's prerogative right of wardship. It was for Charles to dispose of Elizabeth in marriage as he saw fit and he was planning a union with the heir of the Earl of Argyll, reconciling two important families with a history of hostility to one another.[2] Henrietta pleaded with Charles to release Arundel, who was Catholic, but it was only when the House of Lords intervened that he was set at liberty. The affair highlighted the growing conflict between the different religious and political factions as well as the discord between the monarch and his queen.

The strains in Charles' marriage reached breaking point in July when he banished the queen's French servants to Somerset House before sending them back to France. Just prior to the episode the king took the step of appointing four English women as ladies of the queen's bedchamber. Henrietta opposed their appointments because they were Protestant, but when her new first lady of the bedchamber, Susan Feilding, Countess of Denbigh, Buckingham's sister, used her influence so that the queen's childhood nurse, Marguerite Courtin, Madame de Vantelet could remain in Henrietta's household, the queen relented. In reality there was little the queen could do. She was not crowned, England was hostile to Catholic France, and she had not yet provided an heir to the throne. Yet, by the time the Duke of Buckingham was murdered in 1628 the couple had reached a compromise and with the death of the duke, the queen, who showed compassion to both Buckingham's womenfolk and to her husband, became Charles' closest companion.

On 13 May 1629, Henrietta gave birth to a premature baby boy who was baptised Charles in the hour between his birth and death. By the beginning of 1630 she was pregnant again. Fearful that she might lose another infant, the queen ordered a French midwife to arrive in England in time for her lying-in. During the voyage across the Channel, the woman and the party she was travelling with were captured by pirates and only released upon payment of a large ransom. Henrietta Maria withdrew to St James's Palace and, on 29 May, she gave birth to another boy, also named Charles after his father, who was handed to his wet nurse, Christabella Wyndam. The infant was not swaddled as it had fallen from fashion in France. The queen wrote to her mother describing him as 'so dark that I am ashamed of him'.[3]

The queen proposed that the nursery should be overseen by Jean Drummond, Countess of Roxburghe who cared for both Prince Henry and Charles for a time during their infancies. Anne of Denmark's former lady-in-waiting and mistress of the robes was well used to managing a royal household. However, the countess, controversially, was a Catholic. During the reign of James I, she received an annual pension of 1500 ducats from Spain at the request of the Spanish ambassador, Don Juan de Taxis. It has been suggested that she was the conduit for communication between the Stuart Crown and the Catholic monarchies in Europe.[4] She may have been involved in discussions about the possibility of a Spanish match for Henry to the Infanta of Spain before his death and was responsible for concealing Anne of Denmark's faith from the wider public.[5] When Jean married Roxburghe in 1614, Anne paid for the wedding celebrations which were held at Somerset House. The close bond between mistress and servant only ended in 1617 when Lord Roxburghe sought to become Charles' lord chamberlain, in the place of Robert Carey, without either he or his wife telling Anne of their intention. Carey retained his post and the Spanish pension was stopped when the countess returned to Scotland. Now, any hopes of Jean returning to court were thwarted because of her religious beliefs. It broke the agreement made in Charles and Henrietta's marriage treaty which gave the queen control over her children until the age of 12, but the king maintained that their children were to be raised as Protestants and he was not prepared to risk a Catholic governess. It was Mary Sackville, Countess of Dorset who was appointed to oversee Prince Charles' nursery. Her Protestant credentials were impeccable as were those of her husband, Edward, 4th Earl of Dorset. He was part of the force who served under Sir Horatio Vere in 1620 in the defence of Bohemia and had pleaded with Parliament to vote a subsidy for the recovery of the Palatinate in 1621. By 1628 he was appointed as Henrietta Maria's lord chamberlain, ensuring a conduit of information between the queen's household and the royal nursery.

The king's heir was equipped with his own household at St James's Palace. In the summer the household was moved out of London to Oatlands, Hampton Court or Greenwich depending on where the queen was residing. His companions included a daughter and two sons of the Duke of Buckingham, George, Francis and Mary who would marry Charles Herbert in 1634 when she was 12 years old. The boys, who were only slightly older than the prince, would share his lessons. The royal nursery expanded the following year when Henrietta Maria gave birth to a daughter on 4 November 1631. She was named Mary after her great grandmother and her baptism was hastily expedited as it was feared that she would not survive; less kind observers declared it was to save money. Her godmothers were the countesses of Carlisle and Denbigh. Lucy Hay, the Countess of Carlisle was better known for her scandalous love affairs with Thomas Wentworth, 1st Earl of Strafford and his political opponent John Pym. Mary's godfather was William Laud who, as well as being Bishop of London since 1628, was also Dean of the Chapel Royal. More usually godparents were selected to create social and political connections which might one day be of use to both the king and to the State. Mary's godparents were selected by necessity but Laud and Wentworth were political allies. They both supported the king's personal rule following his dissolution of parliament in 1629. During the eleven years when Charles ruled as an absolute monarch, using royal prerogative rights to gather taxes, his realm appeared to be both peaceful and prosperous but it was a decade of increasing political tension and growing opposition to the Crown.

In the royal nursery the king's children flourished. Despite fears for Mary, in the care of her nurse, Mrs Griffin, she began to thrive. The nurse would remain part of the princess' household for the rest of her life, fulfilling the role of surrogate parent. Her household, overseen by the Countess of Roxburghe, despite her Catholic beliefs, included a lady of the bedchamber, a nurse, three rockers and a physician as well as a laundress, a seamstress, four footmen and five kitchen servants. Later a French tutor, Monsieur d'Aranjon joined the household. Each of the king's children were provided with chaplains to ensure that they were raised in the Protestant faith. As well as learning their letters and their prayers, Charles wanted to ensure that their knowledge of scripture was as thorough as his own and James I's. However, Henrietta Maria never gave up hoping that her children would become Catholics. She tried to appoint Catholics to the royal nursery, gave her children crucifixes and even took them to her own chapel to hear Mass.

In 1633 the king travelled north for his coronation as king of Scotland. Henrietta Maria was pregnant once again so she remained in England. James, Duke of York, was born on 14 October 1633 and handed into the care of his wet nurse. Concern was expressed because the woman was a Catholic and it was feared that the infant would take in papistry with her milk. However, when he was baptised on 14 November by William Laud, newly created Archbishop of Canterbury, his godparents, Elizabeth, Queen of Bohemia and Frederick Henry Prince of Orange, were faultlessly Protestant. James joined his brother in the royal nursery under the care of Mary Sackville rather than coming under of the Countess of Roxburghe's influence. Charles I ensured that his two eldest sons were raised without taint of papistry but was more sympathetic to his queen's wishes in the matter of his daughters.

As well as overseeing the care and education of its occupants, it was the Countess of Dorset's job to oversee the management of the nursery and its staff. On 1st August 1637 she wrote to the Earl of Strafford to ask that one of James' servants be excused from undertaking an expedition to Ireland because the Duke of York, who was in his fourth year, could not spare any of his servants.[6] For the children's lessons, exercise and games began each morning with prayer and was finished each day with supper. When the younger children were sent to bed, if they were at Whitehall, the older children might dine with their parents. They were expected to understand the importance of protocol and how to behave with formality as members of the royal family.

The royal children were joined in their nursery by another sister, Elizabeth, born on 28 December 1635. Like her elder siblings, she was born at St James's Palace. Anne arrived two years later and was baptised at St James's Palace. It was a happy childhood under the oversight of the Countess of Roxburghe for the girls and the Countess of Dorset for the boys, and King Charles proved to be a devoted father. While the family was at Richmond, George Coneo, a papal agent, described seeing the family dine together with Charles and James on either side of their father and Mary sitting next to her mother.[7] The king even kept a measuring rod to mark the heights of his children. In 1636, Prince Charles and his Villiers companions took part in their first royal masque at Windsor. The boys were required to sing, dance and to recite verses. In 1637, Van Dyck was commissioned to paint a portrait of the children. It broke with the tradition of painting princes and princesses as miniature adults. On the right-hand side of the picture, 2-year-old Elizabeth supports baby Anne. James, still in long skirts, stands next to his brother who rests his arm on a mastiff. Charles, clad in breeches, was about to leave the care of women.

As Charles' heir left his nursery behind him, the political atmosphere across Scotland and England darkened. The king introduced a new *Book of Common Prayer* in Scotland which placed an emphasis upon ceremony and in England a tax, known as ship-money, was levied across the whole country rather than the coastal counties where it was usually raised. In Buckinghamshire, John Hampden preferred to go to prison rather than pay what many believed to be an illegal tax. To make matters even worse, in the autumn of 1637 Henrietta Marie began a campaign to persuade the king to allow her own mother, Marie de Medici, to come to England. Charles regarded the idea with alarm, not only because of what his Protestant kingdom might think about the arrival of another Catholic into his inner circle, but because of her disagreement with Charles I's brother-in-law, King Louis XIII of France. Aside from her politics and religion being unpopular within his realm, there was the matter of financing another royal household. Instead, he offered to send Marie vessels to carry her from Brussels to Italy or Spain. However, on 18 October she arrived unexpectedly at Harwich. At Romford, she was met by the king who escorted her to St James's Palace where she was reunited with her daughter and met her five grandchildren for the first time. In November

Anne, who was a sickly child, possibly due to tuberculosis, became ill and died. By the end of the year, Mary Villiers was gone as well, having married, on 3 August, to James Stewart, 4th Duke of Lennox.

In 1638 young Charles was created a Knight of the Garter and officially recognised as Prince of Wales. At the same time, he was given his own household and court at Richmond; George and Francis Villiers remained with him. Like princes before him, Charles' new staff more closely mirrored the structure of the king's household than the royal nursery. It was essential, as it was for his predecessors, to maintain royal dignity at all times and to understand the ways in which protocol enhanced his sovereignty. His governor was William Cavendish, Earl of Newcastle, who was considered to be England's most outstanding horseman as well as being a musician, poet and swordsman. Newcastle entertained Charles I at his homes at Welbeck in 1633 and again, at Bolsover Castle, in 1634 with a masque. The Little Castle, decorated as an allegory reconciling pleasure and virtue, revealed Cavendish's love of horses, music and art. Whether the king recognised that the frolicking female nudes in the Marble Closet reflected another of the earl's passions is a matter for speculation. Certainly, it seems that the prince took to heart Newcastle's later advice about being civil to women and avoiding being too devout. However, it was now Newcastle's duty to drill the prince about good manners and civility. He emphasised the importance of a kind word to everyone and the necessity that Charles should guard his tongue. Whereas Charles I, who was shy, often seemed stand-offish with his subjects, his son possessed the common touch.

The earl was an intellectual but his academic skills were overshadowed by his sporting prowess. He took the view, so far as his supervision of the prince was concerned, that too much book learning could be a dangerous thing. In 1660 he would complain there were too many grammar schools, students, lawyers and clerks for his liking. Charles' education at the hands of Newcastle would see him become a young man who enjoyed physical sports, like his uncle, Henry, and a horseman like his own father. Cavendish taught the prince that it was the responsibility of the rider to observe the way his horse moved and to know the animal's limits; they should move as one. Newcastle understood the necessity of winning a horse through kindness and thorough training rather than cruelty. It was a novel idea in an era that often brutalised horses to gain compliance. Cavendish wrote his first manual on horsemanship in 1658, in French. The English version followed in 1667. As well as riding, Newcastle ensured that Charles knew how to dance and how to fence. Master Fawcett was appointed to teach the prince archery. Charles thrived in the earl's care, once writing, 'I ride every day, and am ready to follow any other directions from you. Make haste back to him that loves you'.[8]

Both Charles and, later, James were tutored by their father's chaplain, Brian Duppa who until his royal appointment served as Vice-Chancellor of the University of Oxford. Like their father and grandfather before them, their programme of study was a humanist one. Duppa recognised that his charges were not diligent scholars in the way that their father had been but chose not to demonstrate his own learning or to force the princes into their books, preferring more gentle methods of persuasion. Charles, who rushed to his former tutor's death bed in 1662 to ask for Duppa's blessing, proved to be an able but idle student. He was poor at both Latin and Greek and it was only during his exile in the aftermath of the First English Civil War that he was forced to become fluent in French as well as being able to understand both Italian and Spanish. The prince was also required to learn to play the viols, to read music and to draw. His drawing master was Wenceslaus Hollar, who fled Prague in 1621 but having come to the attention of the 21st Earl of Arundel, who spent two years in the Tower, had returned to England with the earl in 1637.

In January 1639, the younger children were joined by a short-lived sister, Katherine. That summer, King Charles sent out a commission of array. He was going to war against his Scottish subjects who were angered by the king's attempts to reform the Scottish Kirk, despite the fact that the Anglican liturgy he favoured was contrary to Calvinist beliefs. Presbyterians felt that they were being forced to accept a liturgy devised by Archbishop Laud which smacked to them of Catholicism. One of the outcomes of the First Bishops' War, was the so-called Short Parliament which lasted only three weeks in the spring of 1640. Like earlier parliaments it had less interest in voting subsidies for the king's war than redressing royal abuse of power. Inevitably the king dissolved the sitting and the security that his children had known throughout their early lives began to dissolve.

In March, the Earl of Strafford, who was Charles' principal advisor and Lord Deputy of Ireland, held a parliament in Ireland to secure subsidies and to raise an Irish army to be used against the Presbyterian Scots. Tensions between the king's Protestant and Catholic subjects boiled over. Many of London's citizens blamed Thomas Wentworth, the newly created Earl of Strafford, who tried to force prominent merchants to lend the king money and threatened to debase the coinage. Others blamed William Laud who was forced to flee to Whitehall to escape rioters on 11 May. At Richmond a guard of 200 militiamen was placed over the royal nursery[9] but by 14 May the civil unrest was still not quelled and anger now turned-on Henrietta Maria and her Catholic priests. In Whitehall, someone scratched a prayer on a pane of glass hoping that God would save the king but confound his wife and children. Charles smashed the window with his fist[10] but was forced to make a show of arresting Catholic priests and searching houses of known recusants.

On 8 July 1640, amid continuing rumours and arguments between his parents about the best course of action, Prince Henry, Duke of Gloucester, was born at Oatlands. He joined his sisters in the royal nursery, under the care of the Catholic Countess of Roxburghe, and at about the same time the king released the newly imprisoned Catholics. The prince was baptised in the chapel at Oatlands and the king is thought to have planted a cedar tree in the grounds there in celebration of the birth of another son. There were no funds for anything more lavish. Marie De Medici's allowance was halved and Henrietta Maria dismissed many of her household.

In August 1640, subsequent to a Scots invasion and occupation of the north of England, there were calls for Parliament to be summoned. The Earls of Hertford and Essex were among the sixteen commissioners chosen to negotiate with the invaders at Ripon. Later they would both be among twelve signatories who described the necessity of summoning Parliament and called upon the king to do so. The queen and her children moved to Windsor, which was safer and better defended, while Charles went to York to arrive at terms with the Scots against a background of anti-Catholic propaganda.

Chapter Fourteen

The Road to War

King Charles sought to win influence with the men who wished to restrain him by making some concessions to the parliamentary party. He appointed seven new peers to the privy council. Their number included the Earls of Bedford, Essex and Hertford. The king also began to consider the marriages of his children, looking for allies to bolster his position. However, Europe remained torn by the Thirty Years War and any alliances sealed by a marriage would feed into the existing conflict.

Writs were sent out to summon a new parliament to meet on 3 November. Princess Anne, whose cough grew steadily worse that autumn, died on 5 November. The king and queen ordered a post mortem to be carried out by Sir Theodore Mayerne who diagnosed a 'suffocating catarrh, with inflammatory disposition of the lungs'.[1] Her ailments suggest that she probably died from tuberculosis. It has been estimated that almost a third of children died before the age of 15 years during the seventeenth century.[2] In common with other god-fearing men and women of the period, Anne's staff prepared the little girl for death. The 3-year-old knew her prayers, even though she was too exhausted to repeat the Lord's Prayer. There was comfort in the thought of salvation, reassurances for the child and for the gathered family. For Anne's siblings, the grief of losing a beloved sister was accompanied by a lesson in the acceptance of mortality.

There was little time for the king to withdraw from the world to mourn the loss of his daughter. Three days after Anne's death, the House of Commons accused the Archbishop of Canterbury of treason. Among the accusations was that Laud desired to reunite the Church of England with Rome and that he worked at the behest of the queen to that end. At about the same time, Henrietta was ordered by Parliament to dismiss all her Catholic servants, which was contrary to her marriage treaty. The king might have done well to accept the inevitability of the failure of divine right and lay aside his personal approach to monarchy for a more conciliatory approach to Parliament, but he was alarmed by the attack on his wife. On 11 November 1640, the Earl of Strafford was impeached for his actions in Ireland and arrested for treason. At about the same time, Brian Duppa wrote that Prince Charles was likely to turn into 'an excellent man if my presage deceive me not, and flattery and humouring, the bane of Princes, do not spoil him'.[3] It must have seemed to the boy that he was at little risk of being flattered by his father's subjects, especially having witnessed outbursts against his mother, but it was his sister, Mary, who felt the repercussions of the political upheaval first.

In 1640, Charles I received a proposal of marriage for Elizabeth from Frederick Henry, Prince of Orange for his surviving legitimate son, William, who was in his tenth year. It was a good match and of benefit to Britain's trading relations with Holland, but when Elizabeth was shown a miniature of her potential spouse, she suggested that Mary would make a better bride. The news that either Elizabeth or Mary would marry the Dutch heir became public on 12 December. By February 1641 a dowry of £40,000 was agreed and it was decided that the Princess Royal would be the bride. On 6 February, 9-year-old Mary and the Countess of Roxburghe received the Dutch ambassadors while Henrietta Marie watched unobserved from behind a screen. Mary would remain in England until she was 12 years old before making the journey to The Hague.

In March 1641, the Prince of Wales and his companions, including Charles' cousin James Stuart, Duke of Richmond, were sent to Cambridge with their tutor, Dr Duppa, where the prince received an honorary Master of Arts degree before joining the king at Newmarket. As well as providing Charles with an opportunity to rehearse a royal visit, it may also have been a stratagem to provide the Puritan university town with a positive perception of monarchy. The publication of *The true effigies of our most illustrious soveraigne lord, King Charles, Queen Mary, with the rest of the royall progenie*, including a picture of the recently deceased Anne clutching a ball between her hands, was designed to have the same effect. Each of the images of the royal family was accompanied by a verse; Mary's emphasised her upbringing to be the model of a virtuous young woman, 'mild, modest, affable, beloved, and loving'.[4] The king wished to remind his subjects that he and his children were raised according to godly principles and that the alliance he made with the Prince of Orange was in recognition of his regard for Mary's Protestant beliefs.

That same month, Strafford was tried in Westminster Hall where it was decided to find him guilty by Bill of Attainder. The king was often present to witness the debates around the trial. Since he also began keeping his 10-year-old heir more in his own company, not only to provide practical lessons in statecraft but to reduce the possibility of the prince being seen as over influenced by his mother, Charles also witnessed Parliament's actions. Mary, at 9-years-old, also learned first-hand that the authority of the king was something which Parliament might challenge when she accompanied her parents to the Lords to watch proceedings, from a private gallery.

Mary's young groom arrived in London in April 1641 where he was met by her brothers, Charles and James, who escorted him to meet their mother before going to Somerset House where he met the princess for the first time. It was an opportunity for the Prince of Wales and the Duke of York to demonstrate their courtliness when they welcomed their future brother-in-law and when they dined with him. The wedding, a quiet affair, conducted by the Bishop of Ely, took place on 2 May 1641 at Whitehall. For once, Henrietta Maria attended a Protestant ceremony, watching from a gallery with Marie de Medici while the Countess of Roxburghe stood by Mary's side. The celebrations that went with the union were followed by a ritualised bedding ceremony that saw the children placed in bed together, Mary wrapped in a sheet, under the supervision of the queen, the countess and the ever-loyal Mrs Griffin. Charles hoped that the marriage demonstrated his Protestant credentials but Elizabeth of Bohemia's eldest son, Charles Louis of the Rhine, had wished to marry his cousin and refused to attend the service. His anger stemmed not only from his failure to achieve closer ties with England but because there was no Anglo-Dutch treaty for his restoration to the Palatinate. His failure to attend events detracted from the king's claim that the union would help his sister and her family.

The following day a London mob demanding the execution of the Earl of Strafford broke into Westminster Abbey. A week later, the king, despite his misgivings, signed Strafford's death warrant. The next day, 11 May, he sent Prince Charles, who was still only 10 years old, dressed in robes of State, to plead with Parliament for the earl's life. It was to no avail; Wentworth was executed the following day. It was an early, and dramatic, lesson in the fallibility of royalty. Mary's young groom, who feared civil unrest, began to agitate for his bride to accompany him home to Holland rather than waiting until she was older. At first, King Charles refused to contemplate his daughter's departure. She would continue her education in England but in her own household under the guidance of a new governess, Katherine Stanhope, the widow of Philip Stanhope and daughter of Lord Wotton of St Mary's Cray.

In London the royal family deemed it sensible to leave Whitehall for Oatlands while Henrietta Maria's mother, fearing for her safety in the increasingly troubled times, returned to Europe. Parliament demanded that the royal nursery remain in London in the custody of officials appointed by them. Instead, Henrietta sent her children to Richmond. The Earl of Newport reported that she and Prince Charles were to be taken into the supervision of Parliament in order to guarantee the king's behaviour. In response, the queen instructed that her younger children should return to Oatlands while her two older sons remained at Richmond which was about fifteen miles distant. The staffing of Charles' household changed as well. Duppa was appointed Bishop of Salisbury and departed. Cavendish, who was unpopular with the Parliamentarian faction, resigned his governorship shortly before this episode and retired to his home at Welbeck Abbey in Nottinghamshire.

Cavendish was replaced by William Seymour, Earl of Hertford on his predecessor's recommendation as a man 'of honour, of unquestionable fidelity to him [the Prince], and above the reach of popular disapprobation'.[5] Edward Hyde thought him unsuited to the task but his academic credentials suggested otherwise. Parliament demanded that Prince Charles be given more suitable attendants and voted two Puritan peers be appointed joint governors alongside Hertford. William Russell, 4th Earl of Bedford and William Fiennes, 1st Viscount Say and Sele, who were among the most vociferous opponents to the king in the Lords, were both nominated.

They feared that Henrietta Maria wielded too much influence. In Scotland it was felt that the heir to the throne should spend more time there. It was also rumoured that John Hampden aspired to the post of governor.[6] The arguments about who should be admitted into the Prince of Wales's household, where it should be based and who should educate the prince rumbled on. In June, Hertford was elevated to the title of marquess in recognition of his many virtues. It seemed that the prince's new governor had not only the approval of Parliament but also the monarch. It was an accord that could not last. Parliament demanded that the Prince of Wales have no contact with his mother and by October 1641 there was a demand that no Catholics should be allowed to have a hand in his education.

Hertford did not have the vigour of his predecessor. Clarendon described the marquess as 'of an age not fit for much duty and fatigue, who loved, and was even so much wedded to his ease, that he loved his books above all exercises'.[7] Parliament was not concerned about the prince's broader education or the relationship between tutor and pupil. It was troubled only about the religion of those around him. The household at Richmond remained under Hertford's control. He was instructed that 'no such persons as may give either cause of distrust of meddling with him [the prince], either in any point against his religion or against the security of his person, be admitted about him'.[8] However, it became apparent that when Charles returned to Oatlands to visit his family there was no chamber for Hertford, so he had returned to Richmond. When Parliament got wind of the stay, they demanded an explanation from Henrietta Maria, since they wished Hertford to remain with the prince at all times. The queen replied that her son, who had been staying with her since the summer, was celebrating one of his sisters' birthdays and promised that Charles would be returned into his guardian's care at Richmond. While her reply was conciliatory, those reading her letter may have wondered at the length of the festivities given that Mary, whose birthday was nearest the episode, did not celebrate her tenth birthday until 4 November.

Duppa's replacement, John Earle, was a fellow of Merton College Oxford before becoming chancellor of the university there as well as chaplain to Philip Herbert, 4th Earl of Pembroke, who was a favourite both of Charles' father and grandfather. The earl was known to be sympathetic to Puritanism and he opposed the elevation of William Laud to the archbishopric of Canterbury in 1633. However, Earle, like Duppa, was a moderate and his personable nature led Clarendon to describe him as a 'so very innocent and so very facetious, that no man's company was more desired and more loved'.[9] So far as Parliament was concerned, the Prince of Wales was in the best possible hands.

When King Charles returned to England at the end of November and made his state entrance to London, his sons, Charles and James, rode beside him while the queen, Mary and their younger children rode behind in an open carriage. The animosity that Londoners exhibited to the Crown earlier that year was absent and the family were hailed by cries of 'God save the king'. The children knew what their parts were and how to play them. A banquet was held at the Guildhall where the whole family dined in state. What they did not realise was that Parliament's demands were becoming more extreme and that the king was encouraged by the growth of support for him to confront his unruly subjects.

On 4 January 1642, the king attempted to arrest five Members of Parliament in the House of Commons. The attempt was unlawful and, even worse, Charles failed. Six days later, he left Whitehall and retired to Hampton Court with his wife and three eldest children, leaving the younger children, Elizabeth and Henry, in the care of their governess, the Countess of Roxburghe. The king feared that if they remained in London that Henrietta Maria would be arrested but in leaving his younger children behind, he demonstrated that he believed that he would be able to reach an accommodation with Parliament even though there were people who argued that the queen was not above the law and that legal action should be taken against her. It was widely believed that she intended to bring about a rebellion in Ireland to raise support for Charles. The royal family spent an uncomfortable night at Hampton Court, on 10 January 1642, sharing the same bed, because no one expected them there. The five men who escaped arrest were welcomed in triumph back to Westminster.

The royal family then moved to Windsor where they planned their next move. Wagons carrying ammunition arrived from the Tower of London and the Earl of Newcastle was ordered to take command of Hull and its arsenal. On the very same day, Parliament directed Sir John Hotham to do the same for them and put a guard around the Tower of London. Inside it, Sir John Byron was under the king's orders to blow everything up rather than surrender to Parliament. But, because he was not yet able to confront his rebellious subjects, Charles was forced to concede to the Commons.

Byron was replaced and the case against the Parliamentarians accused of treason was dropped.

It was time, the king decided, for Mary to join her husband since it would also give Henrietta Maria cause to leave the country. The queen's departure as part of the bridal party was an opportunity, so far as Parliament was concerned and should they enquire, for Charles' wife to travel to a spa in Belgium. No one need know that she would also take quantities of jewellery to exchange for men and munitions so that the king could fight a war against his own people. As it happened, Parliament made no objection to the queen's departure. They believed, or so the Venetian ambassador thought, that without his wife the king would be more willing to work with his parliament.

It was Lady Stanhope's responsibility to prepare Mary for life as the consort of William, who would become Prince of Orange and Stadtholder of Holland following the death of his own father, Frederick Henry. Katherine who was appointed Grand Superintendent was granted full authority over Mary's household as well as being provided with a list of instructions by the king. She was always to have a place in Mary's coach, was empowered to purchase robes for the princess' wardrobe and that any old dresses were perquisites of the countess. On 25 February 1642, Mary made her farewells to her father, who rode along the cliffs until her vessel, the *Lion,* and its escort of fifteen Dutch warships disappeared from sight. The Princess Royal was accompanied by the queen, Lady Stanhope, Lord Heenvliet, who had helped to negotiate the match, her ladies-in-waiting and, as ever, by Mrs Griffin. The Countess of Denbigh and the Duchess of Richmond also formed part of the group. Henrietta's baggage contained some of the crown jewels as well as plate which she intended to sell in order to raise funds for her husband's campaign against Parliament and it is thought that the Countess of Roxburghe made the journey, as part of the queen's retinue, to assist with the sale.

When Mary arrived in the Netherlands, she and her mother were met by Mary's aunt, Elizabeth of Bohemia, and two of her daughters, including her youngest daughter Sophia, as well as William and his father, before journeying to the Hague by coach. Mary, now a married woman, would continue her education in the care of the Princess of Orange, Amalia van Solms, who had once been one of Elizabeth of Bohemia's ladies-in-waiting. For the time being, though, she remained at The Hague, under the supervision of Lady Stanhope after a tearful farewell to the Countess of Roxburghe. A new list of rules was compiled by the Prince of Orange, to ensure that Mary was groomed as a future consort to his son and that she would conduct herself at all times with the decorum expected by a Calvinist nation. Among the ordinances for the regulation of his daughter-in-law's household was one which stated Mary was not to make a public appearance unless Lady Stanhope, or some other suitably qualified person, was by her side. It was the governess' responsibility to ensure that sufficient respect was shown to the princess at all times.[10] It was only in 1646 that Mary began to cohabit with her husband, by which time she was 15 years old and her siblings in England had lived through a civil war.

Chapter Fifteen

'The Souls and Bodies of His Majesties Children'

In April 1642, Charles and James were with their father in Yorkshire. Among the men who gathered at the court in York was the Earl of Dorset, while his wife remained in London with Elizabeth and Henry. The king, who wished to secure the arsenal at Hull, sent the Duke of York, who was 8 years old, to visit the governor of the city, Sir John Hotham. He and the mayor entertained the prince and his entourage, which included the Elector Palatine, with a tour of the port and a feast that evening. When a letter arrived from the king the following morning announcing his intention of dining with Hotham that same day, the governor gave orders for the town gates to be closed. By the time Charles arrived outside Hull, the guns were all loaded and the town's trained band of men lined the walls. The king demanded entrance but Hotham declared that he held Hull for Parliament. Even more embarrassing, Charles was forced to retire to nearby Beverley and negotiate the release of his son and nephew. For James, it was a lesson in humiliation and the importance of a surprise attack. He described proceedings, which more effectively began the civil war than the lifting of the royal standard at Nottingham that August, in his memoirs. He felt the whole situation to be disastrously mishandled by his father and his advisors.

At the beginning of August, Charles appointed commissioners of array to gather a Royalist army. On 22 August both the king's elder sons were with him, as they had been throughout the summer, when the royal standard was raised over Nottingham Castle. For the next three years Charles kept the Prince of Wales and Duke of York close to him. Both of them drew conclusions about the king's dignity and, less happily, about his skills as a tactician. To begin with though there was the excitement of a gathering army, cheering crowds and the opportunity to get to know their glamourous cousins, Rupert and Maurice of the Rhine. James and Rupert were both appointed Knights of the Garter at the same time. The king's aim was that his nephew, already an experienced soldier, would become a mentor to York. Charles Louis, the Elector Palatine, could not be called upon to act as a role model for his young cousins, being reliant on Parliament for financial aid and having left England after the debacle at Hull.

On 23 October, the princes were at the Battle of Edgehill in the care of Dr William Harvey, the royal physician, whose responsibility it was, when things became too dangerous, to move them to safety. James, who had celebrated his ninth birthday the week before, together with the Prince of Wales, Harvey and Sir John Hinton, another of the royal physicians, were forced to take refuge in a barn that was being used as a field hospital before leaving the field as evening approached. Harvey, who spent the battle reading his book, and who narrowly missed being hit by a cannon ball, helped to care for the injured. Nearly captured by a troop of Parliamentarian cavalry, and having witnessed the deaths of friend and foe alike, Hinton led the two boys from the field, barely avoiding an encounter between Charles, who drew his pistol, and a Parliamentarian trooper who was hacked down by the fortuitous arrival of another Royalist officer. The two princes remembered the experience for the rest of their lives.

Afterwards Harvey, who is more famous for his discovery of the circulation of the blood, accompanied the princes to Oxford where he took up his studies once more, becoming the Warden of Merton College in 1645. James, who missed his home, spent the war in Oxford along with the royal court but the atmosphere was far too febrile to spend much time learning. Flamboyant Royalists, gentry with their wives and daughters, camp followers and soldiers flocked to the city. Scholars and their masters were called upon to help dig defensive fortifications to protect the city which was packed with people who had little thought for improving their minds.

The king sought to ensure that his sons applied themselves to their lessons, even though James had barely left the care of the Countess of Dorset before the war began. Thomas Howard, 1st Earl of Berkshire was released by Parliament for having attempted to execute the king's commission of array in Oxfordshire; he joined the royal court and, in 1643, became the Prince of Wales's governor. Sir George Radcliffe, a friend of the Earl of Strafford, was appointed as James' custodian. Howard's distinction was to have been the king's master of horse while Radcliffe was a lawyer. The governors were supported in their task by Brian Duppa who was also resident at Oxford, although there was not much time for learning as the king kept his heir by his side following the Royalist army.

It would be July 1643 before Charles and his sons were reunited with Henrietta Maria and she took up residence in Merton College just as the tide of war began to tip in favour of Parliament. In September, Gloucester was relieved from its royalist besiegers and on the 20 September, following the inconclusive encounter at the First Battle of Newbury, the relieving force led by the Earl of Essex retreated to London. Although it marked the closest point in the Royalist advance to the capital, the battle was a crucial element that led to the signing of the Solemn League and Covenant between Parliament and the Scottish Covenanters which brought the Scots into the war against the Royalists. It meant that the North, which was in Newcastle's hands, was open to attack. The series of Royalist defeats that followed left the court at Oxford more vulnerable.

Elizabeth and her brother, Henry, remained in London where Parliament took responsibility for their maintenance. In May, Archbishop Laud, still in custody since his arrest in 1641, complained that £70 of rents belonging to him had been requisitioned to maintain the royal nursery[1] which was in the care of the Earl of Pembroke at that time. Lord Say and Sele lent Parliament £780 for the care of the family and a further sum of cash was confiscated from the King's Receiver out of the revenues from Cornish tin.[2] When plague broke out, the children were moved from St James's Palace to Lord Cottingham's house on Broad Street along with the Countess of Roxburghe who re-joined the pair when she returned from Holland.[3] Once there, Elizabeth became unwell but it was only after the countess petitioned for the household's return to the palace, and it had been discussed by both houses of parliament, that they were permitted to go home. The countess, under the burden of caring for the children who were often unwell, became increasingly ill herself. On 17 February, Parliament granted permission for her husband, Robert Kerr, 1st Earl of Roxburghe, to travel from the royal court at Oxford to visit the countess on the understanding that he should remain in London for only three days. Afterwards the licence was extended for a week.

That winter the countess insisted that only familiar medical staff were to care for her charges and Parliament issued further licences. As it happened, the royal apothecary was under arrest and although he was allowed to travel to St James's, he was required to have a guard with him at all times. In May 1643, the countess died, a messenger was sent to Oxford to inform her husband and permission given for her remains to be transported to Scotland for burial. At the same time the king was informed that his children's governess was dead.

While Parliament debated who should replace the countess as governess, her young charges were grieving the loss of Lady Roxburghe who was a figure of stability in their lives. Initially the choice fell to Lady Mary Vere, the widow of Horace Vere, a professional soldier who fought in Europe for the Protestant cause at the side of Elector Frederick of the Palatinate during the Thirty Year's War; she was already in her sixties when the suggestion was made. She was the mother of four daughters including Anne Vere, the wife of Parliamentarian commander, Sir Thomas Fairfax; Elizabeth married to John Holles, 2nd Earl of Clare, the Recorder of Nottingham who affected neutrality in his interactions between the adversaries; Mary married to Mildmay Fane, 2nd Earl of Westmorland; and Catherine who was married to John Poulett. Both Fane and Poulett were Royalists. Despite the discord within her extended kinship network, Lady Vere, who had lived in Holland with her husband, was an advocate of civil and religious liberty as well as being a Puritan.[4] The House of Lords preferred the Countess of Dorset, of whom the king also approved. Her position secured her maintenance payments from her husband's estates which were considerably more than the fifth part usually allocated to the wives and children of Royalist 'delinquents' as Parliament described them.[5] It meant that she was able to retain the earl's estates in Sussex as well as Knole House near Sevenoaks, Kent and Dorset House in London. It was, according to Smith, a unique arrangement based entirely upon the countess' status as governess.

Unfortunately, as well as debating the identity of a potential governess, providing the children with appropriate mourning dress and ordering the Mint to provide for them, it was also decided by the Commons that in future

Elizabeth and Henry's household must swear the covenant oath. Failure to do so would result in immediate dismissal. It meant that men and women who cared for the prince and princess since their infancy were removed from their posts. It felt to Elizabeth, still aged only 7 years, as though she was being punished by Parliament, so she wrote to the Lords, sending the letter in the hands of the Earl of Pembroke:

> My Lords,
> I account myself very miserable that I must have my servants taken from me, and strangers put to me. You promised me that you would have a care of me, and I hope you will show it in preventing so great a grief as this would be to me. I pray, my lords, consider it, and give me cause to thank you, and to rest, Your loving Friend, Elizabeth.[6]

The Lords responded with sympathy to the princess' distress and formed a committee to investigate for itself what was happening at St James's without their prior approval. Even so, a total of eleven members of the household were dismissed because of their failure to take the oath. Among them was Elizabeth's French tutor. Elizabeth's household would consist, in the future, of the Countess of Dorset, Lady Southcote, Mrs Lee (a cofferer), four chamber women, a launderess, a starcher, two physicians and six chaplains as well as menial staff. For fear that the children should be rescued by Royalists and taken to Oxford, Parliament gave orders that the gate to the palace were to be locked at 10:00 pm each evening.

Directions were also given for the removal of pictures from the walls of St James's which offended Puritan sensibilities. The king's younger children were to live in a residence free from the taint of anything remotely Catholic. Parliament directed the religious instruction of their royal wards by appointing men they believed to be more godly ministers than the chaplains employed by the king to 'instil holy and wholesome principles into the princely hearts' of their charges.[7] Puritan clerics including Obadiah Sedgwick, William Spurstow and Stephen Marshall took up residence in the royal nursery. Household ordinances stipulated that a chaplain would read prayers both at night and in the morning as well as preaching two sermons on a Sunday. Marshall delivered lectures to the children in their schoolroom to provide them with a thorough grounding of scripture. For Elizabeth this was no hardship. It was reported that she spent each morning in the study of the Bible. By the time she was 9 years old she could read and write Latin, Greek and Hebrew and was used to translating verses from the Bible for her better understanding. William Greenhill, a Non-Conformist minister who became a member of the Westminster Assembly in 1643, and, in 1649, chaplain to James and Henry, as well as Charles' youngest daughter, dedicated an exposition of the first five chapters from the *Book of Ezekiel* to the princess in 1644 stating that she had expressed a desire to become proficient in the different languages for a better understanding of the Bible.[8] In 1648, Alexander Rowley dedicated a dictionary of Latin and Hebrew words contained in the Bible, called the *Schollers Companion*, to the princess citing her interest in scripture study as the reason for his dedication.[9]

During the summer of 1643 Elizabeth fell during a game and broke her leg. She was temporarily housebound and turned to her books for solace. By the following year the princess was recovered from her injury but when she became ill, as she was prone to do, her physicians recommended a change of air. In July the royal siblings were moved, without fanfare, to the Chelsea home of Sir John Danvers with its Italianate architecture and gardens.[10] Samuel Pepys described it as 'the prettiest contrived house that I ever saw in my life'.[11] At that time Chelsea was surrounded by fields but close enough to London to be convenient. The house was spacious, offered views of the river and even boasted a music room with an organ where Elizabeth might practise.[12] Danvers' brother, Sir Henry, was loyal to the king while John sided with Parliament. From Chelsea the children were sent to Whitehall, in September 1644, to escape an outbreak of plague. They remained there throughout the winter with their governess.

Elizabeth practised mathematics under the guidance of Bathusa Makin, sister of John Pell the linguist and mathematician who published *An Idea of Mathematics* in 1638 suggesting that all theorems and methods be collected into one text. Makin, whose husband lost his post at court in 1640, taught the princess modern languages – French, Spanish and Italian – classical languages and mathematics. It is unlikely that her grandfather would have approved in the return to the provision of a liberal humanist education for a female member of the royal family. Makin, the daughter of a schoolmaster, believed that girls and women should be taught the same academic curriculum as their male counterparts. She would go on, by 1673, to begin a school for gentlewomen at Tottenham High Cross, where as well as domestic and artistic skills, girls learned classical and modern languages and could, if they wish, also discover how to keep accounts. She argued that for a woman to receive a humanist education was of benefit to a Protestant state in terms of religion and effective household management, especially at a time when males might be away fighting. With little real power of their own, Makin also argued that the female population needed to be adept in the art of persuasion.

The Countess of Dorset became unwell at the start of 1645 and died at St James's Palace. The House of Commons prevailed upon the Earl and Countess of Northumberland, formerly Elizabeth Howard, to take on the roles of governor and governess. Until terms were reached, Lady Vere temporarily assumed the task. Algernon Percy, 10th Earl of Northumberland, and friend of the king, was a reluctant guardian. He became Lord High Admiral of Charles' navy in 1638, was openly critical of royal policy in November 1640, testified against the Earl of Strafford in 1641 and was the most important member of Charles I's government to side with Parliament at the outbreak of the civil war. By April 1645 he was one of the strongest supporters of the New Model Army in the House of Lords and as the summer drew on, he became increasingly committed to Parliament's designs. He spent little time in the company of Henry or Elizabeth, leaving their care and learning in the hands of their staff.

Chapter Sixteen

An Exeter Princess

In April 1644, an army of Scots allied themselves with the Parliamentarian army in the north. Another hostile force, led by the Earl of Essex, targeted Oxford. King Charles I decided that the queen, who was now heavily pregnant, should leave his side once more before she found herself under siege and unable to escape. The king and her two elder sons travelled with her as far as Abingdon before parting company. Henrietta Maria went west, visiting Bath to take the waters in the hope that it would ease the aches and pains of a difficult pregnancy. It was believed that the warm mineral rich waters would help rebalance her humours if she bathed in them.

From Bath she travelled to Exeter, arriving on 3 May and taking up residence in Bedford House in preparation for the birth of her child. She was tired, anxious and jolted from her journey through a landscape torn apart by war. Rumours abounded that William Waller's Parliamentarian army was poised to strike at the king and that the Earl of Essex was intent on capturing Exeter and the queen, who had been declared a traitor to the realm, with it. This would be Henrietta Maria's ninth lying-in but her pregnancy had been very different to the rest and she feared that she would not survive the ordeal. The pain of childbirth, in the queen's mind, was a test of her faith. As well as a cough and myalgia she was suffering from pins and needles which may have been indicative of carpal tunnel syndrome caused by a build-up of fluid or else by pressure upon the nerves in the queen's legs. Fearful of what might happen next, she wrote to Dr de Mayerne, a Huguenot who began his career serving the French royal family before becoming physician to Anne of Denmark. The doctor had treated Oliver Cromwell before the civil war and still retained Parliamentary favour, but he was reluctant to travel from his home in London. Finally, the king ordered the elderly medic to make the journey. He was joined by the midwife, Madame Peronne, who had delivered

Prince Charles, on the instruction of Anne of Austria who also dispatched servants, baby clothing, money and the offer of a home in France.

The queen withdrew from the world, having made her confession and prepared for the possibility of her own death either during labour or soon after the birth of her infant. On 16 June 1644 she was safely delivered of a daughter although her health continued to give cause for concern. She found it hard to breathe on occasion, experienced episodes of paralysis in one arm, as well as losing the sight in one eye. She also suffered from abdominal pain and a swollen belly. It is possible that she was experiencing symptoms of puerperal sepsis[1] known at the time as childbed fever. If so, despite the presence of her experienced attendants the queen's symptoms were caused by a streptococcal infection, probably resulting from examinations during labour by her physician or midwife, who did not wash their hands. Classical writers, including Hippocrates, understood the importance of cleanliness and the risk of infection but death caused by childbirth remained commonplace. Approximately one in every forty births concluded with the death of the mother.[2] There was no shared understanding of the causes of infection at that time. Remedies included bloodletting and, on occasion, the medieval cure for fever which recommended live pigeons being placed on the patient's feet. Margaret Godolphin was treated with both these 'cures' in 1678 when she developed childbed fever after giving birth to a son.[3] Unlike Margaret, Henrietta did not advance to the next stage of the illness which manifested itself in the form of a painful rash.

Soon afterwards, while she was still recovering, the Earl of Essex and his army arrived to besiege the town and to take the queen to London, even though she asked for a safe conduct back to Bath. Determined not to become a pawn in Parliament's efforts to force her husband to accede to their demands, Henrietta decided that she would depart Exeter. On 1 July, leaving her newborn daughter in the care of Anne, the wife of Robert Douglas, Lord Dalkeith, the queen made her escape, carried in a litter. It was less than a fortnight after giving birth. She was attended only by a small group of loyal supporters including her physician, Sir John Winton, who left an account of the episode. When the party arrived at Falmouth, word arrived that the baby was suffering from convulsions, so Winton returned to care for the infant while the queen set sail for France, on 14 July, where she was treated for a fever and an abscess in her breast.

The king's northern army, commanded by the Marquess of Newcastle, was defeated on 2 July 1644 at the Battle of Marston Moor but in Devon, the Earl of Essex's siege of Exeter was raised by the Royalists ten days after the queen departed. The princess was baptised Henriette in Exeter Cathedral on the instruction of the king, who arrived there on 26 July. Charles took up residence in Bedford House while the Prince of Wales was given accommodation in the deanery. The following day, the king and his forces departed, in pursuit of the Earl of Exeter's Parliamentary army, scoring a victory at the Battle of Lostwithiel. Before he left the king nominated Sir John Berkeley, governor of Exeter and Henriette's godfather, to be responsible for the baby. Berkeley began his career as the king's ambassador to Christina of Sweden and had negotiated on behalf of Charles' sister Elizabeth and her husband, Frederick of the Palatinate, prior to serving in the king's wars against the Scots in 1638. Now, as well as defending Exeter, his task was to look after the small household of Charles' youngest daughter who was sickly and subject to fits. At the time it was thought that infantile convulsions were caused by bad milk, or even worms. Today neonatal seizures are understood to be due to more serious underlying conditions ranging from infection and metabolic disorders to brain abnormality.

The king returned to Exeter on 17 September, on his way back to Oxford, and spent a week with his daughter. Before he departed, he made arrangements for the support of his daughter's household which were based on the excise duties received by Exeter. Having appointed Thomas Fuller, who was then Lord Hopton's chaplain, to be the princess' priest, the king resumed his campaign against Parliament. Fuller, whose services were not yet required as a tutor to the princess, took the opportunity to write a book entitled *Good Thoughts in Bad Times* which he dedicated to Lady Dalkieth. A copy of the book, decorated with the princess' cypher, was presented to the infant for her use when the time was right. Whatever the Puritan population of his kingdoms might have thought about him, Charles was determined that all his children should be raised as Protestants.

The Prince of Wales was at the Battle of Newbury in October 1644 before returning to Oxford. The Parliamentary victory would prove to be decisive as it left the Royalists only in control of the southwest. The king decided to allocate his son a new governor, Thomas Howard, 1st Earl of Berkshire, who once chastised the teenage prince for laughing at a sermon in St Mary's Church by hitting him over the head with his staff. As the fortunes of war turned against the Royalists, Charles I also recognised that it was essential that he and his eldest son should separate for the sake of the monarchy. He believed that while the Prince of Wales was free, Parliament would not dare harm him, even if he was captured, because in removing him, it would only mean that his son succeeded to the throne as Charles II. The king considered that James was still too young to leave the relative safety of Oxford.

The Prince of Wales was not yet 15 years old but his childhood was far behind him when his father sent him to Bristol with his governor, in early 1645, having been appointed General of the Western Association Army. One of the king's aims was for his son to make the transition from school boy to active participant in the war rather than watching from the side lines. It would also, perhaps, stop Charles I's commanders in the southwest from arguing with one another about who was in control of the region if the Prince of Wales was nominally in charge of operations. He was accompanied on his journey by a single regiment of cavalry and a regiment of foot, both paid for by Arthur Capel of Raine Hall in Essex who was in command of the force. It was all that was available and there was no money to set up a palatial residence, even if the Prince of Wales's household now operated as an adult court, shadowing the one at Oxford. On 4 March 1645, the prince said farewell to the Duke of York and to the king. It was the last time Charles would ever see his father.

The acting governor of Bristol, Sir Ralph Hopton, was appointed to the prince's council, as its chief military officer, to advise him. It was Hopton's responsibility to defend the western counties and to protect Charles. Alongside Hopton was Sir Edward Hyde (later the Earl of Clarendon) who would command the army in the prince's name, Sir John Culpepper and Patrick Ruthven, 1st Earl of Forth. The king had no intention that his son would command an army but once Charles arrived in the southwest, he found that Sir Richard Grenville and Sir John Berkeley were incapable of agreeing with one another, let alone one taking orders from the other. The only thing upon which both of them agreed was their refusal to recognise the pre-eminence of George, Lord Goring, who secured overall command of the region from them in April 1645 after he and his men relieved the king at Oxford.

The prince and his household stayed for the most part in Tiverton and Exeter, where he represented royal authority. In April, Prince Rupert summoned a meeting at Bridgewater with the aim of coordinating Royalist forces. Charles met with Mrs Christabella Wyndham, his former wet nurse, who, if rumours are true, seduced the prince.[4] Certainly Hyde believed that Christabella distracted Charles from his duties, which is something of an understatement as on one occasion he forgot etiquette and demonstrated his open affection for the woman by publicly covering the lady's face in kisses. Hyde recorded that the prince had little intention of improving his mind and did not understand the business of ruling, although even Hyde admitted that the prince applied himself when it came to his council.

The arrival of the New Model Army under the command of General Sir Thomas Fairfax changed the balance of power. The Siege of Taunton was lifted on 4 July and by 23 July the town and castle at Bridgewater were in Parliamentary hands. All that Royalist Exeter could do was to prepare for the inevitable siege. The arguments between the prince's commanding officers about seniority remained unrelenting. Charles was finally forced to commit Sir Richard Grenville, a man known for his brutality, to jail for refusing to obey orders from Prince Rupert and from Lord Goring. In July, Grenville resigned his command and the Cornish levies in the Royalist army deserted. Prince Charles arrived in Exeter on 29 August 1645 and spent some time in the company of his sister, whom he called Minette, as well as persuading Lord Goring to leave the military governorship of the city in the hands of Berkeley.

That autumn the prince made his way to Cornwall where he overwintered at Launceston and Truro. It was an unhappy Christmas. The king wrote to his son warning him to make plans for his escape as Parliament closed in. All that the Prince of Wales and his household could do was to retreat further west. Henrietta Marie wrote to Lady Dalkeith commanding her to ensure Henriette's safety but the Royalists were too busy ensuring Charles avoided capture, so the princess stayed where she was. Exeter was besieged for a second time in December 1645 by a Parliamentarian army. In Paris, the queen wrote angrily that her daughter's governess should have removed Henriette from Exeter into Cornwall before it was besieged. The princess' chaplain, Fuller, who was accompanied by his own young son, spent the time writing educational tracts for use by his small charge when her schooling began and to record the events inside the besieged city. In February, Thomas Fairfax won the Battle of Torrington against the Royalists commanded by Sir Ralph Hopton. It marked the end of Prince Charles' campaign in the southwest. The prince boarded the *Phoenix,* on 15 March, and sailed to the Isles of Scilly where he stayed for the next six weeks.

In Exeter, Berkeley surrendered on 9 April but only after Fairfax agreed that Henriette and her household should be permitted to leave Exeter with all their belongings. The party was to be conducted in transport provided by Parliament, to a property of Lady Dalkeith's choosing where they would await direction from King Charles as to the care of his youngest daughter. Berkeley, who admired Anne, escorted the royal party to Salisbury before making his farewells. Lady Dalkeith elected to take her charge to Richmond Palace which was refused. Instead, the household made its way to Oatlands, where Henriette's governess believed that, according to the terms of the agreement between Fairfax and Berkeley, Parliament would pay the princess' expenses. When financial support failed to materialise, Anne paid for the necessities of the household for the next three months out of her own pocket and wrote a series of letters to General Fairfax, to Parliament and even to the Committee of Justices for the County of Surrey at Kingston reminding them of their agreement.

Instead of providing the required revenue, the latter demanded, on 24 May, that the princess' household should be dissolved and the toddler be sent to join her elder siblings at St James's Palace, where she would be placed in the care of the Countess of Northumberland. Lady Dalkeith, who had received instructions from the king to remain with Henriette, sent another letter to the House of Lords reminding them of the terms of the agreement made at Exeter and stating her own importance to Henriette's well-being:

> ... have preserved Her Highness, not without many cares and fears, from a weak to a very hopeful condition of health, that I am best acquainted with her condition and constitution... All my desire is now to be continued about her

> person, quitting all power, without being any kind of burden to the Parliament, or inconvenience to my Lord and Lady of Northumberland.[5]

She asked only for permission to stay with Henriette and for a return of her own money. Having sent the letter, all Lady Dalkeith could do was await a response. On 14 June 1645 the Royalist army were brought to battle at Naseby. It was comprehensively defeated and Charles I was forced to retreat to Oxford, where he remained that winter. Lady Dalkeith penned her plea to remain with Henriette, who she had nursed through a sickly infancy, on 28 June.

When Parliament did not reply to her letter, Anne, the niece of the Duke of Buckingham, began to lay her own plans, believing that the Commons intended to separate her from her charge. Sir John Berkeley, being resident in the area, was privy to Lady Dalkeith's plans. At around the same time, Prince Rupert of the Rhine and his younger brother Maurice, stopped at Oatlands on their way to Dover. Blamed for the defeat at Naseby as well as the loss of Bristol, Rupert made the mistake of urging his uncle to sue for peace. King Charles I dismissed him from his command and from service in the Royalist army. Rupert and his brother were exonerated at a court martial held in Newark, but after surrendering Oxford into enemy hands they were no longer welcome in their mother's country of birth. Parliament was delighted to allow the charismatic commander, his brother and their retinue to leave English shores. Now, the brothers paused to pay their respects to Lady Dalkeith and, it would appear, to plot the removal of their small cousin from Parliament's grasp.

On 25 July 1646, as darkness fell, Lady Dalkeith and Henriette went missing. Also absent were two of Anne's trusted servants, Elinor Dyke and Thomas Lambert. Elinor petitioned Charles II, after the Restoration, for six years of wage arrears as well as the loss of her home and furniture as a consequence of following the princess overseas.[6] The household, at the governess' written request, did not inform the authorities for another three days. It meant that Anne, disguised in a threadbare gown with rags stuffed into one shoulder to give her a hunched appearance, was able to make good her escape. She, a French valet masquerading as her husband, and the princess dressed as a poor boy called Pierre, were able to walk to

Dover without incident. Lady Dalkeith carried the child the entire way, a distance of some ninety-five miles. The only threat to their escape was Henriette who objected to her attire and to her assumed name. Fortunately, Henriette's grasp of language was not yet so well developed as to offer cause for concern when she informed passers-by that she was not Pierre, but that she was really a princess and the clothes she wore were not her own. The little party was shadowed throughout their journey by Berkeley. Once at the port, they crossed the Channel on a French vessel. When Parliament discovered the truth of the matter, they were inclined to believe that Anne had done them a service.

Having arrived safely in France, Lady Dalkeith collapsed and was ill for several weeks afterwards. The fugitives joined Henrietta Maria and her growing court of exiles at Saint Germain, where the queen had grown up. Anne, who became the Countess of Morton shortly after her arrival in France following the death of her father-in-law, remained in post as Henriette's governess even though she was Protestant and the queen chose to have her youngest daughter raised as a Catholic, which was in contravention of the marriage agreement made in 1625 between England and France which clearly stated that all of Charles' and his wife's children were to be raised as part of the Church of England. Fuller had departed for London and new patrons at the end of Exeter's siege. In his place, the queen ordered her own chaplain, Father Cyprien, to instruct Henriette. Like his predecessor, he published a manual for the princess' spiritual education entitled, *Les Exercises d'une Ame Royal.* Lady Dalkeith remained firmly Protestant despite her charge's enthusiasm for Catholicism and the queen's desire that the governess should convert. Fortunately, the countess had the support of Henriette's elder brother who was horrified that his mother had broken the agreement that was made with Charles I.

It remained the governess' task to ensure that Henriette knew how to behave as a princess at the French court during formal occasions. Anne remained in exile until her husband, Robert Douglas, died in 1651 when she returned to Scotland where she stayed until her own death in 1654. It was fortunate that Henriette was a winsome child who won over the hearts of her eldest brother, her cousins and the queen's sister-in-law, Anne of Austria. Henriette's mother decided that it was tactful to add Anne to the end of the princess' name in recognition of all that the French Queen Mother had done for her family. Both women were united in wanting the best for Henriette Anne. To the women it seemed that her future lay in France. It was perhaps not unreasonable that she should be raised a Catholic under the circumstances. It was arranged that she would receive a thorough education, which did not include a grounding in written English, by the nuns at Chaillot.

Chapter Seventeen

Princes In Name Only

Prince Charles had no real option other than to flee England after the Royalist defeat at Torrington on 16 February. It was inevitable that Cornwall would fall into Parliamentary hands. He boarded the *Pheonix* on 2 March 1646 at Land's End with John Earle, Edward Hyde, John Culpepper and the Earl of Berkshire. Two days later he arrived in the Scilly Isles at St Mary's. During the journey, the prince discovered the joys of sailing and spent his time on the island learning how to handle a vessel. Henrietta Maria wrote to Hyde telling him that the islands were not safe and that her son should join her in France, despite the fact that the king and the prince's advisors advocated seeking refuge in a Protestant country. Fortunately for Prince Charles when a Parliamentary fleet did appear it was dispersed by a storm.

On 16 April the prince and his household, including Berkshire, boarded the *Proud Black Eagle* and sailed to Jersey where the queen's chamberlain, Henry Jermyn, was governor. Charles set up a court at Elizabeth Castle in St Helier, held state dinners, and set about winning the support of his father's subjects. He was described as '*un prince grandement benin*',[1] by Jersey's chronicler. The prince was able to continue his passion for sailing by commissioning a boat at St Malo which was paid for by Sir George Carteret, who was Charles I's controller of the Navy prior to the outbreak of civil war. Later he would accompany Charles II into London at the Restoration and be made the treasurer of the Navy. For two months Charles continued to learn how to sail around the island as well as enjoying hunting and hawking expeditions. Other aspects of the prince's extra-curricular education, and growing passion for women, lay in the hands of Marguerite Carteret who was four years older than him. But the halcyon days of Charles' youth were short lived.

By the end of April, the king made the decision to leave the Duke of York in Oxford while he went to give himself up to the Scots at Southwell, hoping to persuade them to join with him against the English Parliamentarians. However, he was moved to Newcastle and was put under pressure to sign the National Covenant which swore to defend Presbyterianism against Laud's Anglican reforms. Charles I wrote to his heir telling him to join Henrietta Maria and to obey her in all things except religion. The prince's council were not so convinced about the benefits of the queen's influence nor did they think it wise that the Prince of Wales leave his father's realm. However, Prince Charles left Jersey on 25 June for life as a penniless exile in the company of Jermyn leaving Edward Hyde, who advocated exile in Protestant Denmark or in Ireland rather than Catholic France. Berkshire also chose not to accompany the prince. Instead, he first went to Holland before returning to England where he compounded for his estates in 1649. His eldest son, Charles Howard, chose exile and became a gentleman of the king's bedchamber in 1658.

King Louis XIV did not officially meet his cousin for several weeks after Charles' arrival. Instead, the prince joined his mother, and youngest sister, at Saint-Germain-en-Laye, about twelve miles from Paris. Henrietta Maria, who did not wish Charles to take part in council meetings, or even read the documents that were presented to him to sign, expected the Prince of Wales to become a schoolboy once more, despite having experienced four years of war and taken the first of his many lovers. Duppa resumed his task as Charles' tutor, as did Earle. The latter refused a place as one of the Westminster Assembly of Divines in 1643 and whose loyalty to the Church and the Crown saw him deprived of his living at Bishopston as a malignant. Inevitably the Prince of Wales, who always preferred an active life to his books, tried to avoid the hour he was supposed to spend each day with Earle.

Despite a reputation for idleness, Charles was an able student if he was interested in the topic. He acquired knowledge about mathematics, physics and chemistry during his time in exile, catching up on the tuition he missed during the English Civil War. The prince was taught the principles of mathematics by Thomas Hobbes. The philosopher left England in 1641, the week after the Earl of Strafford's execution. Prior to his departure he was a client of Charles' former guardian, the Marquess of Newcastle. Charles was joined in his lessons with Hobbes, in 1651, by George Villiers, 2nd Duke of Buckingham, the prince's childhood companion. Buckingham was excused his involvement in the First English Civil War because of his youth. He and his brother were placed under the tutelage of the Earl of Northumberland and undertook the Grand Tour spending time in Paris, Florence and Rome before they returned to England. His participation in the Third English Civil War, or Wars of the Three Kingdoms as it should perhaps more appropriately be called, saw his younger brother, Francis, another member of the royal nursery, killed and George forced into exile, while his lands were given into the keeping of his father-in-law, General Fairfax. Charles' enjoyment of mathematics and the sciences would lead to the foundation of the Royal Society in 1662, to the construction of the Royal Observatory at Greenwich in 1675 and his patronage of men including Isaac Newton and Robert Boyle. He also awarded Hobbes an annual pension of £100.

In 1646, when Charles, who was 18 years old at the time, did meet his 8-year-old cousin, Louis XIV, it was with all the pomp of the French court but no funds were forthcoming other than a pension, which Henrietta Maria insisted should be paid to her. Even though the queen was a *fille de France,* Charles was a stranger to the culture and etiquette at Fontainebleau. Despite the fact that her eldest son was not fluent in French or an accomplished performer in the stiff and formal world of the French court, the queen hoped that Charles, despite the parlous state of the Stuart throne, would make an advantageous marriage. A bride with money and connections might help to regain the Crown. Henrietta Maria's niece, Anne Marie d'Orléans, described as the richest woman in Europe, was, in the queen's opinion, an ideal choice. Charles, who did not wish to marry his cousin, found himself wooing her anyway, although Prince Rupert was called upon to act as translator. Anne Marie had no intention of marrying a prince with no money, no kingdom and a poor grasp of French. However, there were other opportunities for Charles to rehearse his French and practise the kind of gallantry for which he would become famous as the Merry Monarch.

That summer James, Duke of York, now 13 years old, wrote to his captors and asked to be removed as soon as possible from Oxford. He described the 'solitariness of this place, and the daily increase of the plague in this city'.[2] He also noted that it was his staff who paid for 'several necessaries, and now of late my servants have engaged themselves for the expenses of my household and stables, without which I had not means to eat'.[3] On 28 July

1646, James arrived in London where he was met by his new guardian, the Earl of Northumberland. The retinue that accompanied York from Oxford were immediately dismissed but Parliament did grant Northumberland £7500 a year for the duke's maintenance. Hyde would later write that the earl treated the prince 'in all respects as was suitable to his birth and his own duty'.[4] That summer the three children, who had not seen one another for almost five years, were removed from St James's Palace to Northumberland's home at Syon House, near Richmond for their health.

On 30 January 1647, the Scots handed Charles I to the English in exchange for £400,000. The first instalment was delivered by the 3rd Earl of Pembroke who also collected the king from Newcastle. The prisoner travelled to Holdenby House, the property in Northamptonshire given to him by James I, in the company of General Fairfax. Parliament and the New Model Army were increasingly at loggerheads about pay arrears, further conflict in Ireland and the possibility of the army being disbanded. When a rumour circulated that the king was to be removed to London, Cornet George Joyce, together with 500 cavalrymen, moved Charles from Northamptonshire to Newmarket and into the hands of the army. For the king it was proof that if he waited long enough his enemies would tear themselves apart because their aims were so divergent. By 25 June, he was in Hatfield House and from there he was taken to Windsor, where he asked to be reunited with his children. Parliament, fearing that the army might take control over the royal family as well as the king, initially refused the request.

Charles finally asked Thomas Fairfax, at the beginning of July, to intervene on his behalf so that he might see his children. The general wrote to Parliament guaranteeing the return of the king's younger children into the hands of their custodians at the same time that the Duke of York also petitioned for the opportunity to spend some time with his father. Eventually it was agreed on the proviso that the Earl of Northumberland accompany the party to Maidenhead, which was close to Caversham where the king was then detained. James must have realised during the journey, from the response of the people who saw their coach, that there was much sympathy for him and his siblings among his father's subjects. Henry, who had been only 2 when he last saw Charles, did not know that the man who awaited their arrival was his parent, while James, who was now 14 years old, was simply delighted to be reunited with him. The men who were present at the reunion wrote of their sympathy for the little family. That evening General Fairfax, who described the encounter and Elizabeth's gratitude towards him to Sir John Berkeley, joined the king and his children for dinner.

When his children returned to London, King Charles I wrote to the Duke of York encouraging him to return to his studies. The family was also allowed to spend time together at Hampton Court while the king negotiated with the various opposing factions. Charles tried to exploit the divisions within Parliament to gain an advantage for himself. For James, who hated Parliament for the loss of his family and the humiliation of his father, it was another lesson that men who opposed the Crown should be destroyed. This was reinforced when it became clear that James would not be permitted to stay at Hampton Court with his father. At the end of the summer, on 11 September, Parliament, which was increasingly frustrated by the situation, debated the composition of the royal nursery, the amount of money it should provide to maintain it and where it should reside. Northumberland decided on St James's Palace as the most secure location. He also petitioned Parliament for full reimbursement of his expenses for the care of the king's children at the same time as submitting an account for losses of £42,000 from his estates as the result of the war, of which he received £10,000.[5] Charles I took the opportunity to remind James of the divine right of kings and of primogeniture. When the children were permitted to visit, they discovered more soldiers guarding their father. Both James and Elizabeth knew that the king would try to escape from the custody of Colonel Whalley who was responsible for keeping him secure. On the night of 11 November 1647, after his children departed from the palace, Charles escaped and made his way to the south coast. He sent messengers, one of whom was Sir John Berkeley, to Colonel Hammond, who was the governor of the Isle of Wight, with instructions that they should not reveal his whereabouts unless Hammond swore to help the king. Charles' plans were foiled when Hammond accompanied the messengers back to him without having given his oath. Carisbrooke Castle became a place of closer confinement and Hammond was less accommodating than Whalley.

On the mainland, Prince James and his younger siblings were unwanted wards of the State. Northumberland, who was responsible for James, found himself paying for the elder prince's household from his own funds. On 20 March 1648, the king made his first attempt to escape from Carisbrooke. The royal nursery was at Hampton Court, but when news of their father's escape reached London it was swiftly ordered back to St James's. By then Parliament was considering whether to force Charles' abdication, disinherit the Prince of Wales, and crown James. At his father's urging, the Duke of York became determined to escape. He made two unsuccessful attempts, with his sister's help, and was threatened with the Tower when Parliament intercepted messages sent from France by Henrietta Maria. The Earl of Northumberland categorically refused to guarantee the safety of his charges even though James gave his word not to try to escape again. Instead, he occupied himself with his siblings. They played hide and seek almost every day and the duke became so good at the game that his seekers were often unable to find him. It seemed like innocent fun. Eventually his absences became unremarked and, after twenty months in captivity, the prince was able to affect his escape, having first taken the precaution of locking his sister's dog away and securing the key to a side gate.

Colonel Bampfield, a professional spy who was in the confidence of the king, awaited him and arranged for James to be disguised as a girl before taking a barge from Billingsgate to Tilbury where he boarded a Dutch merchant vessel as Bampfield's sister. Fortunately, the master of the vessel was a Royalist because the pair of fugitives made unlikely siblings.

James arrived in the Hague where he was reunited with his eldest sister, Mary, who wished him to stay with her, but nine months after his escape from England the prince departed for France.

For Elizabeth and Henry, besides the loss of their brother, it meant another change of staff although the Earl of Northumberland was able to persuade Parliament that he had not failed in his duty and remained as guardian. The news Elizabeth received during this period of her life became steadily worse. The earl went as part of a parliamentary commission to Carisbrooke to persuade the king to accept a compromise but Charles refused. The increased clamour of radical voices in Parliament and the army now demanded a more drastic solution.

Chapter Eighteen

The Fortunes of an Exiled Duke

In England, negotiations having finally stalled, Charles I was tried for treason and condemned on 27 January 1649, despite the Prince of Wales's appeal to Parliament, to General Fairfax, and to various of Europe's courts for aid. The king wrote several letters to his heir justifying his own actions and ensuring that Charles would better understand what his duties were. On 29 January, the king made his farewells to Elizabeth and Henry who had last met with their father before his escape from Hampton Court. It had fallen to the Earl of Northumberland, who moved Elizabeth and Henry to Syon House before the trial, to tell his charges the outcome of the deliberations. The king explained to his 8-year-old son the fate that would befall him the following day and made the boy promise not to allow Parliament to crown him in his brother's stead. He also asked Elizabeth to remind James that his older brother was now his monarch. Little wonder that she broke down in tears and the king feared she would forget her instructions and the messages she needed to pass on.

Charles II was staying in the Hague as his sister's guest when his father was executed but the Duke of York had not yet arrived in Paris when news arrived of Charles I's execution at Whitehall.[1] No one knew how to tell Henrietta Maria that she was a widow so it was 9 February before Harry Jermyn, the queen's chamberlain and long-time favourite, found a way to tell her the truth. The new, 19-year-old, king remained in ignorance of Charles I's fate until one of his chaplains, Stephen Goffe, called him 'Your Majesty'. His distress at the news of his father's end demonstrated that while Charles I had his flaws as a monarch, as a parent he was beloved.

On the same day that Henrietta Maria learned she was a widow, *Eikon Basilike, The Pourtraicture of His Sacred Majestie in His Solitudes and Sufferings* was published. Like his father before him, it seemed that Charles I was determined to leave some last instruction for his heir. Written as a journal containing prayers that counselled forgiveness of his executioners, the work was a justification of the decisions that led to civil war. In it, Charles admitted his weaknesses, the main one being in permitting the execution of the Earl of Strafford, but adhered to his motives and religious principles. After the Restoration, the Bishop of Worcester claimed that it was he who wrote the book, although this was refuted by William Levett, a groom of the bedchamber, who was with the king on the Isle of Wight and swore he saw the king writing the diary.[2] In 1649, the work went into thirty-six editions and created much sympathy for the beheaded monarch.

When James arrived in Paris in February 1649, it was to a tense atmosphere. Anne of Austria and Louis XIV had been driven from their capital the previous month by rebellious nobles and a Paris mob and had fled to the relative safety of Saint-Germain. Henrietta Maria and Henriette Anne were left at the Louvre when the French royal family escaped on the night of 6 January 1649 in total secrecy. There was nowhere else for them to go and they were soon playing host to members of the court who did not flee. The queen's household were cold from lack of firewood and scared by the rioters in the streets around the palace. Cardinal de Retz discovered Henriette Anne in her bed because it was too cold for her to do anything else. The civil wars fought between 1648, starting as a parliamentary protest against taxation, and in 1653 became known as The Fronde. During that time Henrietta Maria's pension of 30,000 livres a month was often unpaid. It meant Royalist refugees arriving in Europe faced additional hardship since the queen was unable to pay her own servants.

James was expected to resume his education, although the first lessons that he and his exiled siblings learned was about lack of money and prestige. John Byron, 1st Baron Byron of Newstead Abbey was appointed as his governor. The prince was familiar with the Byron family from his time at Oxford. John, Richard, Robert and William Byron were all present at court there in the winter of 1642–1643 when they were rewarded for their services to the Crown. The following year, Thomas Byron, who commanded the Prince of Wales's regiment at Edgehill, was killed at Oxford by one of his own men in a dispute over pay and buried in the city's cathedral. The baron fought throughout the First English Civil War for the Royalist cause, securing Oxford for the king on 28 August 1642 before advancing on Worcester and taking part in the cavalry charge at the Battle of Edgehill. He would go on to fight at Newbury, in the West Country and the North-West as well as at Marston Moor in 1644. One of his brothers, Sir Richard Byron, held Newark while another, Sir Robert, held Liverpool. The brothers spent their own funds to support the royal cause but the war took its toll on them. Newstead Abbey was plundered by a force of Parliamentarians from Nottingham, and their uncle was sent to the Tower of London and only released upon payment of a large fine. Sir John's part in the conflict concluded with the long-drawn-out defence of Chester which surrendered to Parliament in February 1646. After Byron and his garrison were permitted to leave under the terms of the surrender, he made his way into exile.

Byron was not given the option of compounding for his estates as other Royalists were permitted to do. Instead, he and six other men, including Newcastle, who had been created a marquess in 1643, were exempted from pardon by Parliament and prohibited from returning to England upon pain of death. All of Byron's estates were sequestered. The appointment to James' household was a fortuitous one for the impoverished Royalist. The king concluded that his brother no longer needed a governor by 30 April 1651 but Byron was appointed superintendent-general to the household of the Duke of York. He died unexpectedly on 23 August 1652 in Paris. He left behind a wife, Eleanor Kilmorey, who he married during the Siege of Chester. Pepys reported that she became one of Charles II's mistresses.[3]

Sir John Berkeley, who was a relative of Henry Jermyn, assumed the role of superintendent of James' household, having served as a temporary governor to the duke when Byron was sent to Wales during the Second English Civil War to raise troops. Berkeley introduced his sons and his nephews to the prince's impoverished household and sought to marry the recently widowed Countess of Morton. The former Lady Dalkeith was a close friend of Edward Hyde who argued with Berkeley, and his proposal was rejected. James and his household had little to recommend him to the French court even if he did speak French well. For three years he remained in Paris, apart from the occasional visit to The Hague to see Mary or to Jersey which remained loyal to the Stuarts.

What James really wished for was to be a soldier. At least that way he would have money to buy the essentials. Besides which, it was all he knew during his formative years. Having finally wrung permission from his mother, who had no desire for one of her sons to become a soldier of fortune, he was forced to borrow money to pay for his equipment and enlisted in his cousin's army. Berkeley accompanied the prince, then aged 18 years, on campaign under the command of Vicomte de Turenne, Marshal of France. James was swift to learn about warfare under the tutelage of Berkeley and Turenne who commanded the royal army against the rebellious Prince of Conde and the armies of Spain. The Duke of York proved to be brave, loyal and to have a quick mind when it came to military manoeuvres. James recorded the tactical lessons of seventeenth-century warfare he learned from the marshal, who he greatly esteemed, in his memoirs. For four years he fought in the wars of the Fronde and then campaigned in the north of France against Spanish invaders. The young duke was forced to resign his commission in 1656 and depart for the Spanish Netherlands when the French signed a treaty with the Commonwealth. One of the conditions of the accord was that a number of former Cavaliers, James among them, were to leave France. Cardinal Mazarin offered him a chance to continue serving French interests in Italy but Charles II wished his brother to fight for Spain and James, who had learned the imperative of the divinity of kings as his father required, did as his brother asked.

Chapter Nineteen

Elizabeth and Henry

In April 1649 Elizabeth petitioned Parliament to be allowed to join her sister Mary in The Hague but her request was denied. Instead, she and Henry were transferred from the care of the Earl of Northumberland to the earl's sister, Dorothy, Countess of Leicester on 14 June 1649. Parliament issued instructions that the pair were to be treated as the children of nobility rather than royalty when they arrived at Penshurst Place in Kent. No titles were to be employed and the children should sit at the same table to eat their meals as the younger members of the Sidney family. It meant that Robert Sidney, 2nd Earl of Leicester effectively became their governor even though he was not appointed to the task. He was the younger brother of Sir William Sidney who was dismissed from Prince Henry's household for stabbing his tutor and succeeded to his father's title subsequent to William's unexpected death.

Leicester's long career saw him serve as a professional soldier in the Netherlands before undertaking diplomatic missions on behalf of Charles I to Denmark and to France. During his absence his wife, Dorothy, managed his estates. With the approach of civil war, Leicester remained undecided and was unable to reconcile himself with one side or the other. It meant that although he was appointed as Lord Lieutenant of Ireland by the king in June 1641, Charles I forbade him to go there and ordered him to the court at Oxford in 1642. It was James Butler, 12th Earl of Ormand, whom the king could trust, who was sent to rule Ireland on Charles' behalf, having been appointed in Leicester's place in November 1643. Once at court, Leicester's home at Penshurst was sequestrated by the Kent County Committee, even though the earl refused to become involved with the war. It was the countess, probably with her brother's help, who arranged for the property to be returned to the family. In June 1644 Leicester left Oxford and was reconciled with Parliament before retiring to Penshurst. While his two older sons supported Parliament, like many other families the Sidneys were split in their loyalties. A third son, Robert, was a Royalist who chose exile in the company of Princess Elizabeth's elder brother. Philip and Algernon Sidney were among the 136 commissioners who tried Charles I, although both were absent from the sentencing. They did, however, attend the Commons meeting which abolished both the House of Lords and the monarchy. The earl concerned himself with the running of his estates, intellectual pursuits and managing his finances. He possessed a large library covering theology, politics and history. He was particularly fond of mathematics. Having benefited from a Humanist education, and travelled extensively, his notes were written in several languages.

The library was somewhere that Princess Elizabeth and her tutors might find a wide range of books dating from the sixteenth century onwards to distract her from her grief. She and Henry also had some new companions. They joined the Sidneys' younger children and their grandchildren. Lady Dorothy Sidney, returned to the family home with her children after the death of her husband, Henry Spencer, 1st Earl of Sunderland, at the First Battle of Newbury in 1643. Even so it was a troubled household with its own sadness. Dorothy's daughter Mary died in 1648 as did her grandson, Algernon. Six weeks after the king's execution, Henry Spencer, the Countess of Sunderland's son, who was aged only 5, died at Leicester House in London. The day afterwards, the countess' sister, Lucy, Countess of Carlisle, was arrested and taken to the Tower for her part in raising funds, by selling a necklace worth £1500, on behalf of Henry Rich, Lord Holland the leader of the Royalist militia and Lucy's current lover, during the Second Civil War. Lucy was also accused of acting as an intermediary between the rebels, Henrietta Maria and Prince Charles, despite having disclosed to Parliament, in 1642, the king's intention to arrest five members, including her lover, John Pym. It would be September 1650 before she was released.

The Countess of Leicester was granted expenses of £3000 a year for the care of her new charges and their servants, of whom there were about ten, but the earl decided that he had 'less liberty'[1] in his home and that to 'be obliged to attendance which would be troublesome to me, I thought it very reasonable to...take off £400 a year'[2] from the £700 that the earl gave to his wife for her annual housekeeping expenses. Unsurprisingly this caused some friction between the couple whose marriage was already strained, partly because of the family's political difficulties but also because of quarrels within their extended kinship network. Despite this, the children's new governess was warm hearted and understood something of Elizabeth's plight. Her own father, the 9th Earl of Northumberland, was implicated in the Gunpowder Plot and remained in the Tower of London from the end of 1605, when Dorothy was 7 years old until she was 23. The Duke of Gloucester was placed in the charge of her son Robert's tutor, a man named Richard Lovell, or Lovel, who also taught Elizabeth. He purchased books for Henry as well as a globe and thirteen maps, costing £2 2s. Henry was also encouraged to hunt, to learn to shoot a pistol and to practise his archery. As well as Elizabeth's academic lessons, accounts of the period show the purchase of pins and silk for sewing and shuttlecocks and a game of battledore to encourage the princess to be more active.

Nor did the Countess of Leicester intend that the king's children be treated as anything other than royal. She set about acquiring some of the royal furniture and plate from Parliament so that the children would feel more at home. When William Lenthall, who served as Speaker of the House of Commons both before and after Charles I's execution, arrived to see whether Dorothy was obeying Parliament's instructions for the care of the executed king's younger children, he discovered them dining at a table, separate from the Sidney family. Whether the countess might have been dismissed from her post following his discovery is another matter.

The arrival of Charles II in Scotland in June 1650 and his acceptance of the Covenant, pledging support of Presbyterianism, alarmed the English Parliament. They determined that Elizabeth and Henry should be removed from Penshurst to Carisbrooke. Elizabeth petitioned to remain with the countess and her family in Kent because of poor health but the pair were moved to Carisbrooke in the care of Sir Anthony Mildmay in August 1650. Before she left, Elizabeth gave Dorothy a necklace as a token of her affection.

Mildmay had been a gentleman usher and carver to Charles I in happier times. He waited on Charles I during his imprisonment and had escorted the body of the king to Windsor for burial. Now though, he was given instructions that Henry, who was accompanied by Lovell, was not to be addressed by a title, just plain Henry Gloucester, while the princess was to be addressed only as Lady Elizabeth. The royal household was reduced still further. Eight servants were allowed to accompany Elizabeth and Henry to the Isle of Wight. Elizabeth retained only her lady's maid and her launderess. There were to be no more governesses.

The 14-year-old princess became increasingly unwell after being caught in a shower of rain while playing bowls at Carisbrooke. It was Richard Lovell who was sitting at Elizabeth's bedside when she died a month after her departure from Penshurst. Before her death, she made a verbal bequest that Lady Leicester keep the necklace and that Lady Sunderland should be given other of Elizabeth's belongings in memory of her kindness. It came to be believed that Elizabeth's grief over Charles I's execution exacerbated her ailments. She was buried in St Thomas' Church, Newport beneath a plain slab bearing the initials E.S. By the nineteenth century, Elizabeth's death had acquired a pathos of its own and Queen Victoria commissioned a new tomb for the king's daughter representing a beautiful girl and carrying the queen's inscription remembering her long dead relative.

The necklace that Elizabeth gave to the Countess of Leicester, valued at £600, was claimed by Parliament who required the countess to yield it up. Instead, Dorothy took the case to Canterbury's Prerogative Court while the earl made the following statement, 'I hope Parliament will not deny a young and innocent lady the liberty which every subject hath, to dispose of her goods'.[3] Parliament did not agree and the necklace was seized in 1659. After the Restoration, the Crown reimbursed the Sidneys with a sum equal to the necklace's value.

Henry remained at Carisbrooke, a prisoner of the state, with a small staff in the care of Richard Lovell while the Wars of the Three Kingdoms played out with the defeat of a Scottish army by Parliament at Dunbar. The Battle of Worcester, fought on 3 September 1651, was the final battle of the wars. Charles II was famously forced into hiding at Boscobel House, spending six weeks on the run before making his escape. Henry was released from Carisbrooke in December 1652 and travelled to join his sister, Mary, in The Hague.

Henrietta Maria demanded that her youngest son join her in Paris in April 1653. The following year, in August, Cardinal Mazarin offered King Charles II a pension on the proviso that he left France within ten days.

The king departed for Cologne, never to return to Paris, leaving Henry and Henriette Anne with their mother. He was unable to support Henry and, in Holland, Mary was forbidden to offer the boy a home in case it damaged trading relations with England. The king told his younger brother, just as their own father had ordered him, to obey his mother in all things except the matter of religion. All Charles could hope was that Henry's tutor, Richard Lovell and John Cosin, the Dean of Peterborough, would be able to protect his brother and continue to teach him scripture in a Protestant format. As a final obstacle, Henry was told to let Charles or James, who was still resident in Paris, know if any attempt was made to convert him.

In October, Henrietta, who promised that she would abide by Charles' wishes, sent Henry to Pontoise under the guardianship of Wat Montagu, abbé de St Martin. The abbé had been part of the group who arranged the marriage of Henrietta Maria to Charles I, worked as a secret agent and wrote masques for the court before converting to Catholicism and eventually becoming a priest. As well as gaining Henrietta Maria's favour, Montagu was also a favourite of Marie de Medici who arranged for him to be made an abbot. He had spent time in the Tower during the First Civil War, having been detained at Rochester. Lovell was dismissed from his post. Now, the queen, who told her elder son that Henry was not studying hard enough and that she feared he was being led astray by the young men of the riding academy he attended, planned that Montagu would convert Henry to Catholicism. Her aim, apart from her son's salvation, was the potential of a career in the Church or a rich French wife. She also believed that it would help gain Charles II more assistance from Catholic Europe if the family converted. In order to ensure her goal, she attempted to prevent correspondence from going between Paris and her son's court.

Christopher Hatton, a relative of Queen Elizabeth I's favourite, acted as comptroller of Charles I's household during the civil war and preferred exile in Paris to compounding for his estates in England. He agreed with Henrietta Maria that Prince Henry was ill-taught and needed to learn some manners but he wrote to Edward Nicholas, who was one of Charles II's advisors, informing him that plans were being made for Henry to attend the Jesuit College at Clermont. The king was furious when he was told. He understood all too well that it was essential for him and his siblings to remain

Protestant if he wished to improve his chances of regaining his realm. There was also the matter of financial support from Europe's Protestant rulers to consider. Even worse, his mother had defied him and also the wishes of Charles I. Hyde told Charles II's sister, Mary, 'I have never in my life seen the king so great trouble in mind'.[4] The king recognised that his mother's main occupation was her family but that she was, and always had been, a devout Catholic. He was not alone in his concern; Mary of Orange was equally alarmed by the thought of Henry becoming a Papist.

On 20 November, James Butler, Marquess of Ormond since 1642, who was with King Charles I at Hampton Court in the summer of 1647, and who had fought Oliver Cromwell in Ireland in 1649, was sent to either persuade Henrietta Maria to abide by the terms of her marriage treaty in the matter of her children's beliefs, or to remove Henry from her care. When it became clear that the queen had no intention of obeying either the wishes of her husband or her eldest son, Ormond took the prince from the abbé's care, placing him with Hatton before Henry left France in December 1654 to join his brother in Cologne. Thwarted, Henrietta Maria refused to allow Henry to visit her and declined to pay for his keep during the interval he remained in Paris. Ormond was forced to pawn his garter star to help feed and house the boy. It was a war of wills that Charles II and his supporters could not afford to lose. During the English Civil War no one close to Charles I could be ignorant of the extent to which Henrietta Maria advised her husband. Since his arrival in France, Charles II had disagreed with his mother over everything from religion to his choice of adviser. He knew that he had to impose his authority on his own family, particularly Henrietta, before he could hope to execute it upon three realms.

Chapter Twenty

Lessons For a Monarch

In 1660 King Charles II was invited back to England. He had spent fifteen years in exile. William Cavendish, the Marquess of Newcastle, who chose to go into exile in 1644 after the defeat at Marston Moor sent his former charge a lengthy epistle titled, *Advice to King Charles II* [1] on the eve of the Restoration. He set out the ways in which Charles I's government failed and listed ten causes of the civil war. He listed strategies that his former pupil should now adopt if he wished to remain in power. Newcastle believed in the supremacy of the monarchy and thought that if Charles controlled the Church and legal system it could only be for the betterment of the king's regained realm. He advised the returning monarch to control the Church through a hierarchy that included bishops, prohibit excess sermonising and reduce the number of academics. Newcastle suggested Charles avoid the use of prerogative rights or illegal taxes to raise funds as it would only serve to alienate his subjects. His advice went on to include the risk of rewarding enemies but not favouring friends and the dangers of appointing people to offices that they were unqualified to fill. Newcastle appointed a gentleman of the bedchamber, would soon be elevated to a dukedom but was not appointed as one of the king's political advisers. Cavendish, who retired to his home at Welbeck Abbey, came to feel that he was being undervalued and grew to resent Charles, who did not help him to recoup the debts that he accrued fighting on behalf of the Royalist cause.

Many of Newcastle's views corresponded with the political philosophies of Thomas Hobbes. Cavendish was Hobbes' patron[2] so it is not surprising that they should both make similar pronouncements. The king's mathematics tutor published *Leviathan* in 1651, focusing on society and legitimate government. He gave a copy of his work to Charles while he was still in Paris. In it, Hobbes argued that subjects tacitly agreed to surrender some of their freedoms in exchange for social order under the rule of an absolute monarch.

The book offended Charles because of the principal of consent whereby kings ruled because their subjects agreed to it not because God ordained it. Logically, this also meant that if a monarch failed to keep the peace or to protect his people as he should, that they had the right to transfer their loyalty to someone who would fulfil the social contract between governor and governed. Royalists, who regarded Charles I as a martyr, were horrified and Hobbes returned to England to make his peace with Oliver Cromwell's government. Charles II may have disliked some of the contents of his former tutor's work but he emerged from the experiences of his childhood and his exile as something of a cynic, and besides which he liked the philosopher. At the Restoration, Hobbes was granted a pension and welcomed back into favour to the extent that the king hung his portrait in the Royal Closet.

The king's state apartments took on the Baroque flavour of the French court. When Sir Christopher Wren was called upon to redesign Whitehall Palace, he was sent to Paris to study the Louvre before submitting his design. The apartments at Windsor which were only completed in 1684 reflected the suites of rooms that Charles saw at the court of his cousin. The Royal Closet was the last of these rooms so it was not used as a corridor like the other chambers. It meant that it was the king's private space because access to it could be controlled. Charles had come to admire the French court's aristocratic way of life from architecture to fashion. He soon adopted some other of Louis XIV's practices including dressing in public and using his bedchamber as a place where his subjects might have an audience with him. When Charles II dined, he often did so under the gaze of his subjects. However, he had no desire to be as closely monitored as Louis was and made sure there were plenty of opportunities to escape public gaze. The so-called Merry Monarch also adopted the French approach of promoting royal mistresses. Some of them, like Barbara Villiers, wielded political and social power akin to a French *maîtress-en-titre*, or an officially recognised mistress. Most importantly, the new king understood that public spectacle would help win over his subjects as well as giving him something to hide behind while he negotiated the difficulties of Britain's religious differences. For Charles, avoiding armed insurrection followed by exile, or death – even if no one was happy with the outcomes of his policies – was the most important of the lessons he learned from his father.

The Duke of York, who betrothed himself to Edward Hyde's daughter, Anne, in 1659, when he had few prospects, was now in a position to marry an heiress. However, within a few months of the Restoration, Anne fell pregnant. Henrietta Maria was sceptical about the infant's paternity and did not wish James to marry the girl[3] but, somewhat ironically given the number of natural children he fathered himself, Charles insisted that the marriage go ahead. The baby, named after its uncle, died soon after it was born from an outbreak of smallpox which killed Henry, Duke of Gloucester and Mary of Orange, who both arrived back in England to see their brother crowned. Although Charles married Catherine of Braganza in May 1662, he had no legitimate heirs. The Duke of York and his children would succeed to the throne. James' daughter Mary was born at St James's Palace on 30 April 1662. Anne Hyde provided her husband with eight children but only Mary and her younger sister, Anne, survived infancy.

The king required that they be educated as Protestants. Their tutor was Dr Henry Compton, the Bishop of London who was tasked with teaching Charles II's nieces scripture and Anglican orthodoxies. He was assisted by their chaplain, Edward Lake, who wrote the *Officium Eucharisticum*, an introduction to the Eucharist, for Mary to ensure that she was well versed in Anglican practices. The Duke of York, who never learned that divine right was a tightrope that required careful balance, converted to Catholicism before 1670. Eventually, the religious differences between him and his daughters would become insurmountable. Charles II understood, just as his own father did, that it was essential that prospective heirs to the throne should be untainted by Catholicism if Parliament was going to accept a future Stuart monarch.

After their mother's death in 1671, Mary and Anne moved to Richmond Palace under the guardianship of Colonel Edward Villiers, who was the Keeper of the Park and his wife, Frances, where there would be no doubt about their faith. Their household included the Villiers six daughters and other companions who shared their lessons. Three of them would accompany Mary to Holland when she married her cousin, William of Orange. It was not thought necessary for the girls to receive a classical education of the kind enjoyed by Mary, Queen of Scots, or even Charles II's sister and cousins. Instead, they were equipped with accomplishments to become wives and mothers rather than rulers. They were taught French by Peter de Laine as well as English, art, music (which was taught by Anthony Robart), singing and dancing. Anne received elocution lessons from Mrs Barry, an actress of the period. Their art master was Richard Gibson the miniaturist who also accompanied Mary to Holland when she married in 1677.

Both girls suffered from poor eyesight but Anne suffered from a condition that left her with a squint and eyes that watered. As a result, she avoided reading and rarely attended the theatre. However, when she was sent to stay with her grandmother, Henrietta Maria, in an attempt to cure her, she became fluent in French. When the dowager died in 1699 Anne was still with her, so she joined her cousins, the children of Henriette Anne, only returning to England in July 1670.

Afterword

The earlier Stuarts were correct that the prospect of a Catholic succession was an alarming one. Even so, when Charles II died in 1685, James was acclaimed to widespread support. His subjects believed that a Catholic monarchy, and Stuart rule, would die with him. Both his daughters were Protestant. When James prorogued Parliament and began to use royal prerogative to bypass penal laws against all Nonconformists there was alarm.

The birth, in 1688, of James' son, by Mary of Modena, changed the succession to the throne and raised the prospect of a Catholic dynasty. The Glorious Revolution of November 1688 saw James' eldest daughter, Mary, and his nephew, William, installed as joint monarchs. Although she was devoted to her husband, Mary was unable to have children and it was her sister, Anne, who succeeded to the throne in March 1702. Anne, married to George of Denmark, is known to have given birth to at least twelve stillborn infants. Of her five children who survived birth, four died before the age of 2 while her son, William, Duke of Gloucester, born in 1689, was a sickly infant troubled by hydrocephalus that delayed his motor skills and speech development. He died from an infection in 1700.

Almost a century after James VI of Scotland became James I of England, the Act of Settlement of 1701 excluded Catholics from the throne. Although Queen Anne had other, nearer relations, including her Catholic half-brother, James Stuart, who came to be known as the Old Pretender, it was the youngest of Elizabeth of Bohemia's daughters who was heir to the throne for much of Anne's reign. Unlike her younger Stuart relatives, Sophia of the Palatinate, by then Electress of Hanover, was exceedingly well educated, although all that mattered to Parliament was the fact that she was a Protestant. She died less than two months before Queen Anne in 1714 and the Stuart dynasty was replaced by Sophia's Hanoverian son, George who ascended the throne as King George I.

A Who's Who of Governesses Who Raised the Stuarts

Governesses

NB – it was usual for Scottish women in the sixteenth and seventeenth centuries to retain their maiden names after their marriage.

Margaret Beaton, Lady Rires, or Reres

Married to Arthur Forbes, 4th Lord of Rires, Margaret was one of Mary, Queen of Scots' ladies-in-waiting as well as being an aunt of Mary Beaton, one of the queen's four Marys. She was present when the queen gave birth at Edinburgh and was appointed to oversee the royal nursery. When James was moved to Stirling, the Countess of Mar became the prince's governess although Lady Rires remained part of the household there for a time. Margaret and Helen Little, James' wet nurse, were provided with gowns for the prince's baptism.

Her family fought on the side of Mary, Queen of Scots during the war that followed her deposition. Hostility between the opposing factions led to stories that Lady Rires was involved in the murder of Lord Darnley. *Bannatyne's Memoriales* go so far as to accuse her and the Countess of Atholl of employing witchcraft to ease Mary, Queen of Scots' labour pains.[1]

Elizabeth Carey née Trevannion, Countess of Monmouth (d.1641)

Elizabeth was the widow of Sir Henry Widdrington when she married Robert Carey in 1593 within five months of her first husband's death, much to the irritation of Elizabeth I. After James I ascended the throne in 1603, she went to Berwick to meet Anne of Denmark along with other women who hoped to gain preferment.

Elizabeth, who was the mother of three children, was appointed governess to Prince Charles and cared for him between 1604 and 1611. She was not afraid to disagree with the king about the care of his youngest surviving son and, in 1607, petitioned for a review of the prince's household because she believed it was insufficiently financed. In 1611, Elizabeth returned to court and when Charles I ascended the throne, she became a countess.

Frances Cobham née Howard, Countess of Kildare (b.*c.*1573–1628)

Frances was a daughter of Catherine Carey and Charles Howard, Earl of Nottingham. She was Elizabeth I's cousin and a royal favourite. She served as one of the ladies of the privy chamber until the queen's death. When she was 16 years old she married Henry FitzGerald, 12th Earl of Kildare, who was appointed as vice-admiral for Ireland soon afterwards. The marriage, which produced two daughters who lived to adulthood, was a troubled one and Frances spent much of it at court on the orders of Elizabeth I who remonstrated with the earl for his behaviour. After Kildare's death in 1597 fighting in Ireland against the Earl of Tyrone, when she was 24, Frances returned to Ireland to take possession of the estates to which she was entitled before returning once again to the queen's side. Back in England she petitioned the Court of the Exchequer to grant her an annual pension in exchange for some of her jointure lands in Ireland. She also set about becoming financially independent by petitioning the privy council for several important wardships.

Frances, and the whole Howard family, became involved in a feud between the Earls of Nottingham and Essex. The Earl of Essex may have described Frances' influence over the queen and her council as being like 'the spyder of the Court'.[1]

In 1601 she married Henry Booke, 11th Baron Cobham who had inherited his title a few months previously. Following Cobham's arrest for his involvement in the Main and Bye Plots in 1603, Frances was discharged from her office as Princess Elizabeth's governess and Cobham's possessions were seized. The following year, on 13 May 1604, James leased the forfeited estates, including Cobham Hall and a house at Blackfriars, back to Lady Kildare for her lifetime under the trusteeship of her father, the Earl of Nottingham and her cousin Thomas Howard, Earl of Suffolk. James continued to show the countess favour when he placed her granddaughter Mary under royal protection.

Anne Douglas née Villiers, Lady Dalkeith, Countess of Morton (*c.*1610–1654)

The niece of the Duke of Buckingham by his half-brother, Edward, Anne married Robert Douglas in 1627. The couple had three children by the time Lady Dalkeith, who was one of Henrietta Maria's ladies-in-waiting, was left in Exeter to care for the queen's last child, Henriette. After the fall of Exeter, she took her charge to London but rather than hand her into the care of another governess, she escaped with the princess to France.

Her friendship with Edward Hyde, subsequent to the death of her husband in 1649, was the cause of some speculation. She was betrothed to Sir John Berkeley, who was the governor of Exeter during the siege, although the marriage never went ahead, possibly because of the animosity that existed between Berkeley and Hyde.

Jean Drummond, Countess of Roxburghe (d.1643)

Jean, sometimes known as Jane, was one of Anne of Denmark's Catholic ladies-in-waiting prior to her appointment as Prince Charles' governess in 1602. Following James VI's succession to the English throne as James I, Jean first accompanied her mistress to Stirling to gain custody of Prince Henry before travelling with Anne to England. Evidence suggests that Jean was a royal favourite. She wrote letters on Anne's behalf, was responsible for the queen's finances, and men and women seeking favours from Anne often used Jean as an intermediary. Drummond was so influential that she was awarded a pension of 1500 ducats by the Spanish to work on their behalf.

In 1614 Jean married Robert Ker, 1st Lord Roxburghe but in 1617 she was dismissed from her place because of her husband's ambition, and failure to consult with the queen beforehand, to be appointed to the post of lord chamberlain in the household of Prince Charles. Jean retired to Scotland until 1630 when she hoped to be appointed as governess to King Charles I's eldest son. However, it was not until 1631 when she was recalled to court to care for Princess Mary and, later, her younger siblings.

In 1642, Jean accompanied Henrietta Maria to Holland but on her return to England, remained as governess to Henry and Elizabeth. She died the following year.

Françoise d'Estamville, Dame de Paroy (d.1557)

The dame became Mary, Queen of Scots' governess in 1551 and held the position until 1557 despite tensions with her charge. It was Françoise's duty to teach Mary feminine skills, to act as a chief lady-in-waiting and to manage the queen's household. When she fell ill in 1556, she left the French court but was not formally relieved of her post until the following year.

Anne Harington née Keilway (d.1620)

Anne, who came from Oxfordshire, and was her father's sole heir, married John Harington in 1573. The marriage brought him Coombe Abbey in Warwickshire as well as other property. The couple had three children who survived to adulthood including Lucy, Countess of Bedford who was a patron of Ben Jonson and the poet, John Donne. She and her daughter were among the women who made the journey north in 1603 in the hope of gaining favour and position from the new queen. Although Anne was appointed as a lady of the bedchamber, it was only after the outcome of the Main Plot that she and her husband were appointed as Elizabeth's protectors.

Anne remained with the princess until her marriage in 1613 when she and her husband accompanied Elizabeth to Heidelberg. She returned home, widowed and financially ruined by expenses incurred looking after the king's daughter. She returned to the Palatinate and served as one of her former ward's ladies-in-waiting. Upon her subsequent return to England, in 1616, she made a bequest to All Saints Church in Oakham to provide for the parish's poor and to equip a library for use by the vicar.

Eleanor Hay, Countess of Linlithgow (d.1627)

Eleanor, Helen or Helena, Hay married Alexander Livingston in 1584. Even though her husband was Protestant, Helen came from a steadfastly Catholic family. Despite this, James VI chose to place his daughters in her care. She and her husband had five children, so Eleanor was more than capable of overseeing the early education of Elizabeth and Margaret. Helen faced numerous difficulties with the Kirk because of her beliefs but converted on her deathbed to Protestantism, leaving a testimonial written by the minister, John Livingston.

Françoise d'Humières, Dame de Contay (d.1557)

Françoise de Contay married Jean d'Humières in 1507. She bore her husband a large family. The couple were appointed governor and governess to Henri II's eldest son, François, in 1546. It was her responsibility to supervise the royal nursery under the direction of Diane de Poitiers. Although her husband died unexpectedly in 1550, she remained as governess. When the Dauphin was provided with his own household Françoise remained with Mary, Queen of Scots and the Dauphin's sisters.

Elizabeth Knyvett née Hayward (d.1622)

Elizabeth, the widow of Richard Warren, married Sir Thomas Knyvett in 1597. Listed as a gentlewoman in 1600, she gave Elizabeth I 'one long cushion of cloth of silver with branches of flowers with silkwomans work'[1] as a New Year's gift. Two years later she took part in a court masque. She remained at court when James I ascended the throne and was made governess of his daughter, Mary, in 1605, before the infant was two months old. Despite the care that she gave the infant, Mary died while still a baby as did her younger sister, Sophia.

In 1624, Elizabeth, who was Sir Thomas' executor, oversaw the building of a free school at Stanwell and its endowment of lands worth £20 a year.[2] After her death, she was buried at Stanwell Church in Surrey alongside her husband.

Annabell Murray of Tullibardine, Countess of Mar (1536–1603)

Murray, sometimes known as Annabella, was one of Mary of Guise's ladies-in-waiting as well as well as Mary, Queen of Scots' women. The countess was entrusted with the care of James VI at Stirling while he was still an infant and Mary was queen. She remained royal governess after her husband, the Regent Mar, died in 1572. Following James VI's marriage, she became one of Anne of Denmark's ladies, although she was not a favourite of the new queen. In 1594 she was appointed to care for the king's heir, Henry and tended him until her death in 1603.

Elizabeth Percy née Howard, Countess of Northumberland (d.1705)
Elizabeth, a daughter of the 2nd Earl of Suffolk, married Algernon Percy, 10th Earl of Northumberland, who was a widower, in 1642. Their son Jocelyn, who would become the 11th earl, was born two years later in July 1644. When the earl became the reluctant guardian of King Charles I's younger children, Elizabeth assumed the role of governess with day-to-day oversight over the royal household as well as looking after her own family and her husband's two daughters, Anne and Elizabeth, from his first marriage to Anne Cecil. After the execution of King Charles I, which Algernon opposed, the earl and his wife retired to their home at Petworth.

Diane de Poitiers (1500–1566)
Diane spent part of her childhood in the household of Anne of France, Duchess of Bourbon where she received a Humanist education which included classical languages and rhetoric. After her marriage she served as a lady-in-waiting to the wives of King François I. She was widowed in 1531 and wore mourning colours of black and white for the rest of her life.

In 1529, when François' son, Henri, was 11 years old, she became the boy's tutor but in 1534 she began a relationship with him while he was still only 15 years old. It was Diane who insisted that Henri begin to sleep with his wife, Catherine de Medici, once her lover became heir to the throne in 1536. When Henri became king, in 1547, Diane became the most powerful woman at the French court as the king's official mistress – the *maîtress-en-titre*. She had control of the royal nursery, wrote official correspondence on Henri's behalf and it was to her that he turned for advice rather than his wife. After Henri's death in 1559, Diane was banned from the court and lived the rest of her life at Anet.

Mary Sackville née Curzon, Countess of Dorset (1585–1645)
The sole heiress of Sir George Curzon of Croxhall, in Staffordshire, it was arranged that Mary would marry Edward Sackville, a younger son, in 1606. The wedding took place in 1612 and ten years later she inherited her father's estates; in 1624, when Sackville's elder brother died unexpectedly, Mary's husband became the 4th Earl of Dorset.

The earl became a member of the privy council when Charles I ascended the throne and was appointed Henrietta Maria's lord chamberlain in 1628. In 1630, Mary became governess to Charles I's heir for a term of twelve years. She also assumed responsibility for James, Duke of York. Despite the fact that her husband and sons were Royalists, Mary remained in London and was appointed by Parliament as governess to the princes' younger siblings in July 1643. She died two years later.

Dorothy Sidney née Percy, Countess of Leicester (1598–1659)

Dorothy, the eldest daughter of the 9th Earl of Northumberland, and a descendent of Mary Boleyn, was married to Robert Sidney in 1615. Her family were among the most powerful men and women in the realm but she understood all too well the pitfalls of Tudor and Stuart politics. Her uncle, the Earl of Essex, was executed in 1603 for treason while she was still in the nursery and her father, the so-called Wizard Earl, spent almost sixteen years as a prisoner in the Tower of London due to his alleged involvement in the Gunpowder Plot of 1605. Her grandfather and great grandfather both intrigued on behalf of Mary, Queen of Scots and died for their support of her cause.

The countess would have fifteen children, three of whom died in infancy and a further five of them pre-deceasing their mother. As well as raising her family, Dorothy managed her husband's estates at Penshurst and oversaw the building of Leicester House in London while the earl served as an ambassador in France. Dorothy's extensive correspondence illustrates how aristocratic women supervised their children's education, managed family estates, attended court functions and cultivated social connections, and used kinship network for the purposes of politics and patronage. When the earl returned to England, the couple's relationship became strained.

The countess was appointed as governess of Charles I's younger children, Elizabeth and Henry, by Parliament, in 1649 but they were removed to the Isle of Wight the following year when Charles II was crowned in Scotland, despite Princess Elizabeth's plea that they should remain at Penshurst.

Katherine Stanhope née Wotton, Countess of Chesterfield (1609–1667)

Katherine was married three times. On the first occasion she married Henry Stanhope, the second surviving son of the 1st Earl of Chesterfield. He predeceased his father and elder brother, so it was Katherine's son, born in 1634, who succeeded to the earldom after his grandfather's death in 1656.

The young widow was courted by several suitors but in 1641 she wed for a second time to Jehan van der Kerchhove, Lord of Heenvliet who came to England to negotiate the marriage between the Princess Royal and William of Orange. He died in 1660, shortly after Charles II was restored to the throne. Katherine's royal mistress died the same year. For a short time afterwards, Katherine became governess to Mary's son, William III of Orange[1], but she chose to return to England to take a place as one of Anne Hyde's ladies-in-waiting. The king, who was grateful to Katherine for her care of his sister as well as the financial and political support that she had provided, both to his father during the civil war and to himself during his time in exile, created her Countess of Chesterfield *suo jure*, or in her own right. In June 1663 a warrant was issued to the lord chamberlain for her to be admitted as a lady-in-waiting to the household of Charles II's queen, Catherine of Braganza.[2] Katherine subsequentially married for a third time to David O'Neill, a royal favourite, and another agent, who held the office of postmaster general as well as being a groom of the bedchamber and MP for St Ives in Cornwall. Charles II rewarded the former spy generously with lands, offices and a pension. The pair built themselves a new home at Belsize Park in Hampstead. After O Neill's death in 1664, the countess became postmaster general, the first woman to hold the office, and continued her husband's work not only of ensuring that the post was delivered but of intercepting and copying important correspondence on behalf of the Crown. Little is known about the extent of her espionage work on behalf of the Stuarts but it is evident from the rewards showered upon her that Charles II valued her contribution.

Janet Stewart, Lady Fleming (1502–1562)

The illegitimate daughter of James IV and Agnes Stewart, the king's cousin, was married to Malcolm Fleming, 3rd Lord Fleming in 1524 or 1525 after gaining a papal dispensation because they were closely related. The couple had at least seven children before Fleming's death in 1547 at the Battle of Pinkie. Janet was appointed, the following year, to be Mary, Queen of Scots' governess at Stirling while her daughter, Mary Fleming, became one of the queen's companions and ladies-in-waiting.

Lady Fleming accompanied the queen to France where she became known as *la Belle Écossaise* and was, for a short time, the mistress of Henri II. When she gave birth to the king's son, Henri de Angoulême, she was sent back to Scotland. She re-joined the household of Mary of Guise and was at Edinburgh Castle when the dowager died. Afterwards she petitioned Henri II to be permitted to join her son in France.

Margaret Stewart, Lady Ochiltree (d.1627)

Margaret who married Andrew Stewart, the heir of 2nd Lord Ochiltree, in 1567 was the sister-in-law of John Knox's second wife, also called Margaret. Following Stewart's death in 1578 she married for a second time but continued to be recognised as Lady Ochiltree.

She was appointed to Anne of Denmark's household shortly after her arrival in Scotland along with her three daughters. In 1603, when the queen departed for England, she received an annual pension for her care in looking after the king's younger children.[1]

Marie Stewart, Countess of Mar (1576–1644)

The daughter of Esmé Stewart, 1st Duke of Lennox arrived in Scotland in 1588 with her sister, Henrietta. In 1590, she became one of Anne of Denmark's ladies-in-waiting. Numerous matches were suggested for the daughter of James VI's favourite but, at the end of 1592, she married the 2nd Earl of Mar who was a widower. Following their wedding, the earl arranged for his new bride to be taught the tenets of the Presbyterian faith.

James' son, Henry Frederick, was officially in the care of Marie's mother-in-law, Annabell Murray, but following her death at the beginning of 1603, Mar's countess assumed responsibility in the absence of both the prince's governess and her husband, who travelled to England with the king when he succeeded Elizabeth I. She, and her eldest stepson, refused to allow Anne of Denmark to remove Henry from Stirling Castle without James' assent.

The countess had many children including her eldest son James, who was one of Charles I's gentlemen of the bedchamber while her youngest son, Will, was Charles II's cupbearer. Despite the Erskine family's close association with the royal family, Marie signed the Solemn League and Covenant in support of the Scottish Kirk. Three of her sons fought against Charles I during the First Bishop's War.

Mary Vere née Tracy (1581–1671)

Mary's second husband, whom she married in 1607, was Horace Vere who was some thirty years older than her. She already had two children with her first husband, William Hoby, who died in 1603. Both her sons, Philip and William, would die young. The following year Mary accompanied her husband to the Netherlands where she would give birth to two daughters before returning home to England. Her younger daughters, of whom there were four, would be born in London.

Horace was a professional soldier who fought in Europe for the Protestant cause for three decades during the wars in the Netherlands against Spain and then in the Thirty Years War. Mary followed her husband to the Netherlands while he was on campaign. The couple were both Puritans and Lady Mary was known for her piety both in public and at home. Her personal motto, inscribed into her books, was 'God will provide'. Her servants were expected to be able to give an account of the sermons they heard within the household[1] and she was a patron of godly ministers. As a consequence, when Parliament sought an appropriate governess for Princess Elizabeth and Henry, Duke of Gloucester, it was to her that they turned. However, it was only after the death of the Countess of Dorset in 1645 that Lady Mary assumed the role for a short time. By then, Mary had been a widow for ten years.

Frances Villiers née Howard (1633–1677)

Frances was the youngest sister of Elizabeth Percy, Countess of Northumberland. Their parents Theophilus Howard, 2nd Earl of Suffolk and Elizabeth Home were courtiers and patrons of the arts. Elizabeth was one of Elizabeth of Bohemia's companions during her childhood at Coombe Abbey. She married her husband, Edward Villiers, in 1646 and went on to have a large family. Her husband's political connections to Edward Hyde, Earl of Clarendon and his work against Parliament during the Commonwealth ensured that the couple were well rewarded at the Restoration including, in 1669, governorship of James, Duke of York's daughters, Mary and Anne.

Three of Frances' daughters accompanied Mary to Holland in 1677 as part of her household but Frances died of smallpox the same year and was succeeded by Henrietta Hyde née Boyle, the Earl of Clarendon's daughter-in-law, in November as royal governess to James' younger daughter, Anne.

A Who's Who of Governors Who Raised the Stuarts

Berkeley, John, 1st Baron Berkeley of Stratton (*c.*1607–26–August 1678) Berkeley was the youngest of five sons. After completing his education at Queen's College, Oxford he was sent, in 1637, to serve as Charles I's ambassador in Sweden. In 1638 he returned to serve in the king's Scottish wars. Somerset born, he joined the Marquess of Hertford, in 1642, at Sherbourne in answer to the king's commission of array, before being sent to Cornwall as Sir Ralph Hopton's second in command. In 1644 he attended the baptism of Charles I and Henrietta Maria's youngest child, Henriette, at Exeter and in 1645 he became the colonel-general of Devon and Cornwall, securing Taunton for the Crown before being forced to surrender at Exeter, in April 1646, to Thomas Fairfax.

After his surrender he joined the court in exile in Paris before becoming involved in Charles I's escape from Hampton Court in November 1647. Returning to Paris following the failed escape, he was made temporary governor of James, Duke of York, due to the influence of Henry, Lord Jermyn to whom he was related. During his time in control of the prince's household he attempted to arrange a match between James and Marie de Longueville, daughter of Henri II, d'Orléans. He accompanied James into service in the French army under Marshal Turenne and when the prince was forced to resign his command, he joined the Spanish army with James in 1656. Two years later he was awarded, on James' recommendation, with a baronetcy with a title taken from a civil war victory as he had no land of his own.

Following the Restoration, he gained a post in the Navy and he was rewarded for his loyalty to the Crown with a seat on the privy council. In 1670, he went to Ireland for two years as its Lord Lieutenant. He was also granted interests in Carolina and New Jersey. During his time in office there were complaints about his corruption and it was suspected that he was Catholic. Even so, he did not forfeit royal favour.

John Byron, 1st Baron Byron (d.1652)

In 1641 Byron was the Lieutenant of the Tower of London but was forced to resign his post the following year. He fought at Edgehill and at Marston Moor before becoming governor of Chester, which he held for the Royalists until February 1646 when he was forced to surrender. His service to the Crown meant that he was not permitted to compound for his estates in the way that other Cavaliers were permitted to do. Instead, he remained in exile with the royal family until his death.

Robert, Carey, 1st Earl of Monmouth (*c.*1560–1639)

Carey, cousin to Elizabeth I and descended from Mary Boleyn, was married to Elizabeth Trevannion, the widow of Sir Henry Widdrington, whom he wed for love rather than fortune. The couple would have three children, Henry, Thomas and Philadelphia. As a younger son of Henry Carey, 1st Baron Hunsdon, he served in various capacities in the borders between England and Scotland, including as deputy warden for the West March, as well as taking part in several military expeditions, including in the Netherlands, France and against the Spanish Armada.

It was Carey who, on 26 March 1603, delivered the news to James VI at Holyrood, two days after he set off from London, that James was now king of England. His desire for preferment was initially thwarted but in September 1604, he and his wife were appointed to care for James' youngest surviving son, Charles. In 1617 he became Charles' chamberlain, an event which he seems to have celebrated with the commission of a family portrait, and in 1622 he was created Baron Carey of Leppington. The following year, he was ordered to follow Charles and the Duke of Buckingham to Spain for what was ultimately an unsuccessful attempt to bring about a marriage between the prince and the infanta. In 1626, at Charles' coronation, he was rewarded by his former charge with the title Earl of Monmouth as well as receiving an annual pension of £500. He also gained the lease on Kenilworth Castle where he wrote his memoirs, describing his life during the last ten years of

Elizabeth I's reign when he was closely associated with the borders and the reivers who lived there. In 1631 he moved to Moor Park near Rickmansworth where he lived until his death.

William Cavendish, 1st Duke of Newcastle (1593–1676)

Cavendish, a grandson of Bess of Hardwick, was married in 1618 to Elizabeth Howard by whom he had five children. William gained a reputation as a courtier and something of a playboy as well as serving in various administrative capacities in the Midlands, including as MP for Retford. He was created Earl of Newcastle in 1628 but was unable to acquire the government office which he sought despite entertaining Charles I at Bolsover Castle in 1634. The castle, which included an indoor riding school where Cavendish trained his horses, was the earl's lavish hideaway. It was 1638 before he was appointed as governor to the king's eldest son and then made a privy counsellor.

When the English Civil War broke out, Cavendish was made military commander in the north, mainly because he paid his troops from his own pocket. He was widowed the following year but his victory at the Battle of Adwalton Moor in 1643 led to him being created a marquess. Newcastle knew that his forces were stretched and did not want to take to the field against Sir Thomas Fairfax and the Earl of Manchester's Parliamentary army in 1644. Overruled by Prince Rupert, the defeat at Marston Moor on 2 July 1644 led to the loss of the north to the Royalists and to Cavendish's self-imposed exile.

While Cavendish was in Paris, he met and married Margaret Lucas, one of Henrietta Maria's ladies-in-wating. He encouraged his new wife to pursue her education as a natural philosopher as well as to publish what she wrote. Rather than relying on anonymity, as was usual, she wrote under her own name and the marquess wrote a sonnet that was included at the front of one of the books. It expressed his deep love for her and his admiration of her writing.

In 1648 the couple left France, and moved to Antwerp where they remained in the house previously owned by the artist Rubens until the Restoration. It was there that the marquess, who was without funds at the time but an acknowledged expert on horsemanship, wrote and published his first work on the subject. In 1650 he was appointed to Charles II's privy council, against the advice of Edward Hyde who had little time for the king's former governor.

Cavendish was able to return to England only after the Restoration and in 1665 was rewarded with a dukedom. Increasingly marginalised at court, he retired with Margaret to his home at Welbeck Abbey in Nottinghamshire where he set about restoring his estates, breeding horses, patronising the arts, writing and rebuilding Nottingham Castle, which he purchased in 1663, in the style of a baroque mansion. When Margaret died unexpectedly in 1673, the duke was devastated. He published all her poems and letters as well as erecting a monument to Margaret in Westminster Abbey. The duke, who died three years later, elected to be buried next to her and be commemorated alongside her.

Thomas Chaloner the Younger (1559–1615)

The son of Sir Thomas Chaloner and Ethelreda Frodsham, he was raised after his father's death in 1565, as a ward of William Cecil, Lord Burghley. After completing his education, he travelled extensively and is credited with bringing alum manufacture to England following a visit to Italy. Despite his allegiance to the Cecil family, he found employment in the household of Robert Dudley, Earl of Leicester where he was employed as tutor to the earl's illegitimate son, the explorer, Robert Dudley. By that time, he was married, at Lord Burghley's instigation, to Elizabeth Fleetwood who gave her husband eleven children. When she died in 1603, Chaloner married for a second time and became father to a further seven children. One of his sons, Thomas, would sign King Charles I's death warrant and be forced to flee England, in 1660, as a regicide.

Before Elizabeth I's death Chaloner went to Scotland at the behest of Cecil's son, Robert, where he found favour with James VI. He was with the king when he travelled from Edinburgh to London after his accession to the English throne in 1603. He also managed Anne of Denmark's private estates on her behalf and was responsible for Prince Henry's household and education. When Henry was created Prince of Wales in 1610, Chaloner became the prince's chamberlain. Chaloner used his links with Italy and the Tuscans, in particular, to encourage Henry's interest in art and sculpture.

The courtier's career ended with the death of the Prince of Wales in 1612. He became personally liable for debts owed by the prince's household as well as for the purchase of Kenilworth Castle from Robert Dudley. Even so, it was only after his death that the extent of his monetary difficulties became apparent.

Alexander Erskine of Gogar (d.1592)
A younger son of John Erskine, 5th Lord Erskine, he was appointed as governor to James VI at Stirling after the death of his older brother, the Earl of Mar, in 1572. An opponent of the regent, James Douglas, Earl of Morton, Erskine wielded considerable influence because of his custody of the king. In 1578, Erskine's nephew, the 2nd earl of Mar, was persuaded to try and overthrow his uncle. During the skirmish that followed, James VI's young companion, and Gogar's eldest son, Alexander, was killed.

When James VI transitioned to an adult household, Erskine was appointed as a gentleman of the king's bedchamber and received income from Crown lands as a reward for his care of the king during his minority.

John Erskine, 5th Lord Erskine (1487–1555)
Erskine, who was a claimant to the earldom of Mar, was appointed as James V's governor and Custodian of Stirling Castle following James IV's death at Flodden in 1513. During the course of his duties, he travelled to England and met with Henry VIII on the king's behalf and later took part in negotiations for James' marriage. His daughter,

Margaret, became one of the king's mistresses. His claim to Mary, Queen of Scots' care during her infancy lay in his custodianship of Stirling and ancestral claim to governorship of Scotland's minority kings. His extended family benefited from Erskine's governorship of the queen as a young child including in 1562, the elevation of his son, John, to the earldom of Mar.

John Erskine, 1st Earl of Mar (d.1572)
Erskine was the son of the 5th Lord Erskine who was the guardian of both James V and Mary, Queen of Scots. He had two older brothers and may have been destined for the Church. In 1547 he became Commendator of Dryburgh Abbey and of Inchmahome Priory. Following the deaths of

Robert, who was killed at Pinkie, and Thomas, he was released from any vows he had taken and became his father's heir. He was sympathetic to Scottish reformers during Mary of Guise's regency but was moderate in his beliefs and refused to take sides because of the damage it would do to Scotland. He held the castles at Stirling and Edinburgh. It was in the latter that Mary of Guise died in 1560.

When Queen Mary returned to Scotland in 1561, he was appointed to her privy council, while his wife, Annabell Murray, became a lady-in-waiting. Although he was hostile to the Earl of Lennox and supported an English alliance with marriage to Robert Dudley, he did not rebel against the queen. The murder of Lord Darnley and the queen's subsequent remarriage to Bothwell strained Mar's relations with Mary. She relieved him of command of Edinburgh Castle but, on the same day, made him guardian of her son James at Stirling. This was insufficient to win Mar's support and he continued to disapprove of the queen's third marriage. Instead, he ensured that Stirling could withstand any attempt by Bothwell to seize the prince. Like Mary of Guise before him, he recognised that custody of the heir to the throne gave him political capital. When Mary was deposed, he retained custody of the new king. It was Mar's wife who carried James to his coronation at the Church of the Holy Rude but the earl who held the king once he was crowned. Mary wrote to Mar from Bolton Castle accusing him of ingratitude but he refused to be swayed in his loyalty to the regent, Moray. After Moray's murder he was equally faithful to James' grandfather, the Earl of Lennox, until Stewart was mortally wounded by men loyal to the queen who attacked Stirling.

He was elected regent of Scotland on 5 September 1571 and chose to appoint James Douglas, 4th Earl of Morton to assist him in the task. Historians are divided about the effectiveness of Mar's rule and the extent to which Morton dominated the relationship. The earl sought assistance from Elizabeth I and from her representative in Berwick, Henry Carey, Lord Hunsdon but took a moderate approach towards Marian supporters and to the relationship between Church and State. He died the following year after being taken unexpectedly ill on 29 October at Stirling and was buried at Alloa.

John Erskine, 2nd Earl of Mar (*c.*1558–1634)

Erskine, the eldest son of the 1st earl and his wife Annabell Murray, was still a minor when his father, who was regent of Scotland, died in 1572. He remained in the custody of his mother and continued to be educated alongside James VI with his cousins Thomas and George Erskine. The king, who respected him, often referred to Erskine in later years by his nickname John Slaitis. As the earl grew to adulthood, he began to take his place as part of Scotland's political elite. When he was 16 years old he claimed his hereditary right to the keys of Stirling Castle and in the aftermath of the affair took his place on the privy council where he was known for his pro-English stance.

While Esmé Stewart, Duke of Lennox was high in the king's favour, Mar lost much of his influence over the king which led to his involvement in the Ruthven Raid on 23 August 1582 and the overthrow of Lennox. The king escaped the following year and the regime which Mar helped shore up during that time began to disintegrate. Several of his supporters were dismissed from James' household and Mar was himself declared an outlaw and ordered to leave the country for three years because of non-payment of taxes. Instead of obeying the king, Mar, having gone first to Ireland, returned to Scotland and attempted to capture Stirling in March 1584 in an attempt to overthrow the Earl of Arran who was the new leader of James' government. However, the royal army was stronger than Mar's so he and his supporters were forced to flee to England. Mar chose to remain in Newcastle to agitate his supporters against Arran. His patience was rewarded in December 1585 when he was able to raise an army to capture Stirling without bloodshed. With James once again in Mar's hands, it was Arran's turn to flee.

Mar's position, with James adopting a pro-English approach, was a secure one. James arranged for the earl, who was a widower, to take Esmé Stewart's daughter, Mary, as his second wife in 1592 but warned him that Mary should have Protestant companions as her faith was suspect. In 1594 when James VI's heir, Henry, was born at Stirling Castle, Mar was immediately appointed to care for the prince to the exclusion of James' wife, Queen Anne.

John Harington, 1st Baron Harington of Exton (1539–1613)
Harington, who was nephew to John Harington of Cheshunt, counted himself friend to both Henry VIII and Elizabeth I, and began his career in service to Robert Dudley, Earl of Leicester and his brother Ambrose, Earl of Warwick. His position in Midlands society was cemented by his marriage to Anne Keilway, who was a sole heiress to her father's property in Rutland and Leicestershire. As part of the established gentry, he served as a Member of Parliament for Warwickshire.

Harington's association with the Stuarts began when he escorted Mary, Queen of Scots from Staffordshire to Fotheringhay in 1586. When her son, James VI, succeeded to the English throne, Harington entertained the new king at Coombe Abbey and provided the new monarch with the use of his coach. Harington was rewarded with an elevation to the peerage and governorship of Princess Elizabeth. Harington's cousin, John Harington of Kelston, the courtier, author and inventor of a flushing toilet, described the care that he and Anne took to raise the princess in a godly household. However, the Haringtons' diligent maintenance of the Stuart princess ruined the baron financially.

His hopes for the future preferment of his family through their association with the royal family ended with the death of Prince Henry in November 1612 and the demise of his own heir, another John Harington, in 1614 when he was in his twenty-second year, leaving only his sisters, Lucy and Frances, to inherit what was left of their father's property.

Philip Herbert, 4th Earl of Pembroke (1584–1650)
Herbert, a courtier, patron of the arts and close relation of the Sidney family, succeeded his brother, William, as earl in April 1630. Although he and the king shared an interest in art, and Charles spent several summers at Wilton House, near Salisbury, in the company of the man he regarded as a friend, Herbert was alarmed by the influence that Henrietta Maria exerted over her husband. He was also a Puritan who opposed William Laud and voted in favour of the attainder against Strafford in 1641. Charles could not forgive Pembroke for his role in Wentworth's execution and took the opportunity occasioned by an argument with Henry Howard to dismiss him from his post as lord chamberlain. A moderate man, Herbert chose Parliament over his

loyalty to the Crown during the civil war and was Parliament's initial choice of guardian for King Charles I's younger children, Elizabeth and Henry.

Thomas Howard, 1st Earl of Berkshire (1587–1669)

Howard was a politician and a diplomat. From 1628 he held the post of Lord Lieutenant of Oxfordshire. It was this office that saw him sent to the Tower by Parliament when he attempted to carry out the king's commission of array. Following his release, because Edward Hyde claimed Parliament believed him to be of no threat, he joined the royal court in Oxford where he was appointed governor to Prince Charles. In 1646, the earl accompanied his charge to Jersey but rather than go into exile he went first to Holland and then returned to England, compounding for his estates in 1649. Howard's eldest son, Charles, was one of Charles II's gentlemen of the bedchamber while the king was in exile. He and his eight brothers all supported the Royalist cause. On the Restoration the earl joined Charles II's privy council.

Jean d'Humèires, Sieur de Mouchy (d.1550)

Court official responsible for the oversight of the French royal nursery from 1546 until his death. Prior to his appointment he served as the French ambassador to England in 1527. Remnants of his tomb and its effigy can be found in the Louvre.

William Keith, 4th Earl Marischal (d.1581)

Keith, whose eldest son was taken prisoner at the same time, fought at the Battle of Pinkie in 1547 but initially favoured a marriage between Mary, Queen of Scots and Henry VIII's son, Edward. He was one of the men who accompanied the queen to France, at his own expense, and, in 1561, he was appointed to Mary's privy council. During his time in office, he accrued several debts and chose to retire to his home at Dunnottar Castle, earning himself the nickname William of the Tower. He fulfilled his duty as Mearns sheriff until his death when he was succeeded by his grandson.

Thomas Knyvett, 1st Baron Knyvett (*c.*1545–1622)

Kyvett, or Knyvett, studied at Cambridge before being admitted to Gray's Inn in 1566. By 1572 he was a groom of the privy chamber. His career path was as might be expected for a member of the gentry, with connections at court and the royal household, including becoming a JP for Middlesex as well as being returned to the House of Commons. Knyvett became embroiled in a violent feud with the 17th Earl of Oxford when Knyvett's niece, Anne Vavasour, gave birth to the earl's illegitimate son. It is likely that it was through Knyvett, that Anne and her sister gained a place among the queen's ladies.

As one of Elizabeth I's trusted servants, Knyvett held a lifetime lease on lodgings at Whitehall which he surrendered to James I when the king decided that it would become part of Prince Charles' accommodation. In return Knyvett was granted a lease on another property and an annuity of £20 a year. By 1605 he was the keeper of the palaces at Westminster and Whitehall as well as Warden of the Mint. It was in the last capacity that he was instructed by the king to build parkland with fountains and waterworks to house part of the Tower's menagerie at St James's Park.[1] He is more famous for having led the search which discovered Guy Fawkes in the cellars beneath Westminster in 1605.

In 1605 he and his wife, Elizabeth, were made custodians of James' daughter, Mary, with a grant of £20 per week. After Mary's death, Anne of Denmark made Knyvett her surveyor general. In 1607 he became a baron as well as a privy councillor. When he died in 1622, without heirs, he left instructions for a free school and schoolhouse to be built at Stanwell. His property in London, known as Knyvett House, passed to his niece, Elizabeth Hampden, whose own son was one of the five MPs that Charles I attempted to arrest in 1642.[2] Today, the site of the baron's London residence is better known as 10 Downing Street.

John Lindsey, 5th Lord Lindsey of Byres (d.1563)

Lindsey was present at James V's bedside when he died in 1542. The judge, who was the Sheriff of Fife, was one of eight guardians appointed to the care of Mary, Queen of Scots when she was an infant. He assisted with her movement from Linlithgow to Stirling in 1543. A moderate man, he played an important role in the negotiations between the Lords of the Congregation and Mary of Guise.

Alexander Livingston, 5th Lord Livingston (d.1553)

Livingston was a companion of James V, accompanying the king to Paris in 1537, when he married for the first time to Magdalene of France. As the keeper of Linlithgow Palace, he was named one of Mary, Queen of Scots' guardians during her infancy. He was an opponent of the proposed Anglo-Scottish marriage for the queen advocated by the Earl of Arran. In 1545, Livingston was appointed to the regency council. Two years later, the lord's heir, John, who was married to a daughter of Janet Stewart (an illegitimate half-sister of James V), was killed at Pinkie. In 1548, he accompanied the queen to Paris where he died and was succeeded by his second son, William, who was married to another of Janet Stewart's daughters. Two of his daughters, Mary and Magdalen, served as ladies in waiting to Mary, Queen of Scots. The latter was also part of James VI's and Henry Frederick Stuart's household in Stirling.

Sir Anthony Mildmay (unknown)

In 1640, Mildmay, a courtier, was MP for Westlow in Cornwall. He served Charles I as the king's 'carver'[1] and was with him throughout the war and his imprisonment. By the time Charles was imprisoned in Carisbrooke Castle he was forced to revise his opinion of the monarch he served so faithfully throughout a tumultuous period. He wrote to his brother, Henry, describing Charles as 'the most perfidious man that ever lived, and if he ever gets power, he will make no more difficulty to hang you than I will to eat my dinner this cold day'.[2]

By November 1648, Mildmay had made his peace with Parliament through the intercession of his brother and, following Charles' execution, was involved in inventorying the late king's personal belongings including his horses and the contents of the Jewel House. In July 1650, he and his wife, Anne, received custody of the king's young children and transferred them from Kent to the Isle of Wight. After Princess Elizabeth's death soon after her arrival there, Mildmay remained as governor of the Duke of Gloucester. The captain was reticent about releasing the boy even after Parliament gave its permission for Henry to join his sister in The Netherlands. This may have been as a consequence of being left out of pocket for the care he afforded Elizabeth during her final illness and the cost of her funeral. He also petitioned

Parliament on behalf of the princess' servants describing them as 'very civil and inoffensive, and humbly conceiving them fit objects of the Parliament's compassion'.[3] It is unclear whether Elizabeth's staff received recompense but it is evident that Mildmay did not. Instead, he took matters into his own hands. He was convicted in 1661 for embezzling some of Charles I's plate and hangings which were allocated to Elizabeth and Henry after the king's execution but which Mildmay kept for himself.

Wat Montagu, Abbé de St Martin (d.1677)
A younger son of the 1st Earl of Manchester, Wat began his court career in the service of George Villiers, 1st Duke of Buckingham and was with the duke when he was assassinated in 1628.

He spent much of his career as a diplomat in France as well as travelling to Rome. During his time on the Continent, he converted to Catholicism. As a consequence, when he returned to England and took a place in Henrietta Maria's household, he was asked to absent himself and returned to Rome at the behest of Charles I. By the end of the 1630s Montagu became a Benedictine monk and was ordained a priest. He returned to the French court, and the household of Henrietta Maria's mother. Marie de Medici used her influence to have him appointed as the abbot of St Martin, near Pontoise, as well as appointing him to her council.

In 1643 he returned to England carrying important correspondence but was captured at Rochester and interred in the Tower of London where he remained until 1647. By then the queen was an exile in Paris. He was appointed as her chaplain, only returning to England in 1663 when Henrietta Maria summoned him back. He remained with the queen, whose marriage he helped to negotiate in 1624, and presided over her funeral in 1669.

Algernon Percy, 10th Earl of Northumberland (1602–1668)
The oldest surviving son of the 9th Earl, the so-called 'Wizard Earl', who was imprisoned in the Tower of London for complicity in the Gunpowder Plot in 1605. Percy used some of his time in custody to compose an '*Advice*' for his son instructing him on how to manage his life and the family estates. At 12 years old, Algernon was sent to St John's College, Cambridge before continuing his studies in the Middle Temple, London. In 1618, in something

of a rite of passage, he went on a Grand Tour of Europe with his tutor before returning home to marry Anne Cecil, a daughter of William Cecil against the wishes of the 9th Earl who blamed the Cecil family for his incarceration.

Percy was able to resume control of the family estates in the north as well as taking a seat in the House of Lords in 1626, as Baron Percy, where he became the leader of those opposed to the Duke of Buckingham. In 1632, following the death of his father, he became the 10th Earl of Northumberland and began to re-establish himself at court. He was initially unsuccessful in this attempt but in 1633, when the king went to Scotland for a belated coronation, Northumberland accompanied him there in a bid to gain royal favour. In 1635, by which time he won the approval of Henrietta Maria, he was admitted to the Order of the Garter; in 1636 he was awarded command of the 'Ship Money' fleet. As well as making reforms of the Navy, bypassing the admiralty and going directly to the privy council, he enforced the Oath of Supremacy, removing officers who refused to take it. The influence of the Earl of Strafford and Archbishop Laud saw him promoted to Lord Admiral in 1638. The appointment was intended to last until James, Duke of York, was old enough to assume the responsibility. However, Northumberland disagreed with royal policy towards Scotland and opposed the dissolution of the Short Parliament of 1640. In 1642, Charles I removed Percy's commission.

Despite his support for Parliament his attitude to the king wavered and the earl's health prevented him from fully participating in events. Between 1642 and 1643 his support for the war faltered and he became associated with the party who favoured a peaceful settlement between the warring parties. In April 1643 he retired to his estates at Petworth but following the adoption of the Solemn League and Covenant, the earl returned to London and took the Covenant and served as the chairman of the Committee of Both Kingdoms. By the end of 1644 his attitude to the war had undergone a fundamental transformation. He was recognised as one of the principal supporters of the New Model Army.

In March 1645 he was made governor of Princess Elizabeth and Prince Henry. In July 1646, Prince James joined the royal household. In February 1648 he asked to be relieved of the care of the royal family but, despite his earlier stance, by the autumn of 1648 was the leader of the party in the Lords who wanted to continue negotiations with Charles I and opposed the execution of the king. In May 1649 he was relieved of his official duties, including governorship of the royal children. He withdrew from public life, refusing to take his seat in the Lords.

In 1660 Northumberland was part of the group of men who tried to force Charles II to accept the terms Charles I was offered at Newport in September 1648 which aimed to restore the king to his throne but limit his power. The so-called Suffolk House cabal failed when General Monck decided to support the Convention Parliament which proclaimed that Charles II had been the lawful sovereign since the death of Charles I in 1649. Even so, the earl became part of the privy council on 31 May 1660 and was the Lord High Constable at the king's coronation in 1661. He failed to accrue any significant political power and retired once more to the country, dying at Petworth in 1668.

George Radcliffe (1594–1657)

The lawyer, from near Huddersfield, was an associate of the Earl of Strafford as well as being a relation by marriage. He served as an MP and went with the earl to Ireland although he held no official post there. Radcliffe spent most of the civil war in Oxford where he was given the role of James, Duke of York's governor. The king seems to have intended for Radcliffe to take the prince to Ireland but there was insufficient time to affect the move.[1] Instead, he handed his charge into the care of the Earl of Northumberland and chose exile in France, his Yorkshire lands being sold off in 1651 by Parliament.

He was one of the men who thwarted Henrietta Maria's plans to convert the Duke of Gloucester to Catholicism and who was forced to leave Paris under the terms of the Anglo-French treaty negotiated in 1655. His son regained Radcliffe's Irish estates in the years after the Restoration.

Alexander Seton, 1st Earl of Dunfermline (1555–1622)

The Seton family, a devoutly Catholic family, supported Mary, Queen of Scots, even after she was forced to abdicate. Alexander was educated in Rome where he was reported to excel at mathematics as well as gaining a reputation on his return home for his understanding of law. By 1586, he was both a privy councillor and Lord President of the Court of Session. After James VI's marriage to Anne of Denmark, Seton was responsible for the management of her estates and was given custody of Dunfermline. In 1598 he was created Lord Fyvie and after the birth of Anne's son, Charles, there in 1600, he was appointed by the king as the prince's tutor and guardian. His task was completed in August 1604 when he accompanied the boy to England.

William Seymour, 1st Marquess of Hertford and 2nd Duke of Somerset (1587–1660)

Seymour's descent from Katherine Grey, who was the granddaughter of Mary Tudor, the younger sister of King Henry VIII, gave him a claim to the throne even though his father had been rendered illegitimate. When William made a secret marriage to his cousin, Arbella Stuart, in 1610, he excited the fury of King James I because he believed that their union consolidated their position as an alternative to his own line. Arbella who was the only child of Charles Stuart, 1st Earl of Lennox, was the great-granddaughter of Margaret Tudor, the elder of Henry VIII's sisters as well as being the king's own cousin. Like his grandparents before him, William, then known by the title Lord Beauchamp, was confined to the Tower.

Seymour escaped custody and went into exile in France. Arbella absconded from confinement in Lambeth at the same time but was recaptured just before the vessel she was aboard reached Calais. She died in prison on 25 September 1615 and was buried in Westminster Abbey. William returned from exile in January 1616 having petitioned the king for forgiveness. That year he was rehabilitated at court and in November he received a knighthood. In 1617, he married Frances Devereux, the daughter of the 2nd Earl of Essex and Frances Walsingham. In 1621, he succeeded his grandfather as Earl of Hertford, despite his father's questionable legitimacy. During the following decade he became an opponent of King Charles I's attempts to exclude the Earls of Arundel and Bristol from the House of Lords and by the parliament of 1628 supported the Petition of Right.

Hertford was little at court preferring to live in retirement on his country estates in Somerset and Wiltshire during the twelve years when the king ruled without Parliament. In 1639, the First Bishops' War, fought between forces loyal to the king and Scottish Covenanters as a result of Charles' attempts to reform the Scottish Kirk, led to a commission of array being issued for troops to muster. One of the outcomes of the conflict was the so-called Short Parliament which lasted only three weeks in the spring of 1640. In August 1640, subsequent to a Scots Covenanter invasion and occupation of the north of England, the earl was one of the men who petitioned Charles to summon the lower house which met on 3 November. Before it met, Herford was selected as one of the commissioners to meet with the Scots at Ripon to negotiate with the Covenanters who had gone to war with the king because of the way in which he imposed the liturgy contained in the *Book of Common Prayer* upon them. One of its first acts was to impeach Strafford for his conduct in Ireland.

Charles was prompted to try to achieve a reconciliation with Seymour as one of the twelve signatories of the petition which had asked the king to summon Parliament. The following year Seymour became a privy councillor, a marquess and was appointed, on 10 August 1641, as governor to the Prince of Wales. His new roles led to a change of viewpoint in favour of the Crown. This was signalled by his failure to sit in the Lords when the vote on the Earl of Strafford's attainder was made on 7 May. In April he joined the king at York with his royal charge, ignoring Parliamentary demands that he returned to London with Prince Charles. When the civil war began, he served the royalist cause as a military commander in the south-west of England and south of Wales until disputes with the king's nephew, Prince Rupert, led to him being recalled to court at Oxford.

Throughout the First Civil War, Hertford remained moderate in outlook. He continued to communicate with his brother-in-law, the Earl of Essex, and was among the earls in December 1644 who counselled Charles I to negotiate with Parliament. In October 1647, the earl was one of the advisors permitted to join the king at Hampton Court where he was confined. When it became clear that no further negotiations would prevent the king's trial, Hertford remained by the king's side. On 8 February 1649, he was one of the pall bearers at Charles' funeral at Windsor.

In 1660, at the Restoration, Charles II restored the Dukedom of Somerset to his former tutor, which had been forfeited by his great-grandfather's sentence for treason in 1552. However, Hertford's health was failing and he died a month later on 24 October 1660.

Claude d'Urfé (1501–1558)

D'Urfé, who was a friend of François I, served in France's Italian campaigns before being appointed to the post of governor overseeing the French royal nursery in 1550. Following his time as a soldier and a diplomat in Italy he became a patron of Renaissance art and literature. As well as amassing a large library he was a sponsor of the La Pléiade group of court poets who wrote in their native tongue in the style of classical authors.

Colonel Edward Villiers (1620–1689)

Villiers, whose uncle was the 1st Duke of Buckingham, and whose sister, Barbara, was one of Charles II's mistresses, married Frances Howard at the end of the First English Civil War. A loyal Royalist throughout the war, Villiers remained in England until 1648 when he chose to go into exile with his cousin, the 2nd Duke of Buckingham.

He returned to England in 1651, seemingly having made his peace with Parliament. However, in 1654 he was in correspondence with Edward Hyde and a significant player in the Sealed Knot, plotting for the restoration of the monarchy. He was even arrested in 1654 and held for several months when an assassination plot against Oliver Cromwell was uncovered.

Villiers served Charles II and James II but chose to support William and Mary when James was deposed in the Glorious Revolution of 1688. His daughter, Elizabeth, who accompanied Mary to the Netherlands when she married, was an important figure in the Dutch court, and is alleged to have become William's mistress in 1680. The colonel's son, Edward, was appointed as Mary's master of horse and in 1697, following a successful diplomatic career, was created Earl of Jersey as well as the English ambassador, first at the Hague and then in Paris. By 1700, he held the office of lord chamberlain. Edward did not live to see his family's preferment because of their association with Mary and Anne, or his son's subsequent loss of favour and alliance with the Jacobite cause. He died in 1689 and was buried in Westminster Abbey beside his wife.

Table Identifying the Men and Women Who Raised Stuart Princes and Princesses

	Governors	Governesses	Tutors and Chaplains	Significant others
Parents: King James V of Scotland (1512–1542) = Mary of Guise (1515–1560)				
Mary, Queen of Scots b. 8 December 1542 Ruled Scotland from 14 December 1542 until her forced abdication on 24 July 1567. She fled to England where she remained in captivity until her death. Executed 8 February 1587	John Erskine, 5th Lord Erskine Jean d'Humieres William Keith, 4th Earl Marichal John Lindsey, 5th Lord Lindsey of Byres Alexander Livingston, 5th Lord Livingston Claude d'Urfé	Françoise d'Humieres, Dame de Contay Françoise d'Estamville, Dame de Paroy Janet Stewart, Lady Fleming Diane de Poitiers	Jacques Amyot Joachim du Bellay George Buchanan Pierre Danés Pierre Danjou John Erskine, Prior of Inchmahome Antoine Fouquelin Claude Millot Pierre de Ronsard Alexander Scott	James Hamilton, 2nd Earl of Arran and Duke of Châtellerault Jean, or Janet, Sinclair
Parents: Mary, Queen of Scots (1542–1587) = Henry Stuart, Lord Darnley (1546–1567)				
James Stuart b. 19 June 1566 Ruled as James VI of Scotland from 24 July 1567 and also as James I of England from 24 March 1603. d. 27 March 1625	John Erskine, 1st Earl of Mar Alexander Erskine of Gogar	Margaret Beaton, Lady Rires Annabel Murray of Tullibardine, Countess of Mar	George Buchanan Peter Young Adam Erskine David Erskine William Hudson	Margaret Beaton, Lady Forbes of Rires or Reres James Douglas, 4th Earl of Morton Helen Little David Murray of Gorthly James Stewart, 1st Earl of Moray Matthew Stewart, 4th Earl of Lennox (regent) Esme Stuart, Duke of Lennox

Parents: James VI & I of Scotland & England = Anne of Denmark (1574–1619)				
Henry Frederick Prince of Wales b. 19 February 1594 d. November 1612	John Erskine, 2nd Earl of Mar Thomas Chaloner the Younger	Annabell Murray of Tullibardine, Dowager Countess of Mar Marie Stewart, Countess of Mar Jean Drummond	Dr John Bull Salomon de Caus Alfonso Ferrabosco II John Harington of Exton John Harington of Kelston Thomas Harriot Thomas Lydiat David Murray Adam Newton Richard Preston Walter Quin Edward Wright	George Hakewill Margaret Masterton Phineas Pett Sir Walter Raleigh
Elizabeth, Electress Palatine and Queen of Bohemia b. 19 August 1596 Married Frederick, Elector Palatine of the Rhine, later Frederick V King of Bohemia. Known as 'The Winter Queen'. d. February 1662	John Harington, 1st Baron Harington of Exton Alexander Livingston, 1st Earl of Linlithgow	Frances Cobham (née Howard), Lady Kildare Eleanor Hay, Countess of Linlithgow Anne Harington (nee Keilwey) Margaret Stewart, Lady Ochiltree	Dr John Bull Francis Cardell Thomas Cardell Salomon de Caus Jean de Beau-Chesne Theodore Diodati	Elizabeth Auchmowtie Alison Hay, Lady Dunkerrant Elizabeth Hay Bessie McDowall
Margaret b. 24 December 1598 d. March,1600	Alexander Livingston, 1st Earl of Linlithgow	Eleanor Hay, Countess of Linlithgow Margaret Stewart, Lady Ochiltree		Helena Chichton Marian Hepburn Christian Scrimgeour

Charles b. 19 November 1600 Later King Charles I Ruled 27 March 1625. Executed 30 January 1649	Robert Carey, 1st Earl of Monmouth Alexander Seton, 1st Earl of Dunfermline	Elizabeth Carey, Countess of Monmouth Jean Drummond, Countess of Roxburghe Margaret Stewart, Lady Ochiltree	Norman Lisle Thomas Murray Walter Quin	Marian Hepburn
Robert b. 18 January/February 1602 d. 27 May 1602	Alexander Seton, 1st Earl of Dunfermline	Margaret Stewart, Lady Ochiltree		Isobel Colt
Mary b. 8 April, 1605 d. 16 September or December 1607	Sir Thomas Knyvett	Elizabeth Knyvett née Hayward		
Sophia b. 22 June1606 d. 23 June 1606				
Parents: King Charles I (1600–1649) = Henrietta Maria (1609–1669)				
Charles b. 13 May 1629 d. 13 May 1629				
Charles b. 29 May 1630 d.1685	William Cavendish 1st Duke of Newcastle Thomas Howard, 1st Earl of Berkshire William Seymour, Marquess of Hertford	Mary Sackville, Countess of Dorset	Brian Duppa John Earle Master Fawcett Thomas Hobbes Wenceslaus Hollar	Sir John Culpepper Edward Hyde, Earl of Clarendon Sir Ralph Hopton Patrick Ruthven, 1st Earl of Forth Mrs Walton Mrs Wyndham

Mary Henrietta Princess Royal b. 4 or 29 November 1631 Married William II of Orange 2 May 1641. d. 24 December 1660		Jean Drummond, Countess of Roxburghe Katherine Stanhope née Wotton, Countess of Chesterfield	Monsier d'Aranjon	Mrs Griffin
James **Duke of York** b. 24 October 1633 Ruled as James II from 6 February 1685. Deposed during the Glorious Revolution and deemed abdicated on 11 December 1688. d.16 September 1701	Sir John Berkeley John Byron, 1st Baron Byron William Seymour, Marquess of Hertford Algernon Percy, 10th Earl of Northumberland George Radcliffe	Mary Sackville, Countess of Dorset	Brian Duppa William Greenhill	Vicomte de Turenne
Elizabeth b. 28 December 1635 d. 8 September 1650	Philip Herbert, 4th Earl of Pembroke Sir Anthony Mildmay Algernon Percy, 10th Earl of Northumberland	Jean Drummond, Countess of Roxburghe Elizabeth Percy née Howard, Countess of Northumberland Mary Sackville, Countess of Dorset Dorothy Sidney, Countess of Leicester Mary Vere née Tracy	William Greenhill Richard Lovell Bathsua Makin Stephen Marshall	Sir John Danvers Robert Sidney, 2nd Earl of Leicester

Anne b. 17 March 1637 d. 5 November 1640		Jean Drummond, Countess of Roxburghe		
Katherine b. 29 June 1639 d. 29 June 1639				
Henry Duke of Gloucester b. 8 July 1640 d. 23 September 1660	Philip Herbert, 4th Earl of Pembroke Sir Anthony Mildmay Wat Montagu, Abbé de St Martin Algernon Percy, 10th Earl of Northumberland	Jean Drummond, Countess of Roxburghe Elizabeth Percy née Howard, Countess of Northumberland Mary Sackville, Countess of Dorset Dorothy Sidney, Countess of Leicester Mary Vere née Tracy	William Greenhill Richard Lovell Stephen Marshall	Robert Sidney, 2nd Earl of Leicester
Henriette Anne **'Minette'** b. 16 June 1644 Married Philip of Bourbon, Duc d'Orléans on 31 March 1661. d. 15 or 30 June 1670	Sir John Berkeley	Anne Douglas née Villiers, Lady Dalkeith, Countess of Morton	Thomas Fuller Father Cyprien	
Charles II married Catherine of Braganza, daughter of John IV of Portugal but had no children. He was succeeded by his brother James.				

Parents: King James II = Anne Hyde, daughter of Edward Hyde, 1st Earl of Clarendon (1637–1671)				
Charles b. 22 October 1660 d. 5 May 1661				
Mary b. 30 April 1662 Married her cousin, William III, Prince of Orange on 4 November 1677. Proclaimed joint monarch with her husband William of Orange on 13 February 1689 after her father abdicated. d. 28 December 1694	Colonel Edward Villiers	Frances Villiers née Howard	Dr Henry Compton Richard Gibson Peter de Laine Anthony Robart	
Anne b. 6 February 1665 Succeeded her brother-in-law as Queen Anne on 8 March 1702. d. 1 August 1714	Colonel Edward Villiers	Frances Villiers née Howard	Mrs Barry Dr Henry Compton Richard Gibson Peter de Laine Anthony Robart	

Notes

All the authors referenced in the notes have their works listed in the bibliography.

Chapter One: The Infancy of Mary, Queen of Scots

1. Porter, Linda, *Crown of Thistles*, p.289.
2. Ballantyne, J. W., 'The Byrth of Mankynde, p.246.
3. Chalmers, George (ed.), *The Life of Mary, Queen of Scots,* p.4 fn. h.
4. Scottish History Society, *Rentale Sancti Andree*, p.139.
5. Buchan, P., *An Historical and Authentic Account of the Ancient and Noble Family of Keith* pp.41–42.
6. Erskine is often described as the prior of Inchmahome. Erskine was responsible for overseeing Inchmahome Priory and Dryburgh Abbey, and exercising the functions of a head of a monastic house, but he was only in minor orders. It was a common practice in Scotland when members of the nobility or a monarch secularised monastic land but retained the monastic house rather than dissolving it.
7. Clifford, Arthur (ed.), *Sir Ralph Sadler*, Sir Ralph Sadler report made to King Henry VIII, 23 March 1543, p.88.
8. Ibid., Sir Ralph Sadler, letter to the Privy Council, 8 April 1543, p.122.
9. Ibid., p.123.
10. Ibid., Sir Ralph Sadler letter to the Privy Council, 11 July 1543, p.228.
11. Ibid.
12. Ibid., Sir Ralph Sadler letter to the King, 15 July 1543, p.229.
13. Ibid.
14. *Report on the Manuscripts of the Earl of Mar and Kellie, preserved at Alloa House.* An Ordinance for the Keeping of King James V was issued on 3 August 1522. It instructed Erskine to teach the young king 'all gude vertuis, to reid and write and to speke Latin and French', p.11.
15. Clifford, Arthur (ed.), *Sir Ralph Sadler*, Sir Ralph Sadler to Earl of Suffolk, 6 September 1543, p.286.
16. Thorpe, Markham John (ed.), *Accounts of the Treasurer* no 53, p.66.
17. Durkan, James, 'The Earl of Arran and Queen Mary', p.261.
18. Thorpe, Markham John, (ed.), *Accounts of the Treasurer*, Robert Moffet to Lord Wharton, 2 March 1548, no 64. p.82.

Chapter Two: Mary's French Education

1. Jansen, Sharon (trans.), *Anne of France: Lessons for My Daughter,* p.x.
2. Ibid., pp.39–40.
3. Pollnitz, Aysha, *Princely Education*, p.211.
4. Guy, John, *My Heart is My Own,* pp.71–72.

5. Ibid., p.72.
6. Taylor, William M., *John Knox*, p.164; Carpenter, Sarah, 'Performing Diplomacies', p.194.
7. Guy, John. *My Heart is My Own*, p.79.
8. Jones, Anne Rosalind and Stallybrass, Peter, *Renaissance Clothing and the Materials of Memory*, p.308.
9. Wardle, Patricia, 'The Embroideries of Mary Queen of Scots', p.4.
10. Turnbull, William B. (ed.), *Calendar of State Papers, Foreign series of the Reign of Edward VI*, No. 332, p.97.
11. Ibid., No. 320, p.90.
12. Durkan, James, 'The Earl of Arran and Queen Mary', p.264.
13. Thomson, Thomas and Innes, C. (eds.), *The Acts of the Parliaments of Scotland*, p.535.

Chapter Three: A Stuart Heir to Scotland and England

1. Melville, Sir James and Thomson, Thomas (ed.), *Memoirs of his Own Life by Sir James Melville of Halhill*, pp.158–159.
2. Ibid.
3. McInnes, Charles Thorpe. (ed.), *Accounts of the Treasurer*, Volume 12, p.403.
4. Beveridge, James and Donaldson, Gordon (eds.), *Register of the Privy Seal of Scotland*, No. 3297, pp.297–298.
5. Marshall, Rosalind K, 'Hir Rob Ryall: the Costume of Mary of Guise', p.8.
6. Hume, Martin A. S. (ed.), *Calendar of the Letters and State Papers Relating to English Affairs in the Archives of Simancas*, Volume 2, pp.590 and 612.
7. Ibid., p.427.
8. *Report on the Manuscripts of the Earl of Mar and Kellie, preserved at Alloa House*, 10 March 1567, p.18.
9. Melville, Sir James and Thomson, Thomas (ed.), *Memoirs of his Own Life by Sir James Melville of Halhill*, pp.261–262.
10. Ibid., p.36.
11. Shaman, Julian, *The Library of Mary Queen of Scots*, p.11.

Chapter Four: The Making of a King

1. Moray went to France when Bothwell was acquitted of Darnley's murder in April 1567.
2. Buchanan went so far as to describe Margaret as 'a woman very heavy, both by unwieldy age, and much substance' in Buchanan, George, *A detection of the actions of Mary queen of Scots. p.*9.
3. Juhala, Amy L., *The Household and Court of King James VI of Scotland*, p.20, fn. 10.
4. *Report on the Manuscripts of the Earl of Mar and Kellie, preserved at Alloa House*, pp. 18–21.
5. McInnes, Charles Thorpe, (ed.), *Accounts of the Treasurer*, Volume 13, pp. 275 and 354.
6. Gibson, Craig, J. T., *Papers relative to the marriage of King James the Sixth of Scotland*, p.33.
7. Mackie, J. D. (ed.), *Calendar of the State Papers Relating to Scotland and Mary, Queen of Scots 1547–1603*, Volume 13, No. 108, p.102.
8. Juhala, Amy L., *The Household and Court of King James VI of Scotland*, p.186.
9. Hickey, Julia A., *Raising the Tudors*, p.36.
10. *Calendar of the Cecil Papers in Hatfield House*, Volume 3, 1583–1589, note 97, Fontenay to the Queen of Scots and to Nau (London, 1889), accessed via British History online, https://www.british-history.ac.uk/cal-cecil-papers/vol3/pp47-65.

11. Discussion about the health of James VI/I can be found in Beasely A. W., 'The disability of James VI & I', pp. 151–162 and Garrard P., Stephenson J., Ganesan V., Peters, T., 'Attenuated variants of Lesch-Nyhan disease: the case of King James VI/I', p.153.
12. Strickland, Agnes (ed.), *Letters of Mary Queen of Scots*, Volume 1, Elizabeth I to Sir Nicholas Throckmorton, 14 July 1567, p.53.
13. Ibid.
14. McInnes, Charles Thorpe, (ed), *Accounts of the Treasurer*, Volume 12, p.166.
15. *Calendar of the Cecil Papers in Hatfield House*, Volume 3, 1583–1589, note 97, Fontenay to the Queen of Scots and to Nau, (London, 1889), British History online, https://www.british-history.ac.uk/cal-cecil-papers/vol3/pp47-65.
16. Weldon, Sir Anthony, *The Court and Character of King James*, p.179.
17. Ibid., p.178.
18. Orme, Nicholas, *Tudor Children*, p.49.
19. *Report on the Manuscripts of the Earl of Mar and Kellie, preserved at Alloa House*, p.21.
20. Ibid.
21. Brown, K. M. and Mann, A. J. (eds.), *Records of the Parliaments of Scotland to 1707*, 15 December 1567, accessed at https://www.rps.ac.uk.
22. Row, John, *The History of the Kirk of Scotland*, pp. 33–35 cited in Stewart, Alan, *The Cradle King: A Life of James VI & I*, p.41.
23. *Report on the Manuscripts of the Earl of Mar and Kellie, preserved at Alloa House*, p.21.
24. Ibid.
25. Thomson, Thomas (ed.), *The historie and life of King James the Sext*, p.53.
26. Matusiak, John, *James I: Scotland's King of England*, p.38.
27. Cited in Stewart, Alan, *The Cradle King: A Life of James VI & I*, p.33.
28. Dawson, Jane E. A., 'Jane Stewart, Countess of Argyll: the story behind GD112/39/8/1', based on a Paper given to the Marie Stuart Society, (Edinburgh: The University of Edinburgh, 2006) p.2.
29. Ibid., p.10.
30. The name Stewart became Stuart during Mary, Queen of Scots time in France. Stewart is the Scots version of the name while Stuart became more commonly associated with the royal family from the sixteenth century onwards.
31. Buchanan, George, *A detection of the actions of Mary queen of Scots*, p.52.
32. Ibid.
33. Ibid.
34. Ibid., p.51.
35. Brown, Peter Hume, *George Buchanan, Humanist and Reformer*, p.254.
36. Houston, S. J., *Seminar Studies in History: James I*, p.3; Juhala, Amy L., *The Household and Court of King James VI of Scotland*, p.23.
37. Matusiak, John, *James I: Scotland's King of England*, p. 37.
38. Buchanan, George and Aikman, James (ed.), *The History of Scotland*, Volume 1, p.xxxiii.
39. *Report on the Manuscripts of the Earl of Mar and Kellie, preserved at Alloa House*, p 22.
40. Ibid.
41. Cited in Stewart, Alan, *The Cradle King: A Life of James VI & I*, p.36.
42. Weldon, Sir Anthony, *The Court and Character of King James*, p.178.
43. Cited in Blakewell, Amy, *Regency in Sixteenth Century Scotland*, p.11.
44. *Report on the Manuscripts of the Earl of Mar and Kellie, preserved at Alloa House*, p.26.

Chapter Five: Educating A Protestant prince

1. Gatherer, W. A., (trans. and ed.), *The Tyrannous Reign of Mary Stewart,* p.viii.
2. Hayward, Maria, *Stuart Style: Monarchy, Dress and the Scottish Male Elite*, p.45.
3. Blakeway, Amy, *Regency in Sixteenth Century Scotland*, p.43.
4. McCrie, Thomas, *The Life of Andrew Melville,* p.65.
5. Willson, D. H., *King James VI and I*, p.24.
6. Young, Sir Peter, and Warner, George Frederick (ed.), *The Library of James VI,* p.xii.
7. Willson, D. H., *King James VI and I*, p.25.
8. Stewart, Alan, *The Cradle King: A Life of James VI & I*, p.38.
9. Buchanan, George and Aikman, James (ed.), *The History of Scotland,* Volume 2, p.440.
10. Young, Sir Peter, and Warner, George Frederick, (ed.), *The Library of James VI,* p.lxxii.
11. Melville, James and Pitcairn, Robert (ed.), *The autobiography and diary of Mr James Melvill, with a continuation of the diary*, p.38.
12. Matusiak, John, *James I: Scotland's King of England,* p.32.
13. Young, Sir Peter, and Warner, George Frederick (ed.), *The Library of James VI,* p.xlviii.
14. Bain, J., *et al.*, *Calendar of State Papers relating to Scotland and Mary, Queen of Scots, 1547–1603.* Volume 5 (1907) p.477.
15. Buchanan, George and Aikman, James (ed.), *The History of Scotland,* Volume 1, pp. xxxviii–xxviiv.

Chapter Six: The 'Scotch Urchin'

1. Pollnitz, Aysha, *Princely Education in Early Modern Europe*, p.272.
2. Melville, Sir James and Thomson, Thomas (ed.), *Memoirs of his own life by Sir James Melville of Halhill*, p.260 and p.266.
3. Ibid., p.43.
4. Strickland, Agnes (ed). *Letters of Mary, Queen of Scot*s, Volume 2, Castelnau to Henri III, 9 December 1583, p.34.
5. Juhala, Amy L., *The Household and Court of King James VI of Scotland,* p.43.
6. Strickland, Agnes (ed.), *Letters of Mary, Queen of Scots,* Volume 2, Castelnau to Henri III, 9 December 1583, p.36.
7. Matusiak, John, *James I: Scotland's King of England,* p.53.
8. Calderwood, D. and Thomson, Thomas (ed.), *The History of the Kirk of Scotland*, Volume 3, p.483.
9. Hume, Martin A. S. (ed.), *Calendar of the Letters and State Papers Relating to English Affairs in the Archives of Simancas*, Volume 3, p.124.
10. Cited in Stewart, Alan, *The Cradle King: A Life of James VI & I*, p.59.
11. Strickland, Agnes (ed.), *Letters of Mary, Queen of Scots,* Volume 2, Letter from Mary Stuart to her son, James VI, 29 January 1580–1581, pp.29–30.
12. Ibid.
13. Ibid., Castelnau to Henri III, 9 December 1583, p.34.
14. He resigned his earldom of Lennox in 1580 which he inherited from James VI's uncle, Charles Stewart, in 1578 in favour of his nephew Esmé Stewart. In return, James VI created him Earl of March and Lord of Dunbar.
15. Strickland, Agnes (ed.), *Letters of Mary, Queen of Scots*, Volume 2, Castelnau to Henri III, 9 December 1583, p.65.
16. Ibid., Mary Queen of Scots to Castelnau, 11 March 1585, p.66.
17. Ibid., p.75.

18. Cited in Gatherer, W. A., (trans. and ed.), *The Tyrannous Reign of Mary Stewart*, p.6.
19. Marcus, Leah S., Mueller, Januel, and Rose, Mary Beth (eds.), *Elizabeth I: Collected Works*, Elizabeth to James, June or July 1585, p.262.
20. Ibid., James to Elizabeth, *c.*31 July 1585, p.263.

Chapter Seven: The Value of a Son

1. Meikle, Henry (ed.), *Works of William Fowler*, p.xix fn.4.
2. Strickland, Agnes (ed), *Letters of Mary, Queen of Scots*, Volume 1, letter from Mary, Queen of Scots to Elizabeth, Queen of Spain, 24 September 1568, p.113.
3. Ibid., Volume 2, letter from Mary, Queen of Scots to Mendoza, 23 November 1586, pp.108–109.
4. Ibid., Mary, Queen of Scots to the Duke of Guise, 24 November 1586, p.112.
5. Juhala, Amy L., *The Household and Court of King James VI of Scotland*, p.62.
6. *Report on the Manuscripts of the Earl of Mar and Kellie, preserved at Alloa House*, p.39.
7. MacDonald, Alexander, (ed.), *Letters To King James VI*, appendix, p.lxix.
8. Matusiak, John, *James I: Scotland's King of England*, p.132.
9. Cameron, Annie I. (ed.), *Calendar of State Papers, Scotland*, Volume 11, p.151.
10. Calderwood, D. and Thomson, Thomas (ed.), *The History of the Kirk of Scotland*, Volume 2, p.365; Williams, Ethel C., *Anne of Denmark*, p.53.
11. Bailey, Geoff B., 'The Persecution and Confession of Eleanor Hay, Countess of Linlithgow', p.4.
12. MacDonald, Alexander (ed.), *Letters To King James VI*, p.lxxiv.
13. Cameron. Annie I. (ed.), *Calendar of State Papers, Scotland*, Volume 13, p.997.

Chapter Eight: Sparks of Majesty

1. Pollnitz, Aysha, *Princely Education in Early Modern Europe*, p.324–328.
2. MacDonald, Alexander (ed.), *Letters To King James VI*, p.xxxv.
3. Ibid.
4. Ibid., p.xxxv.
5. Strong, Roy, *Henry, Prince of Wales and England's Lost Renaissance*, p.66.
6. MacDonald, Alexander (ed.), *Letters To King James VI*, p.lxxvii.
7. Ibid., p.xxxvii.
8. Ibid., p.lxxiv.
9. Masson, David (ed.), *Register of the Privy Council of Scotland:1625–1657*, p.201.
10. Ibid.
11. Ibid.
12. Green, Mary Anne Everett, *Calendar State Papers Domestic, Addenda, 1580–1625*, p.467.
13. Nott, George Frederick (ed.), *The Works of Henry Howard, Earl of Surrey, and Sir Thomas Wyatt*, James to Henry Howard, 1st Earl of Northampton, p.475.

Chapter Nine: Princes and Princesses of Both Scotland and England

1. Seton, George (ed.), *Memoir of Alexander Seton*, p.55.
2. Bailey, Geoff B., 'The persecution and Confession of Eleanor Hay, Countess of Linlithgow', p.12.
3. Tweedie, William King (ed.), *Select Biographies*, p. 347, note xxi.
4. Beaumont's Dispatches, Brienne MS. 32, f.158, Bibliothèque National, Paris, cited in Green, Mary Anne Everett, *Elizabeth of Bohemia*, p.6.

5. Teulet, Jean Baptiste Alexandre, *Relations de la France Et de L'Espagne Avec L'Ecosse au xvi siècle*, pp.279–280.
6. Marshall, Rosalind, K. *The Winter Queen*, p.23.
7. Steen, Sara Jayne (ed.), *The Letters of Lady Arbella Stuart*, p.183.
8. Akkerman, Nadine (ed.), *Elizabeth Stuart: Queen of Hearts*, p.37.
9. Clifford, Lady Anne, *The Diary of Lady Anne Clifford*, p.15, fn*.
10. Chambers, E. K., *The Elizabethan Stage*, Volume 1, p.171.
11. *Calendar of the Cecil Papers in Hatfield House, 1604*, Volume 16 (London, 1933), p.432.
12. Spring, Matthew (ed.), *The Lute in Britain*, p.215.
13. Pollnitz, Aysha, *Princely Education in Early Modern Europe*, p.325.
14. Miller, Anthony, '"These Forc'd ioyes": Imitation, Celebration, and Exhortation in Ben Jonsons' Ode to Sir William Sidney', p.170.
15. Ibid., p.168.
16. Perrin, William, Gordon (ed.), *The Autobiography of Phineas Pett*, p.21.
17. Ibid., p. 31.
18. Anderson, Adam, *Letters and State Papers of the Reign of James VI*, p.55.
19. Seton George (ed.), *Memoirs of Alexander Seton*, p.59.
20. It was Elizabeth's duty to ensure that the queen's clothes smelled fragrant.

Chapter Ten: Henry Frederick: the Rising Sun of England

1. Pagnini, Caterina, 'Henry Stuart, "The Rising Sun of England": The Creation of the Prince of Wales' (June 1610), p.262.
2. Laskowski, Eliza Fisher, *Performance, Politics and Religion*, p.102, fn. 69.
3. Ibid.,
4. Braybrooke, *The History of Audley End*, p.41.
5. Watt, A. F. (ed.), *The Essays of Sir Francis Bacon*, XVIII- Of Travel, pp.54–56.
6. Davies, Eloise, 'England's Lost Renaissance?', p.208.
7. Pollnitz, Aysha, *Princely Education in Early Modern Europe*, p.347.
8. Eloise Davies, 'England's Lost Renaissance?', p.205.
9. Displayed by the National Portrait Gallery in 2013 as part of their exhibition entitled *The Lost Prince: The Life and Death of Henry Stuart*.
10. Fraser, Sarah, *The Prince Who Would be King*, p.196.
11. O'Farrell, Brian, *Shakespeare's Patron*, p.vii.
12. Machiovelli, Niccoló, *The Prince*, p.81.
13. Perrin, W. G. (ed.), *The Autobiography of Phineas Pett*, p.100.

Chapter Eleven: Elizabeth: The Winter Queen

1. Cited in Rait, Robert S. (ed.), *Five Stuart Princesses*, p.55.
2. Akkerman, Nadine (ed.), *The Correspondence of Elizabeth Stuart*, Elizabeth to Prince Henry, letter 53, 1610, p.94.
3. Lord Harington's Account of the Expenses of the Lady Elizabeth, 1612–1613, *Exchequer of Receipt Miscellanea*, p.343.
4. Harrington, Sir John, *Nugae Antiquæ*, Volume 1, p.371.
5. Erskine, Lady Frances, *Memoirs Relating to the Queen of Bohemia*, p.123.
6. Ibid., pp.121–124.
7. Ibid., p.350.
8. Ibid., p.349.

9. Ibid., p.353.
10. Ibid, cited in Green, *Elizabeth, Electress Palatine and Queen of Bohemia*, pp.13–14.
11. Green, *Elizabeth, Electress Palatine and Queen of Bohemia*, p.16.
12. Akkerman, Nadine (ed.), *Elizabeth Stuart: Queen of Hearts*, p.67.
13. Broadway, Jan, *ODNB online.*
14. 'Gottfried Wilhelm Leibniz', *Stanford Encyclopaedia of Philosophy*, accessed online.

Chapter Twelve: Charles: A Subject and a Sovereign Are Clean Different Things.

1. Akrigg, G. P. V., (ed.), *Letters of King James VI & I*, p.xxxviii.
2. Pollnitz, Aysha, *Princely Education in Early Modern Europe*, p.355.
3. Ibid.
4. Pollnitz, Aysha, *Princely Education in Early Modern Europe*, p.357.
5. Perrin, W. G. (ed.), *The Autobiography of Phineas Pett*, p.101.
6. Pollnitz, Aysha, *Princely Education in Early Modern Europe*, p.335.
7. De Lisle, Leanda, *White King: Charles I, Traitor, Murderer, Martyr*, p.7.
8. Crust, Richard, 'Charles I and the Order of the Garter', p.343.
9. Porter, Linda, *Royal Renegades*, p.8.
10. Pollnitz, Aysha, *Princely Education in Early Modern Europe*, p.360.
11. Whitaker, Katie, *A Royal Passion*, p.27.
12. Crust, Richard, 'Charles I and the Order of the Garter', p.348.

Chapter Thirteen: Family Man

1. Lee, Sidney, *ODNB online.*
2. Caraccioli, Charles, *The Antiquities of Arundel*, p.205.
3. Falkus, Christopher, *The Life and Times of Charles II*, p.13.
4. Fry, Cynthia, 'Perceptions of Influence: The Catholic Diplomacy of Queen Anna and Her Ladies, 1601–1604', pp.265–285.
5. Payne, Helen, *ODNB online*; Payne, 'Aristocratic women, power, patronage and family networks at the Jacobean Court, 1603–1625', p.251.
6. Smith, David L., *ODNB online.*
7. Green, Mary Anne Everett, *Lives of the Princesses of England,* p.103.
8. Worsley, Lucy, *Cavalier,* p.120.
9. Whitaker, Katie, *A Royal Passion*, p.172.
10. Pearce, Dominic, *Henrietta Maria*, p.168.

Chapter Fourteen: The Road to War

1. Green, Mary Anne Everett, *Lives of the Princesses of England*, p.394.
2. Newton, Hannah, 'The Dying Child in Seventeenth-Century England', pp.218–220.
3. Wyndham, H. A., *A Family History, 1410–1688*. p.19.
4. Green, Mary Anne Everett, *Lives of the Princesses of England*, p.104.
5. Collins, Arthur, 'The English Baronage: Or, An Historical Account of the Lives and Actions of the Nobility' p.34; Clarendon, Edward Hyde, Earl of, *The History of the Rebellion and Civil Wars in England*, p.662.
6. Fraser, Antonia, *King Charles II*, p.26.
7. Murdoch, W. G. Blaikie, 'Charles the Second: His Connection with Art and Letters', p.42.

8. Thrush, Andrew, and Ferris, J. P. (eds.) "'Seymour William, Lord Beauchamp (1587–1660)" of Amesbury House, Amesbury, Wilts. And Tottenham Court, Great Bedwyn, Wilts.; later Essex House, London' in *The History of Parliament 1604–1629*, accessed online.
9. Clarendon, Edward Hyde, Earl of, *The History of the Rebellion and Civil Wars in England*, p.x.
10. Ibid., pp.267–268.

Chapter Fifteen: 'The Souls and Bodies of His Majesties Children'

1. Strickland, Agnes, *Lives of the Queens of Scotland and English Princesses*, p.349.
2. Ibid.
3. Ibid.
4. Clements, Robert Markham, *The Fighting Veres*, p.380.
5. Smith, David L., *ODNB online.*
6. Strickland, Agnes, *Lives of the Queens of Scotland and English Princesses,* p.353.
7. Ibid., p.355.
8. Goodwin, Gordon, revised by Kelsey, Sean, *ODNB online.*
9. Ibid.
10. Thrush, Andrew and Ferris, John P. (eds.) 'Danvers, Sir John (c.1585–1655) of Danvers House, Chelsea, Mdx. And West Lavington, Wilts.' in *The History of Parliament: The House of Commons 1604–1629*, accessed online.
11. Pepys, Samuel, and Bright, Rev. Mynors (ed.), *The Diary of Samuel Pepys*, Monday 30 September 1661, accessed online.
12. Le Lay, David, 'Danvers House', p.36.

Chapter Sixteen: An Exeter Princess

1. Pearce, Dominic, *Henrietta Maria,* p.230.
2. Schwartz, Louis, '17th century childbirth: "exquisite torment and infinite grace"', p.1486.
3. Fraser, Antonia, *The Weaker Vessel*, p.70.
4. Ibid.
5. Ibid., p.12.
6. Ibid., p.15.

Chapter Seventeen: Princes in Name Only

1. Ballantyne, Archibald, *Lord Carteret, A Political Biography,* p.4.
2. Cary, Henry (ed.), Duke of York, 16 July 1646. *Memorials of the great civil war in England from 1646 to 1652*, p.125.
3. Ibid.
4. Clarendon, Edward Hyde, Earl of, *History of The Rebellion and Civil Wars in England,* Volume 5, p.74.
5. Drake, George G., *ODNB online.*

Chapter Eighteen: The Fortunes of an Exiled Duke

1. One of the men who signed Charles' death warrant was Sir John Danvers, whose house was one of the places where Elizabeth and her brother Henry stayed. Danvers is said to have become a regicide because his elder brother disinherited him for his support

of Parliament. Sir Henry Danvers' will was overturned and John did inherit the family estate at Dauntsey.
2. Wood, Anthony and Clark, Andrew (ed.), *Anthony Wood's Life and Times*, p.384 and fn. 4.
3. Pepys, Samuel, and Bright, Rev. Mynors (ed.), *The Diary of Samuel Pepys*, 26 April 1667, accessed online.

Chapter Nineteen: Elizabeth and Henry

1. Ady, Julia Mary Cartwright, *Sacharissa; some account of Dorothy Sidney*, p.117.
2. Ibid.
3. Ibid., p.119.
4. Pearce, Dominic, *Henrietta Maria*, p.271.

Chapter Twenty: Lessons for a Monarch

1. Cavendish's letter is contained in Slaughter, Thomas P. (ed.), *Ideology and Politics on the Eve of Restoration*. An earlier letter containing advice on ruling was penned in 1639 (British Library MS Harley 6988, ff.111r–112v.).
2. For a full exploration of the association see, Sarasohn, Lisa T., 'Thomas Hobbes and the Duke of Newcastle: A Study in the Mutuality of Patronage before the Establishment of the Royal Society', *Isis*, Volume 90, No. 4, (December, 1999), pp.715–737.
3. Earle, Peter, *The Life and Times of James II*, p.52.

A Who's Who of Governesses Who Raised the Stuarts
Margaret Beaton, Lady Rires, or Reres

1. Bannatyne, Richard D., and Pitcairn, Robert (ed.), *Memorials of Transactions in Scotland, A.D. 1569–1573*, p.174.

Frances Cobham née Howard, Countess of Kildare (b.*c.*1573–1628)

1. Hammer, Paul E., *The Polarisation of Elizabethan Politics*, p.387 fn250. Frances had other reasons for her dislike of Elizabeth's favourite. He had argued with the Earl of Kildare and had an affair with Elizabeth Southwell, whose brother was married to Frances' elder sister.

Elizabeth Knyvett née Hayward (d.1622)

1. Nichols, John, *The Progresses and Public Processions of Queen Elizabeth*, p.106.
2. Reynolds, Susan (ed.), 'Stanwell Schools' in *A History of the County of Middlesex*, Volume 3, p.49.

Katherine Stanhope née Wotton, Countess of Chesterfield (1609–1667)

1. Fisher, Deborah, *William and Mary: A History of Their Most Important Places and Events*, p.3
2. Green, Mary Anne Everett and Lawrence, Frances, (eds.), *Calendar of State Papers, Domestic Series, of the Reign of Charles II*, Volume 6, June 1 1663, p.160.

Margaret Stewart, Lady Ochiltree (d.1627)

1. Beveridge, James and Donaldson, Gordon (eds.), *Register of the Privy Council of Scotland:1625–1657*, 2nd series, Volume 1, p.201.

Mary Vere née Tracy (1581–1671)

1. Burder, Samuel, *Memoirs of Eminently Pious Women*, Volume 1, p.128.

Thomas Knyvett, 1st Baron Knyvett (*c.*1545–1622)

1. Grigson, Caroline, *Menagerie: The History of Exotic Animals in England*, p.18.
2. Brown, Colin, *Whitehall: The Street that Shaped a Nation*, p.157.

Sir Anthony Mildmay (unknown)

1. Mildmay, Herbert A. St John, *Brief Memoir of the Herbert family*, p.102.
2. Ibid., p.104.
3. Ibid., p. 111.

George Radcliffe (1594–1657)

1. Thrush, Andrew and Ferris, John P., (eds.), 'Radcliffe (Ratcliffe), George (1594–1657), of Overthorpe, Thornhill, Yorks., and Gray's Inn, Mdx.; later of Dublin Castle and Rathmines, co, Dublin', *In The History of Parliament*, accessed online.

Bibliography

Primary Sources

Akkerman, Nadine (ed.), *The Correspondence of Elizabeth Stuart, Queen of Bohemia, 1603–1631*, Volume 1. (Oxford: Oxford University Press, 2015.)

Akrigg, G. P. V., (ed.), *Letters of King James VI & I.* (Berkeley, Los Angeles and London: University of California Press, 1984.)

Anderson, Adam (ed.), *Letters and State Papers of the Reign of James VI.* (Edinburgh: The Abbotsford Club, 1838.)

Bain, J., *et al.*, *Calendar of State Papers relating to Scotland and Mary, Queen of Scots, 1547–1603*, 8 volumes. (Edinburgh: HMSO, 1898–1969.)

Bannatyne, Richard D., and Pitcairn, Robert, (ed.), *Memorials of Transactions in Scotland, A.D. 1569–1573.* (Edinburgh: The Bannatyne Club, 1836.)

Beveridge, James and Donaldson, Gordon, (eds.), *Register of the Privy Seal of Scotland*, Volumes 1 and 2. (Edinburgh: HMSO, 1957.)

Brennan, Michael G., Kinnamon, Noel J. and Hannay, Margaret P., *The Correspondence (c.1626–1659) of Dorothy Percy Sidney, Countess of Leicester.* (London: Routledge, 2010.)

Brown, K. M. and Tanner, T. J., (eds.), *Records of the Parliaments of Scotland to 1707, Volume 2, Parliament and Politics, 1567–1707.* (Edinburgh: Edinburgh University Press, 2005.)

Brown, Horatio F., (ed.), *Calendar of State Papers Relating to English Affairs in the Archives of Venice*, 1603–1607, Volume 10. (London: HMSO, 1900.)

Bruce, John (ed.), *Calendar of State Papers, Domestic Series, of the Reign of Charles I. 1635–1636.* (London: HMSO, 1866.)

Buchanan, George, *A detection of the actions of Mary queen of Scots: concerning the murder of her husband, and her conspiracy, adultery, and pretended marriage with Earl Bothwell: and a defense of the true lords, maintainers of the king's majesty's action and authority,* (1721).

Buchanan, George and Aikman, James (ed.), *The History of Scotland*, Volumes 1 and 2. (Glasgow: Blackie, 1827.)

Calderwood, D. and Thomson, Thomas (ed.), *The History of the Kirk of Scotland*, Volumes 2 and 3. (Edinburgh: Wodrow Society, 1843.)

Cameron. Annie I. (ed.), *Calendar of State Papers relating to Scotland and Mary, Queen of Scots, 1547–1603,* Volume 11. (Edinburgh: HMSO, 1936.)

Cary, Henry, *Memorials of the Great War in England from 1646 to 1652*, Volumes 1 and 2. (London: H. Colburn, 1842.)

Chalmers, George (ed.), *The Life of Mary, Queen of Scots, Drawn from the State Papers, with Subsidiary Memoirs,* Volume 1. (John Murray, 1822.)

Clifford, Arthur (ed.), *The State papers and letters, to which is added, a memoir of the life of Sir Ralph Sadler, with historical notes*, 1507–1587. (Edinburgh: Constable, 1809.)

Clifford, Lady Anne, *The Diary of Lady Anne Clifford with an Introductory Note by V. Sackville West.* (London: Heinemann, 1923.)

Cornwallis, Sir Charles, *A Discourse of the Most Illustrious Prince, Henry, Later Prince of Wales: Written Anno 1626.* (London: John Benson, 1641.)

Craig, J. T. Gibson, *Papers relative to the marriage of King James the Sixth of Scotland, with the Princess Anna of Denmark.* (Edinburgh: Bannatyne Club, 1828.)

Dickson, Thomas and McInnes, C. T. (eds.), *Accounts of the Lord High Treasurer of Scotland, 1566–1574*, Volume 12. (Edinburgh: Scottish Record Office, 1970.)

Donaldson, G. (ed.), *Scottish Historical Documents.* (Glasgow: Scottish Academic Press, 1970.)

Earle, John and Bliss, Dr (ed.), *Microcosmography or, A Piece of the World Discovered in Essays and Characters.* (London: W. Crofton Hemmons, 1811.)

Gatherer, W. A. (trans. and ed.), *The Tyrannous Reign of Mary Stewart: George Buchanan's Account.* (Connecticut: Greenwood Press, 1978.)

Green, Mary Anne Everett, *Calendar State Papers Domestic, Addenda, 1580–1625.* (London: Trubner & Co, 1872.)

Green, Mary Anne Everett, *Calendar State Papers Domestic, of the Reigns of Elizabeth and James I, Addenda, 1580–1625.* (London: Trubner & Co, 1872.)

Green, Mary Anne Everett and Lawrence, Frances (eds.), *Calendar of State Papers, Domestic Series, of the Reign of Charles II*, Volume 6. (London: HMSO, 1860.)

Harrington, Sir John, *Nugae Antiquæ: being a Miscellaneous Collection of Original Papers in Prose and Verse Written During the Reigns of Henry VIII, Edward VI, Queen Mary, Elizabeth and King James,* Volume 1. (London: Vernor and Hood, 1804.)

Hardy, Sir Thomas, *Syllabus (in English) of the Documents Relating to England and Other Kingdoms contained in the collection known as 'Rymer's Fœdera'*, 1377–1654, Volume 2. (London: Longman's & Co, 1873.)

HMSO, *Report on the Manuscripts of the Earl of Mar and Kellie, preserved at Alloa House.* (London: HMSO, 1904.)

Hobbes, Thomas, *Leviathan.* (Oxford: Oxford University Press, 2008.)

Hollar, Wenceslaus and Merian, Matthaeus (illus.) *The true Effigies of Our Most Illustrious Soveraigne Lord King Charles Queene Mary, with the Rest of the Royall Progenie. Also a Compendium Or Abstract of Their Most Famous Geneologies and pedegrees, Expressed in Prose and Verse. With the Times and Places, of Their Births.* (London: John Sweeting, at the signe of the Angell in Popes–Head Alley, 1642.)

Hume, Martin A. S. (ed.), *Calendar of the Letters and State Papers Relating to English Affairs in the Archives of Simancas.* 1568–1579, Volumes 2 and 3. (London: HMSO, 1894.)

Jansen, Sharon L. (trans.), *Anne of France: Lessons for My Daughter.* (Cambridge: D. S. Brewer, 2004.)

King James II and Sellis, A Lytton (ed.), *The Memoirs of James II: His Campaigns as Duke of York, 1652–1660 with an introduction by Sir Arthur Bryant.* (Bloomington: Indiana University Press, 1962.)

King James VI, *A mediation upon the 27, 28, 29 verses of the xxvii chapter of Saint Matthew. Or a paterne for a Kings in-auguration.* (London: John Bill, 1620.)

MacDonald, Alexander (ed.), *Letters To King James VI from the Queen, Prince Henry, Prince Charles, The Princess Elizabeth and Her Husband Frederick King of Bohemia, and From their Son Prince Frederick Henry.* (Edinburgh: Maitland Club, 1835.)

Machiavelli, Niccoló, *The Prince.* (Norderstedt: Books on Demand, 2023.)

Mack, J. D, *Calendar of State Papers relating to Scotland and Mary Queen of Scots, 1547–1603,* Volume 13. (Edinburgh: HMSO, 1969.)

Mackie, J. D. (ed.), *Calendar of the State Papers Relating to Scotland and Mary, Queen of Scots 1547–1603*, Volume 13, Part 1. (Edinburgh: HMSO, 1969.)

Marcus, Leah S., Mueller, Januel, and Rose, Mary Beth (eds.), *Elizabeth I: Collected Works*. (Chicago & London: University of Chicago Press, 2002.)

Masson, David (ed.), *The Register of the Privy Council of Scotland 1626–1657*, second series, Volume 1. (Edinburgh: HMSO, 1899.)

McInnes, Charles Thorpe (ed), *Accounts of the Treasurer*, Volume 12. (Edinburgh: HMSO, 1970.)

McInnes, Charles Thorpe (ed.), *Accounts of the Treasurer*, Volume 13. (HMSO: Edinburgh 1978.)

Meikle, Henry (ed.), *Works of William Fowler*, Volume 3. (Edinburgh: Scottish Text Society, 1940.)

Melville, Sir James and Pitcairn, Robert (ed.), *The autobiography and diary of Mr James Melvill, with a continuation of the diary*. (Edinburgh: Wodrow Society, 1842.)

Melville, Sir James and Thomson, Thomas (ed.), *Memoirs of his own life by Sir James Melville of Halbill. M.D.XLIX.–M.D.XVIII. From the original manuscript*. (New York: AMS Press, 1973.)

Monmouth, Robert Carey, Earl of and Scott, Walter (ed.), *Memoirs of Robert Carey, Earl of Monmouth, Written by Himself. And Fragmenta Regalia; Being a History of Queen Elizabeth's Favourites by Sir Robert Naunton with Explanatory Notes*. (Edinburgh: James Ballantyne and Co, 1808.)

Nott, George Frederick (ed.), *The Works of Henry Howard, Earl of Surrey, and Sir Thomas Wyatt the Elder*, Volume 1. (London: Longman, Hurst, Rees, Orme and Brown, 1816.)

Pepys, Samuel and Bright, Rev. Mynors (ed.), *The Diary of Samuel Pepys M.A. F.R.S. Clerk of the Acts and Secretary to the Admiralty*. (London: George Bell & Sons, 1893.) Online version at pepysdiary.com.

Perrin, William Gordon (ed.), *The Autobiography of Phineas Pett*. (London: Navy Records Society, 1918.)

Scottish History Society, *Rentale Sancti Andree, Being the Chamberlain and Granitar Accounts of the Archbishopric in the Time of Cardinal Betoun, 1538–1546* (Publications of the Scottish History Society, Second Series, Volume 4, 1913.)

Seton, George (ed.), *Memoir of Alexander Seton, Earl of Dunfermline, President of the Court of Session, and Chancellor of Scotland. With an Appendix*. (Edinburgh: William Blackwood and Sons, 1882.)

Slaughter, Thomas P. (ed.), *Ideology and Politics on the Eve of Restoration*. (Philadelphia: The American Philosophical Society, 1984.)

Steen, Sara Jayne (ed.), *The Letters of Lady Arbella Stuart*. (Oxford: Oxford University Press, 1994.)

Strickland, Agnes (ed.), *Letters of Mary, Queen of Scots, and Documents connected with her personal history in Two Volumes*, Volumes 1 and 2. (London: Henry Colburn, 1842.)

Thomson, Thomas (ed.), *The historie and life of King James the Sext: being an account of the affairs of Scotland, from the year 1566, to the year 1596; with a short continuation to the year 1617*. (Edinburgh: Bannatyne Club, 1825.)

Thomson, Thomas and Innes, C. (eds.), *The Acts of the Parliaments of Scotland, 1424–1707*, Volume 2. (Edinburgh: William Green & Sons, 1814–1875.)

Thorpe, Markham John (ed.), *Calendar of the State Papers Relating to Scotland: The Scottish Series of the Reign of Queen Elizabeth*, Volume 2. (London: Longman, Brown, Green, Longmans & Roberts, 1858.)

Turnbull, William B., *Calendar of State Papers, Foreign series of the Reign of Edward VI 1547–1553.* (London: Longman, Green, Longman and Roberts, 1861.)
Weldon, Sir Anthony, *The Court and Character of King James.* (London: John Wright, 1817.)
Wood, Anthony and Clark, Andrew (ed.), *The Life and Times of Anthony Wood, antiquary, of Oxford, 1632–1695, described by Himself. Volume III: 1682–1695.* (Oxford: Oxford Historical Society at the Clarendon Press, 1894.)
Young, Sir Peter, and Warner, George Frederick (ed.), *The Library of James VI, 1573–1583, from a Manuscript in the Hand of Peter Young, His Tutor For The Scottish History Society.* (Edinburgh: T. and A. Constable,1893.)

Secondary Sources

Ady, Julia Mary Cartwright, *Sacharissa; some account of Dorothy Sidney, countess of Sunderland, her family and friends, 1617–1684.* (New York: E. P. Dutton & Company, 1924.)
Akkerman, Nadine, *Elizabeth Stuart: Queen of Hearts.* (Oxford: Oxford University Press, 2021.)
Anon, *Historic Houses of the United Kingdom.* (London: Cassell & Co, 1892.)
Bailey, Geoff B., 'The persecution and Confession of Eleanor Hay, Countess of Linlithgow', *Calatria*, Autumn 1995: No. 8, pp.1–14. Falkirk Local History Society.
Ballantyne, Archibald, *Lord Carteret, A Political Biography, 1690–1763.* (London: Richard Bentley & Son, 1887.)
Ballantyne, J. W., 'The Byrth of Mankynde', *Transactions of the Edinburgh Obstetrical Society*, 1907; 32, pp.236–294.
Beasely A.W ., 'The disability of James VI & I', *The Seventeenth Century*, 1995, Volume 10, pp.151–162.
Blakeway, Amy, *Regency in Sixteenth Century Scotland.* (Woodbridge: Boydell Press, 2015.)
Braybrooke, Lord Richard, *The History of Audley End.* (London: Samuel Bentley, 1836.)
Broadway, Jan, 'Harington, John, first Baron Harington of Exton (1539/40–1613)', *Oxford National Dictionary of Biography (ONDB) online*, September 2004; this version 2005.
Brown, Alexander, *The Genesis of the United States*, Volume 2. (New York: Houghton Mifflin, 1890), pp.1025–1026.
Brown, Colin, *Whitehall: The Street that Shaped a Nation.* (London: Pocket Books, 2009.)
Brown, Peter Hume, *George Buchanan, Humanist and Reformer: A Biography.* (Edinburgh: David Douglas, 1890.)
Brunton, George and Haig, David (eds.), *An Historical Account of the Senators of the College of Justice, from its Institution to M.D.XXXII.* (Edinburgh: The Edinburgh Printing Co, 1836.)
Buchan, P., *An Historical and Authentic Account of the Ancient and Noble Family of Keith, Earls Marichal of Scotland.* (Peterhead, Edinburgh and London: Clark and Sangster, W. Laing and G. & W. B. Whitaker, 1820.)
Burder, Samuel, *Memoirs of Eminently Pious Women*, Volume 1. (London: J. J. Woodward, 1834.)
Caraccioli, Charles, *The Antiquities of Arundel: The Peculiar Privilege of Its Castle and Lordship; with an Abstract of the Lives of the Earls of Arundel, from the Conquest to this Time.* (London: G Robinson & J. Roberts, 1766.)
Carpenter, Sarah, 'Performing Diplomacies: The 1560s Court Entertainments of Mary Queen of Scots', in *The Scottish Historical Review*, Volume 82, Issue 2, No. 214 (October 2003), pp. 194–225.
Cary, Henry (ed.), *Memorials of the Great Civil War in England from 1646 to 1652*, Volume 1. (London, 1842.)

Chambers, E. K., *The Elizabethan Stage*, Volume 1. (Oxford: Oxford University Press, 1923.)
Clarendon, Edward Hyde, Earl of, *The History of the Rebellion and Civil Wars in England*, Volume 5. (Oxford: Clarendon Press, 1827.)
Clegg, Melanie, *The Life of Henrietta Anne*. (Barnsley: Pen and Sword, 2017).
Clements, Robert Markham, *'The Fighting Veres': Lives of Sir Francis Vere, general of the queen's forces in the Low Countries, governor of Brill and of Portsmouth, and of Sir Horace Vere, general of the English forces in the Low Countries, governor of Brill, master-general of ordnance, and baron Vere of Tilbury.* (London: Sampson Low, Marston, Searle & Rivington, 1888.)
Cressy, David, *Birth, Marriage & Death: Ritual, Religion, and the Life-Cycle in Tudor and Stuart England*. (Oxford: Oxford University Press, 1999.)
Davies, Eloise, 'England's Lost Renaissance? Anglo-Venetian Politics between the Household of Prince Henry and the Court of James VI & I', *The Court Historian*, Volume 28, Issue 3, 2023 online version.
Dawson, Jane E. A., 'Jane Stewart, Countess of Argyll: the story behind GD112/39/8/1', based on a Paper given to the Marie Stuart Society. (Edinburgh: The University of Edinburgh, 2006.)
De Lisle, Leanda, *White King: Charles I, Traitor, Murderer, Martyr*. (London: Penguin, 2018.)
Dobson, Julia, *The Children of Charles I*. (London: Heinemann, 1975.)
Dongsun, Lee, 'Absolutism and Constitutionalism: James VI and the Duty of a King', *European Studies*, Volume 19 (2019), pp.5–15.
Drake, George A., 'Percy, Algernon, tenth earl of Northumberland (1602–1668)', *ODNB online*, January 2008.
Durkan, James, 'The Earl of Arran and Queen Mary', *The Scottish Historical Review*, Volume 18, No. 72 (July 1921), pp. 258–276.
Earle, Peter and Fraser, Antonia (ed.), *The Life and Times of James II*. (London: Weidenfeld and Nicolson, 1972.)
Erskine, Lady Frances, *Memoirs Relating to the Queen of Bohemia*. (1772.)
O'Farrell, Brian, *Shakespeare's Patron: William Herbert, Third Earl of Pembroke 1580–1630: Politics, Patronage and Power*. (London and New York: Continuum, 2011.)
Falkus, Christopher, *The Life and Times of Charles II*. (London: Weidenfeld and Nicolson, 1972.)
Fisher, Deborah, *William and Mary: A History of Their Most Important Places and Events*. (Barnsley: Pen and Sword, 2024.)
Fraser, Antonia, *King Charles II*. (London: Weidenfeld and Nicolson, 1979; this edition 1998.)
Fraser, Antonia, *King James VI of Scotland and I of England*. (London: Weidenfeld and Nicolson, 1994.)
Fraser, Antonia, *The Weaker Vessel*. (London: Weidenfeld and Nicolson, 1979.)
Fraser, Sarah, *The Prince Who Would be King: The Life and Death of Henry Stuart*. (London: William Collins, 2017.)
Fry, Cynthia, 'Perceptions of Influence: The Catholic Diplomacy of Queen Anna and Her Ladies, 1601–1604', in Akkerman, Nadine and Houben, Birgit (eds.), *The Politics of Female Households: Ladies in-waiting across Early Modern Europe*. (Leiden: Brill, 2013.)
Garrard P., Stephenson J., Ganesan V., Peters, T., 'Attenuated variants of Lesch-Nyhan disease: the case of King James VI/I', *Brain*, November 2010, Volume 133, Issue 11. p.153
Goldstone, Nancy, *Daughters of the Winter Queen*. (London: Weidenfeld and Nicolson, 2018.)
Gordon, Peter and Lawton, Denis, *Royal Education: Past, Present, and Future*. (London: Frank Cass, 2003.)

Green, Mary Anne Everett, *Elizabeth, Electress Palatine and Queen of Bohemia*. (London: Methuen & Co, 1855, revised 1909.)

Green, Mary Anne Everett, *Lives of the Princesses of England from the Norman Conquest*, Volume 6. (London: H. Colburn, 1849.)

Greenspan, Nicole, 'Public Scandal, Political Controversy, and Familial Conflict in the Stuart Courts in Exile: The Struggle to Convert the Duke of Gloucester in 1654', *Albion: A Quarterly Journal Concerned with British Studies*, Volume 35, No. 3, (Autumn, 2003), pp. 398–427.

Grigson, Caroline, *Menagerie: The History of Exotic Animals in England, 1100–1837*. (Oxford: Oxford University Press, 2016.)

Grogan, Jane. '"Fatall Turkes" and the Limits of Epic: King James' *Lepanto* (1591)', *Scottish Literary Review*, Volume 13, number 1, Spring/Summer 2021, (Association for Scottish Literary Studies), pp.1–15.

Guy, John, *My Heart is My Own: The Life of Mary Queen of Scots*. (London: Harper Perennial, 2004.)

Hammer, Paul E., *The Polarisation of Elizabethan Politics: The Political Career of Robert Devereux, 2nd Earl of Essex, 1585–1597*. (Cambridge: Cambridge University Press, 1999.)

Handley, Stuart, 'Henry, Prince, duke of Gloucester (1640–1660)', *ODNB online*, September 2004.

Hayward, Maria, *Stuart Style: Monarchy, Dress and the Scottish Male Elite*. (New York and London: Yale University Press, 2020.)

Hervey, Mary F.S ., 'A Lumley Inventory of 1609', *The Volume of the Walpole Society*, Volume 6, 1917–1918, pp. 36–50.

Hickey, Julia A., *Preparing Tudor Kings and Princes to Rule: The Men and Women Who Trained the Royals*. (Barnsley: Pen and Sword, 2023.)

Hickey, Julia A., *The Son That Elizabeth I Never Had: The Adventurous Life of Robert Dudley's Illegitimate Son*. (Barnsley: Pen and Sword, 2021.)

Horsburgh, Davie, 'Young, Sir Peter (1544–1628)', *ODNB online*, September 2004.

Houston, S. J. M, *Seminar Studies in History: James I*. (London and New York: Yale University Press, 1995.)

Hulse, Lynn, 'Cavendish, William, first duke of Newcastle upon Tyne (bap.1593– d.1676)', *ODNB online*, January 2011.

Juhala, Amy L., *The Household and Court of King James VI of Scotland*, 1567–1603, Unpublished PhD thesis, University of Edinburgh, 2000.

Jones, Anne Rosalind and Stallybrass, Peter, *Renaissance Clothing and the Materials of Memory*. (Cambridge: Cambridge University Press, 2000.)

Laskowski, Eliza Fisher, *Performance, Politics and Religion*, Unpublished PhD. University of North Carolina, 2006.

Le Lay, David, 'Danvers House', *The Chelsea Society Report*, (2001), pp.35–39.

Lee, Sidney, revised by McGinley, J. K., 'Quin, Walter (*c*.1575–1641)', *ODNB online* (2004).

Lewis, Anne-Marie, 'A Catalogue of Learned Women in the Latin Schoolroom Letters of Mary Stuart, Queen of Scots' in Steiner-Weber, Astrid and Römer Franz (eds.), *Acta Conventus Neo-Latini Vindobonensis, Proceedings of the Sixteenth International Congress of neo-Latin Studies*, Vienna 2015, (Leiden and Boston: Brill, 2018), pp.423–433.

Loades, David, *The Cecils: Privilege and Power Behind the Throne*. (London: The National Archives, 2007.)

Loomie, A. J., 'Carey, Robert, first earl of Monmouth', (1560–1639), *ODNB online*, January 2008.
Marshall, Rosalind K., 'Hir Rob Ryall: the Costume of Mary of Guise', *Costume*, Volume 12, Issue 1 (1978), pp.1–12.
Marshall, Rosalind, K., *The Winter Queen: The Life of Elizabeth of Bohemia (1592–1662).* (Edinburgh: Scottish National Portrait Gallery, 1998.)
Matusiak, John, *James I: Scotland's King of England.* (Stroud: The History Press, 2017.)
McCrie, Thomas, *The Life of Andrew Melville: Containing Illustrations of the Ecclesiastical and Literary History of Scotland, During the Latter Part of the Sixteenth and the Beginning of the Seventeenth Century*, Volume 1. (Edinburgh: Blackwood, 1819.)
McCullough, P. E., 'Hakewill, George (baptised 1578–d.1649)', *ODNB online*, January 2008.
Miller, Anthony, '"These Forc'd ioyes": Imitation, Celebration, and Exhortation in Ben Jonsons' Ode to Sir William Sidney', *Studies in Philology*, Volume 86, No.1 (Winter, 1989), pp.42–68.
Murdoch, W. G. Blaikie, 'Charles the Second: His Connection with Art and Letters' in *The Scottish Historical Review*, Volume 3, No. 9, (October, 1905), pp.41–52.
Newton, Hannah, 'The Dying Child in Seventeenth-Century England', *Pediatrics*, July 6, Issue 136 (2), 2015, pp.218–220.
Nichols, John, *The Progresses and Public Processions of Queen Elizabeth: Among which are interspersed other solemnities, public expenditures, and remarkable events during the reign of that illustrious princess. Collected from original manuscripts, scarce pamphlets, corporation records, parochial registers, etc, etc. Illustrated with historical notes.* (London: John Nichols and Son, 1823.)
Orme, Nicholas, *Tudor Children.* (New York and London, Yale University Press, 2023.)
Pagnini, Caterina, 'Henry Stuart, "The Rising Sun of England": The Creation of the Prince of Wales (June 1610)', *Drammaturgia*, Volume 16, No. 6 (2019), pp. 261–269.
Payne, Helen, 'Ker (Kerr; neé Drummond), Jane (Jean), Countess of Roxburghe (b. in or before 1585–d.1643)', *ODNB online*, September 2004.
Payne, Helen, 'Aristocratic women, power, patronage and family networks at the Jacobean Court, 1603–1625' in Daybell, James (ed.), *Women and Politics in early modern England* (London: Routledge, 2004), pp.164–180.
Pearce, Dominic, *Henrietta Maria.* (Stroud: Amberley Press, 2015.)
Plowden, Alison, *The Stuart Princesses.* (Stroud: Alan Sutton Publishing, 1996.)
Pogson, Fiona, 'Foulis, Sir David, first baronet (d.1642)', *ODNB online*, September 2004.
Pollnitz, Aysha, *Princely Education in Early Modern Europe.* (Cambridge: Cambridge University Press, 2015.)
Porter, Linda, *Crown of Thistles: The Fatal Inheritance of Mary Queen of Scots.* (London: MacMillan, 2013.)
Porter, Linda, *Royal Renegades: The Children of Charles I and the English Civil Wars.* (London: MacMillan, 2016.)
Rait, Robert S. (ed.), *Five Stuart Princesses: Margaret of Scotland, Elizabeth of Bohemia, Mary of Orange, Henrietta of Orleans, Sophia of Hanover.* (New York: Dutton & Co, 1902.)
Reid, Steven J., 'Of bairns and bearded men: James VI and the Ruthven Raid' in Kerr-Peterson, Miles and Reid, Steven J., (eds.), *James VI and Noble Power in Scotland 1578–1603.* (London: Routledge, 2017.)
Reid Steven J., *The Early Life of James VI: A Long Apprenticeship 1566–1585.* (Edinburgh: John Donald, 2023.)

Reynolds, Anna, *In Fine Style: The Art of Tudor and Stuart Fashion.* (London: Royal Collection Trust, 2013.)
Reynolds, Susan (ed.), 'Stanwell: Schools', in *A History of the County of Middlesex: Volume 3, Shepperton, Staines, Stanwell, Sunbury, Teddington, Heston and Isleworth, Twickenham, Cowley, Cranford, West Drayton, Greenford, Hanwell, Harefield and Harlington.* (London: Institute of Historical Research, 1962.)
Riddell, John, *Stewartiana, Containing the Case of Robert II and Elizabeth Mure, And the Question of the Legitimacy of their Issue, with Incidental reply to Cosmo Innes, Esq.; new Evidence Conclusive Upon the Origin of the Stewarts and Other Stewart Notices, etc.* (Edinburgh: Thomas G. Stevenson, 1843.)
Row, John, *The History of the Kirk of Scotland: from the year 1558 to August 1637.* (Edinburgh: Wodrow Society, 1842.)
Rowse, A. L., *The Byrons and the Trevanions.* (London: Weidenfeld and Nicolson, 1978).
Sarasohn, Lisa T., 'Thomas Hobbes and the Duke of Newcastle: A Study in the Mutuality of Patronage before the Establishment of the Royal Society', *Isis*, Volume 90, No. 4, (December, 1999), pp. 715–737.
Schwartz, Louis, '17th century childbirth: "exquisite torment and infinite grace"', *The Lancet*, Volume 377, Issue 9776, (April 30, 2011), pp.1486–1487.
Scott, Eva, *The King in Exile: The Wanderings of Charles II from June 1646 to July 1654.* (New York: E. P. Dutton, 1905.)
Scott Robertson, W. A., 'Six Wills Relating to Cobham Hall', *Kentish Archaeology*, Volume 2, (London: Mitchell and Hughes, 1877) pp.18–113 with specific reference to pp.36–44.
Seton, George, *Memoir of Alexander Seton, Earl of Dunfermline, President of the Court of Session and Chancellor of Scotland with an Appendix.* (Edinburgh: Blackwood and Sons, 1832.)
Seton, Walter W., 'The Early years of Henry Frederick, prince of Wales, and Charles, Duke of Albany (Charles I), 1593–1605', *The Scottish Historical Review*, Volume 13, No 52 (July 1916), pp.366–379.
Shaman, Julian, *The Library of Mary Queen of Scots: With an Historical Introduction and a Rare Portrait of the Queen.* (London: Forgotten Books, 2019.)
Smith, David L., 'Seymour, William, first marquess of Hertford and second duke of Somerset (1587–1660), *ODNB online*, 2009.
Somerset, Anne, *Unnatural Murder: Poison at the Court of James I.* (London: Weidenfeld and Nicolson, 1997.)
Spence, Richard T., *Lady Anne Clifford.* (Stroud: Sutton Publishing, 1997.)
Spring, Matthew, *The Lute in Britain: A History of the Instrument and Its Music.* (Oxford: Oxford University Press, 2001.)
Stewart, Alan, *The Cradle King: A Life of James VI & I.* (London: Pimlico, 2003.)
Strickland, Agnes, *Lives of the Queens of Scotland and English Princesses Connected with the Regal Succession of Great Britain*, Volume 3. (London: Blackwood, 1852.)
Strickland, Agnes, *Lives of the Tudor and Stuart Princesses.* (London: George Bell and Sons, 1888.)
Stoddart, Jane T., *The girlhood of Mary queen of Scots from her landing in France in August 1548 to her departure from France in August 1561.* (London: Hodder and Stoughton, 1908.)
Strong, Sir Roy, *Henry, Prince of Wales and England's Lost Renaissance.* (London: Pimlico, 2000.)
Sutton, James M., 'Henry Frederick, prince of Wales (1594–1612)', *ODNB online*, January 2008.

Swain, Margaret, *The Needlework of Mary Queen of Scots*. (Carlton: Ruth Bean Publishers, 1986.)

Taylor, William M., *John Knox*. (New York: A.C. Armstrong & Son, 1885.)

Teulet, Jean Baptiste Alexandre, *Relations de la France Et de L'Espagne Avec L'Ecosse au xvi siècle*, Volume 4. (Paris: Libraire de la Société de l'Histoire de France, 1862.)

Thrush, Andrew and Ferris, John P. (eds.), *The History of Parliament: The House of Commons 1604–1629*. (Cambridge: Cambridge University Press, 2010.)

Turnbull, Mark, *Charles I's Private Life*. (Barnsley: Pen and Sword, 2023.)

Tweedie, William King (ed.), *Select Biographies*. (Edinburgh: The Wodrow Society, 1845.)

Wardle, Patricia, 'The Embroideries of Mary, Queen of Scots: Notes on the French Background' in *Bulletin of the Needle and Bobbin Club*, Volume 64, (1981), pp.3–20.

Watt, A. F., (ed.), *The Essays of Sir Francis Bacon*. (London: MacMillan & Co, 1904.)

Weir, Alison, *Britain's Royal Families: The Complete Genealogy*. (London: Vintage Books, 2008.)

Weir, Alison, *Mary, Queen of Scots and the Murder of Lord Darnley*. (London: Pimlico, 2004.)

Whitaker, Katie, *A Royal Passion: The Turbulent Marriage of Charles I & Henrietta Maria*. (Weidenfeld & Nicolson, 2010.)

Williams, Ethel C., *Anne of Denmark*. (New Jersey: Prentice Hall, 1970.)

Willie, Rachel, 'William Cavendish: Virtue, Virtuosity and the Image of the Courtier' in Hopkins, Lisa and Rutter, Tom (eds.), *A Companion to the Cavendishes*. (York: ARC Humanities Press), pp.127–145.

Willson, D. H., *King James VI and I*. (Oxford: Oxford University Press, 1967.)

Woolrych, Humphrey William, *Eminent Serjeants-at-law of the English Bar*, Volume 1. (New Jersey: The Lawbook Exchange, Ltd, 2002.)

Worsley, Lucy, *Cavalier: A Tale of Chivalry, Passion and Great Houses*. (London: Faber and Faber, 2007.)

Wright, Edward, Parsons, E. J. S. and Morris, W. F., 'Edward Wright and His Work', *Imago Mundi*, Volume 3, 1939. pp.61–71.

Wyndham, H. A., *A Family History, 1410–1688. The Wyndhams of Norfolk and Somerset*. (Oxford: Oxford University Press, 1939.)

Index